D0049548

PUSHOUT

Also by Monique W. Morris

*Black Stats: African Americans by the Numbers
in the Twenty-First Century*

Too Beautiful for Words: A Novel

PUSHOUT

THE CRIMINALIZATION OF
BLACK GIRLS IN SCHOOLS

Monique W. Morris

THE NEW PRESS

NEW YORK
LONDON

Requests for permission to reproduce selections from this book should be mailed to:
Permissions Department, The New Press, 120 Wall Street, 31st floor, New York, NY 10005.

Published in the United States by The New Press, New York, 2015
Distributed by Two Rivers Distribution

ISBN 978-1-62097-094-2 (hardcover)
ISBN 978-1-62097-120-8 (e-book)
CIP data available.

The New Press publishes books that promote and enrich public discussion and understanding
of the issues vital to our democracy and to a more equitable world. These books are made
possible by the enthusiasm of our readers; the support of a committed group of donors, large
and small; the collaboration of our many partners in the independent media and the
not-for-profit sector; booksellers, who often hand-sell New Press books; librarians; and
above all by our authors.

www.thenewpress.com

Composition by Westchester Publishing Services
This book was set in Garamond Premier Pro

Printed in the United States of America

For Black girls

CONTENTS

INTRODUCTION

C all my mama!"

This was the cry of fourteen-year-old Dejerria Becton, who in the summer of 2015 was thrown to the ground as well as physically and verbally assaulted by Corporal Eric Casebolt after she refused to leave her friends at the mercy of this law enforcement officer in McKinney, Texas. A video, which later went viral, showed Casebolt pushing Dejerria's face into the ground as she—a slight-framed, barefoot, bikini-clad teenager who presented no physical threat or danger—screamed for someone to call her mother for help. The video showed Casebolt grinding his knee into her bare skin and restraining her by placing the full weight of his body onto hers.

The incident was violent and reeked of sexual assault—overtones that were later deemed inappropriate, "out of control," and inconsistent with the police department's policies, training, and articulated practices.[1] Though Casebolt resigned in response to the public outcry and internal scrutiny associated with his actions, the image of her helpless, frightened body under his has become one of the snapshots that call our public consciousness to examine the overzealous policing and criminalization of Black youth. Though media and advocacy efforts have largely focused on the extreme and intolerable abuse cases involving Black boys, such as seventeen-year-old Trayvon Martin in Florida or twelve-year-old Tamir Rice in Ohio, a growing number of cases involving Black girls have surfaced to reveal what many of us have known for centuries: Black girls are also directly impacted by criminalizing policies and practices that render them vulnerable to abuse, exploitation, dehumanization, and, under the worst circumstances, death. For example, eighteen-year-old Sheneque Proctor died in police custody after she was arrested for disorderly conduct in Bessemer, Alabama.[2] Even in high-profile cases involving boys, we often fail to see the girls who were right there alongside them. After the fatal shooting of Tamir Rice, the officers tackled his fourteen-year-old sister to the ground and handcuffed her. Not only had she just watched her little brother die at the hands of these officers, but she was forced to grieve his death from the backseat of a police car.[3]

Addressing these problematic narratives has proved difficult in the current social and political climate, one that embraces punitive responses to expressions of dissent and increases the surveillance of the homes where our families live, the communities where our children play, and the schools where our children are educated.

The result has been an increasing number of girls in contact with the criminal and juvenile justice systems. Since 1992, girls' share of delinquency cases resulting in detention (the most common form of confinement for girls) has increased, often for charges such as prostitution, simple assault, or status offenses.* For a host of reasons—paternalistic juvenile courts and a lack of community-based, culturally competent, and gender-responsive services among them—diversion away from these systems has been underutilized with girls. These are mostly girls of color (a disproportionately high percentage of girls are Black and/or Latina), and many of them (by some estimates 40 percent) identify as lesbian, gay, bisexual, transgender, queer/questioning (LGBTQ), or gender-nonconforming.[4]

One of the most persistent and salient traits among girls who have been labeled "delinquent" is that they have failed to establish a meaningful and sustainable connection with schools. This miss-

---

* Status offenses refer to those that are only a violation because the person is underage, such as truancy, curfew violations, or running away from home.

ing link is exacerbated by the increased reliance of public schools on exclusionary discipline, at present one of the most widely used measures to deal with problematic student behaviors. Indeed, nearly 48 percent of Black girls who are expelled nationwide do not have access to educational services.[5] Black girls are 16 percent of the female student population, but nearly one-third of all girls referred to law enforcement and more than one-third of all female school-based arrests.[6]

The criminalization of Black girls is much more than a street phenomenon. It has extended into our schools, disrupting one of the most important protective factors in a girl's life: her education.

In May 2013, Ashlynn Avery, a sixteen-year-old diabetic girl in Alabama, fell asleep while reading *Huckleberry Finn* during her in-school suspension. When she did not respond, the suspension supervisor allegedly threw a book at her and ordered her to leave the classroom. As she was leaving the room, a police officer allegedly slammed her face into a file cabinet and then arrested her.[7] In April 2013, sixteen-year-old Kiera Wilmot was charged with a felony offense when what she said was a science experiment went wrong, leaving her subjected to a mandatory suspension and arrest following an unauthorized "explosion" on school grounds.[8] The charges were later dropped after significant public objection and petitioning by advocacy groups; however, after the incident, Wilmot has feared being labeled a "terrorist."[9] In 2008, Marché Taylor was arrested in Texas after she resisted being barred from prom for wearing a dress that was considered too revealing.[10] And in 2007, Pleajhia Mervin was harmed by a California school security officer after she dropped a piece of cake on the school's cafeteria floor and refused to pick it up.[11]

Some of the most egregious applications of punitive school discipline in this country have criminalized Black girls as young as six or seven years old, who have been arrested for throwing tantrums in their school classrooms, yelling and screaming at a teacher, and being disruptive to the learning environment. Six-year-old Salecia Johnson was arrested in Georgia in 2012 for having a tantrum in her classroom.[12] In 2011, seven-year-old Michelle Mitchell was arrested with her eight-year-old brother after they got into a fight on an Ohio school bus.[13] And six-year-old Desre'e Watson was hand-cuffed and arrested at a Florida school in in 2007 for throwing a tantrum in her kindergarten class.[14]

These cases were so extreme that they managed to capture considerable public attention—mostly through social media. However, they were never pieced together to present a comprehensive, national portrait of how school responses to the disruptive behaviors of Black girls push them out and often render them vulnerable to further victimization and delinquency. It turns out that the incidents involving Ashlynn, Kiera, Marché, Pleajhia, Salecia, Michelle, and Desre'e were not isolated ones. Black girls from coast to coast tell stories of being criminalized and pushed out of schools.

For many Black girls, interactions between the justice system and schools often do not begin, or end, in school. The surveillance to which Black girls are subjected, and the punitive responses to either their (sometimes poor, sometimes typical) decision making or their reactions to perceived injustice have made contact with law enforcement a frequent occurrence. The implementation of zero-tolerance policies, as I will discuss throughout this book, has become the primary driver of an unscrupulous school-based reliance on law enforcement and school security guards. People who often know little to nothing about child or adolescent development, and who often lack the appropriate awareness and training for the school environments they patrol, are responding to behaviors that were previously managed by skilled teachers, counselors, principals, and other professionals. While there are plenty of numbers and statistics that paint a troubling picture, the harm done by this shift can hardly be quantified. Black girls are being criminalized in and by the very places that should help them thrive.

Historical Perspectives on the Importance of Educating Black Girls

Long before the Supreme Court handed down its decision in *Brown v. Board of Education*, Black women were clear about the liberative power of education. Under slavery, the education of people of African descent was illegal and considered a punishable offense under state slave codes.* In Georgia, enslaved Africans or other free people of color were fined or whipped, at the discretion of the court, if discovered reading or writing "in either written or printed characters."[15] In this society, to read challenged the oppressive, controlling logic of slavery and the presupposed inferiority of Black people. For many enslaved Black women, learning to read represented a reclamation of human dignity and provided an opportunity to ground their challenges to the institution in scholarship, literature, and biblical scripture. Many a Black woman's commitment to education was so strong that she risked incarceration or other penalties just to attain it.

Why take the risk? Because Black women understood the reward. Having an education would make it much harder for Black people to be relegated to servitude and poverty. Those Black women who became educators and generally learned people were able to renegotiate power relationships that had previously held them in bondage, and recast themselves as directors of their own destinies. Education provided an alternative—and it was tangible. It was tangible in 1793, when Catherine Ferguson, a formerly enslaved young woman, committed her life to corralling "poor and neglected" Black and White children for religious instruction on Sunday.[16]

* States with slave codes that delineated the status of enslaved persons and the rights of their "owners" included Georgia, South Carolina, Alabama, Maryland, Louisiana, Texas, and parts of Missouri, among others.

Though she could not read or write herself, as the founder of New York's first Sunday school, Ferguson was hungry to pass on her faith practice and the important educational lessons that she knew would provide tools for others to secure a better future.[17] It was tangible in 1853 when Sarah Mapps Douglass, an abolitionist and passionate educator, led the girls' preparatory department for the Philadelphia Institute for Colored Youth.[18] It was tangible in 1904 when Mary McLeod Bethune opened the Daytona Educational and Industrial Training School; with just five students, she built the foundation for what would eventually become a co-ed institution of higher learning, Bethune-Cookman College.[19]

In each of these cases, Black women understood that education was a core civil and human right. It was the foundation upon which a life of opportunity stood. It was a critical tool for advancement in a society that regularly practiced discrimination against women and against people of color. But the road was neither easy nor straight. Black women's efforts to establish educational pathways encountered significant backlash. In the South, where efforts to restrict opportunity followed the emancipation of enslaved Black people, education was embraced as a tool for the upward mobility of freemen and freewomen—which meant that to be educated remained a threat to the power structure. Fear of retaliation was warranted and quite palpable.

In October 1871, thirty-five-year-old Carolyn Smith, in testimony before Congress, described the terror that Black communities in Atlanta, Georgia, felt from the Ku Klux Klan in response to their quest for education. In her testimony, she was asked about a beating that she and her husband endured one night from a group of men who identified as Ku Klux Klan members: "They said we should not have any schools . . . They went to a colored man there, whose son had been teaching school, and they took every book they had and threw them into the fire; and they said they would dare any other nigger to have a book in his house."[20]

Historically, to be a scholar was a dangerous proposition for Black Americans and countless Black women and men have died to be able to read and write. The lingering barriers to a quality education and the transgenerational trauma associated with internalized ideas about performance in school have yet to be exhaustively measured. However, the systematic denial of equal access to education for African American children has been documented and successfully challenged in the judicial system,[21] in the social sciences,[22] and in the court of public opinion.[23]

While White students and students of color have continued to experience separate and unequal learning environments over the past six decades, most legal and educational reform advocates recognize *Brown v. Board of Education* (1954) as the landmark case that ended legal segregation in our society.* *Brown* was both a precursor to civil rights laws designed to guarantee equal protection and eliminate de jure segregation as well as an important extension of a growing public will to reimagine the promise of American democracy.† However, while de jure segregation may have ended in many ways with the *Brown* decision, affecting public policy well beyond the issue of education, it did not address the ways in which enduring xenophobia, tribalism, and the intersections between race and poverty would sustain de facto segregation—expanded

---

* The Supreme Court case *Brown v. Board of Education* (1954) was actually a combination of five cases from five different jurisdictions: Delaware (*Gebhart v. Belton*, 1952), Kansas (*Brown v. Board of Education*, 1951), South Carolina (*Briggs v. Elliott*, 1952), Virginia (*Davis v. County School Board of Prince Edward County*, 1952), and the District of Columbia (*Bolling v. Sharpe*, 1952).

† For the purposes of this book, de jure segregation is defined as the practice of forcibly separating people along racial or ethnic lines, using laws, policy, or practice.

residential racial isolation that by extension kept schools highly segregated. The decision also did not anticipate future proxies for race (including class and criminal conviction history) that would later facilitate a resegregation of several public learning spaces that had in fact managed notable progress on integration.

Since the elimination of de jure segregation, Black girls have been subjected to harmful stereotypes about Black femininity that have at least shaped and at worst defined their experiences in classrooms and schools around the country. The ways in which Black girls' educational experiences would be constructed according to a hierarchy that favors White middle-class norms has been floating under the national radar for six decades. As Patricia Hill-Collins wrote, "All women engage an ideology that deems middle-class, heterosexual, White femininity as normative. In this context, Black femininity as a subordinated gender identity becomes constructed not just in relation to White women, but also in relation to multiple others, namely, all men, sexual outlaws (prostitutes and lesbians), unmarried women, and girls."[24]

While not referring specifically to educational environments, these norms permeate and shape how Black women and girls are understood and treated in innumerable aspects of public and private life. The purpose of this book is to interrogate the racial and gender inequality that still prevails in education more than sixty years after *Brown v. Board of Education*. In setting forth some truths that have heretofore been ignored or obscured, my aim is to chart a new path and advocate for efforts that move beyond the "deliberate speed" rhetoric that has for too long underserved low-income girls of color, Black girls in particular.

The central argument of this book is that too many Black girls are being criminalized (and physically and mentally harmed) by beliefs, policies, and actions that degrade and marginalize both their learning and their humanity, leading to conditions that push them out of schools and render them vulnerable to even more harm. We can counter the criminalization of Black girls in schools by first understanding what their criminalization looks like, and then by building a common language and framework for making sure that struggling Black girls are not left behind. We can all get behind a fair and effective education strategy that provides a quality education for every young person.

Expanding the School-to-Prison Pipeline Discussion

In a 2012 report, *Race, Gender, and the "School to Prison Pipeline": Expanding Our Discussion to Include Black Girls*,[25] I argued that the "pipeline" framework has been largely developed from the conditions and experiences of males. It limits our ability to see the ways in which Black girls are affected by surveillance (zero-tolerance policies, law enforcement in schools, metal detectors, etc.) and the ways in which advocates, scholars, and other stakeholders may have wrongfully masculinized Black girls' experiences. It encourages a kind of myopia that leaves everyone involved without a proper understanding or articulation of the school relationships and other factors that put Black girls in "the system" and on paths toward incarceration.

Literature exploring the school-to-prison pipeline is dominated by an investigation of discipline, and in particular, the use of exclusionary discipline (i.e., suspensions and expulsions) among Black males, and largely obfuscates the ways in which Black females and males experience this phenomenon together *and* differently.

While leading a series of focus groups in New York to inform a report by the African American Policy Forum, *Black Girls Matter*, I encountered Tamara, who described her first experience with suspension as follows:*

---

* Tamara is a pseudonym. Descriptive details and the names of group members and research participants have been changed to protect the privacy and ensure the safety of all students whose stories appear in this book.

I was in the 5th grade, and this boy, he kept spitting them spitballs through a straw at me while we was [*sic*] taking a test. I told the teacher, and he told him to stop; but of course, he didn't. He kept doing it. So, I got up and I yelled at him, and he punched me in my face, like in my eye . . . my eye was swollen and everything . . . I don't even remember if I fought him, 'cause that's just how it ended, I think. But I remember that we both got suspended, and I was like, why did I get suspended? I was, like, a victim . . . all the girls rushed to my side, they took me down to the nurse and then, it was just a mess.[26]

Tamara described this incident as the first of many subsequent suspensions. It sent her a powerful signal about whether or not she would be protected in school—and how she needed to behave moving forward. As she understood it, she was likely going to face suspension under most circumstances involving conflict, no matter the particular circumstances. The common approach in schools and outside of them for discussing this scenario would prioritize responding to *his* suspension, rather than equally responding to both. While patterns of exclusionary discipline have been found to produce similar outcomes between Black girls and Black boys, narrative-based research—the sort drawn on throughout this book—uncovers a more nuanced picture.[27]

Through stories we find that Black girls are greatly affected by the stigma of having to participate in identity politics that marginalize them or place them into polarizing categories: they are either "good" girls or "ghetto" girls who behave in ways that exacerbate stereotypes about Black femininity, particularly those relating to socioeconomic status, crime, and punishment.[28] When Black girls do engage in acts that are deemed "ghetto"—often a euphemism for actions that deviate from social norms tied to a narrow, White middle-class definition of femininity—they are frequently labeled as nonconforming and thereby subjected to criminalizing responses.[29]

It has also been speculated that Black girls' nonconformity to traditional gender expectations may prompt educators to respond more harshly to the negative behaviors of Black girls.[30] For example, a 2007 study found that teachers often perceived Black girls as being "loud, defiant, and precocious" and that Black girls were more likely than their White or Latina peers to be reprimanded for being "unladylike."[31] Other research has found that the issuance of summonses and/or arrests appear to be justified by students' display of "irate," "insubordinate," "disrespectful," "uncooperative," or "uncontrollable" behavior.[32] These labels underscore the use of discipline, punishment, and the juvenile justice system to regulate identity and social status. They also reflect a consciousness that refuses to honor the critical thinking and leadership skills of Black girls, casting them as social deviants rather than critical respondents to oppression—perceived and concrete.

Notwithstanding these trends, the narrative arc of the school-to-prison pipeline has largely failed to interrogate how punitive discipline policies and other school-related decision-making affect the well-being of girls. Ignoring their unique pathways to confinement and other contact with the criminal legal system that result from school dropout and delinquency has lasting and transgenerational impacts, particularly for those who have experienced victimization.[33] Being abused and/or neglected as a child increases the risk of arrest among children by 59 percent and among adults by 28 percent.[34] And female foster youth are at a higher risk of arrest (34 percent) by the age of nineteen than females and males in the general population (3 percent and 20 percent, respectively)—a reality that facilitates a "way of life" that is more likely to include surveillance, substance abuse, and participation in underground economies.[35] Failing to interrupt pathways to delinquency for girls has lasting effects not just on their own adult lives but also on the lives of future generations of girls and boys, who are more susceptible to being involved with the judicial system as a result of their *mother's* incarceration.[36] There have been some

notable programs and moderate support for the daughters, partners, and mothers of criminalized men and boys; still, exploring
the deficiencies and investing in the education of Black girls
and the women they become must be about more than whether
their father, brother, son, or partner is struggling or incarcerated. The full inclusion of Black girls in the dominant discourse
on school discipline, pushout, and criminalization is important
simply because it affects *them*—and their well-being is worthy
of investment.

Toward this end, it has to be acknowledged that most Black
girls experience forms of confinement and carceral experiences beyond simply going to jail or prison. Broadening the scope to include
detention centers, house arrest, electronic monitoring, and other
forms of social exclusion allows us to see Black girls in trouble
where they might otherwise be hidden. Therefore, in this book and
in general, I refer to "school-to-confinement pathways" as opposed
to a "school-to-prison pipeline" when describing the educational
factors that impact a girl's risk of confinement.

The criminalization of Black girls in schools is more than just a
function of arrests on campus, or even the disparate use of exclusionary discipline—though those outcomes are certainly important to mapping the impact of punitive policies. Paramount to
shifting our lens is understanding the convergence of actions with
a prevailing consciousness that accepts an inferior quality of Black
femininity. This is what underlies the exploitation and criminalization of Black girls. Historic representations of Black femininity, coupled with contemporary memes—about "loud" Black girls
who talk back to teachers, "ghetto" Black girls who fight in school
hallways, and "ratchet" Black girls who chew dental dams like
bubble gum in classrooms—have rendered Black girls subject to a
public scrutiny that affects their ability to be properly situated in
the racial justice and school-to-confinement narrative. They are
rendered invisible or cast as deserving of the mistreatment

because of who they are misperceived to be. What suffers is not only their ability to shape their identities as young scholars but also their ability to develop agency in shaping professional and personal futures where they can live with dignity, respect, and opportunity.

> The colored woman of to-day occupies, one may say, a unique position in this country. In a period of itself transitional and unsettled, her status seems one of the least ascertainable and definitive of all the forces which make for our civilization. She is confronted by both a woman question and a race problem and is as yet an unknown or an unacknowledged factor in both. . . . May she see her opportunity and vindicate her high prerogative.
> —Anna Julia Cooper, 1892[37]

This book presents narratives that I hope will inspire us all to think about the multiple ways in which racial, gender, and socioeconomic inequity converge to marginalize Black girls in their learning environments—relegating many to an inferior quality of education because they are perceived as defiant, delinquent, aggressive, too sexy, too proud, and too loud to be treated with dignity in their schools.

As I discuss in Chapter 1, while Black girls have been able to achieve a certain degree of academic success, they have also been subjected to powerful narratives about their collective identity that impact what they think about school, what they think about themselves as scholars, and how they perform as students. In Chapter 2, I look at how Black girls are disproportionately represented among those who experience the type of discipline that renders children vulnerable to delinquency and future incarceration. This chapter also brings into focus why their experiences are important to understanding the full impact of zero-tolerance policies, and to developing classroom-, school-, and community-based interventions for high-risk youth. The intention is to demonstrate through narratives the importance of Black girls' educational conditions and to improving the socioeconomic conditions of Black communities, and ultimately to decreasing the institutional and individual risks that fuel mass incarceration and our collective overreliance on punishment.

Chapter 3 addresses critical questions of sexual and gender identity among Black girls and the ways in which they are affected by policies, practices, and a prevailing consciousness that seek to regulate their bodies in the learning environment. Chapter 4 explores Black girls' educational experiences in correctional facilities, and Chapter 5 examines how Black girls can be supported in repairing their relationships with school and how institutions can better support their educational and career objectives. Finally, Appendix A offers a Q&A highlighting the most common questions that advocates receive from Black girls, their parents, educators, and community service providers about how to combat school pushout and the criminalization of Black girls, and Appendix B lists some innovative approaches that schools and facilities are currently testing out. The epigraphs to Chapters 1–4 are pulled from childhood rhymes and songs that have been recited by African American girls and others for several generations. While their origins and lyrics vary by the region of the country in which they were learned, they remain a fixture in Black communities.

This work is intended to encourage a robust conversation about how to reduce the criminalization of Black girls in our nation's learning environments. The pathways to incarceration for Black youth are worthy of our most immediate inquiry and response. Using gender *and* racial lenses to examine school-to-confinement pathways allows for an appreciation of the similarities and differences between females, males, and nonconforming students that is essential to shaping efforts that interrupt the pathways to confinement for *all* youth.

This book is written with love. We're in this struggle against racial oppression and patriarchy together, and unless we examine everyone's experiences, we lose the ability to support our girls and young women as they seek to bounce back from adversity, to be in their best health, to demand the best education, to earn a decent living, to be healthy partners, to help raise strong children who will thrive, and to play an integral part in shaping strong communities and a better world.

1

STRUGGLING TO SURVIVE

Mama's in the kitchen, burnin' rice,
Daddy's outside, shootin' dice,
Brother's in jail, raisin' hell,
Sister's on the corner, sellin' fruit cocktail . . .

There were fewer than ten girls in the facility that day, and all of them had been assembled into a small group for a book discussion I'd come to facilitate. Typically, girls there were between fifteen and seventeen years old, but as our exchange got under way, I noticed that some of the girls were younger. About halfway through the discussion, the youngest-looking face among them raised her hand.

I invited her to speak.

She nodded and then slid from behind her desk to stand. She adjusted the oversized county sweatshirt covering her petite frame and looked at me.

"Well, my name is Danisha, and I'm eleven years old," she said. "And I'm a ho, that's what I do."

Danisha had a baby face. Her dark brown skin was flawless— not yet touched by acne—and her coarse hair was frizzy around the temples but otherwise neatly pulled back into a small bun. I remember her as a quiet girl who kept staring at the Marcus Garvey T-shirt I was wearing, her eyes examining with interest the words printed on it: SCHOOL OF LIBERATION. Her apparent interest in my shirt made me curious about her even before her arm shot up to declare how she had come to define herself.

She continued, sharing how the novel I had written inspired her to think about "leaving the life." I was happy to hear that she was willing to consider alternative ways to circumvent the poverty and abuse she faced.

But she was eleven years old. *Eleven*. And she was already referring to herself as a "ho."

In some communities, girls learn early on that selling "fruit cocktail" is one of the few options they have to escape poverty. It's an idea effortlessly absorbed by the psyche of young girls from the moment they can play patty cake. In the absence of safer, healthier ways to connect—and in the presence of multiple factors that reinforce harmful thoughts and choices—sex can and often does become a type of conditioned response that is rarely interrogated. Danisha should have been telling us about her teachers or her fifth-grade homework; instead, she was describing her sex hustle. Not only was her tone unapologetic, but it elicited confirming nods from the group, as if everyone was in agreement that what she was engaged in was actually "ho'ing"—or prostitution—rather than rape or sexual exploitation.

That exchange still haunts me, mostly because since that day, I have encountered many more Danishas in and out of detention facilities—girls struggling to overcome the exploitative conditions of poverty and abuse, who roam hallways and streets wondering if anyone really cares about their well-being. That was in 2001, and the sexual exploitation of children was just beginning to emerge as an issue for justice reform advocates, behavioral health professionals, and other adults concerned about the girls in the Bay Area who could be seen—day or night—strolling the streets as scantily clad sex workers.

I had been to this particular juvenile facility many times before, watching the boys and the girls walk by in orderly lines, their hands clasped behind their backs and their hair disheveled.

During these visits, I'd spoken to young people in focus groups and invited them to think about and discuss what might reduce their risk of reoffending. Even as a researcher trained to preserve objectivity, I hoped that my presence would somehow show these children—who were mostly Black at the time—that some of "us" could make it. So I was excited to find out that my novel about a family's ordeal with prostitution had grown popular among the youth confined in this facility, thanks in part to a very dedicated librarian who ran a robust literature and speaker series in various juvenile correctional facilities. Returning as an author this time, I could shed my research posture and relate to the young people differently. I could tell them what was on my mind, share my own experience of what it means to be Black and female in America, and open new conversations to support and inspire them. Then I met Danisha, and I was stuck.

Good Girls and Bad Girls

In her book *Between Good and Ghetto: African American Girls and Inner-City Violence*, Nikki Jones poses the following question: Why is it that inner-city girls must struggle so hard simply to survive?[1]

The question of survival among Black girls has always been about *whether* they are seen, and if so, *how* they are seen, particularly in economically and socially isolated spaces. Are they "background noise" in a larger view of urban life that prioritizes men and boys? Are they disruptive forces in the exploitation of Black communities? Are they loyal "ride-or-die chicks" who sacrifice their own safety and well-being in the name of love? Are they willing participants in their own oppression? Are they making a way out of no way at all? Are they good girls? Are they bad girls? These are not yes-or-no questions. The answers are anything but simple, and too often no one stops to ponder whether the questions themselves create or even worsen the very problems they seek to illuminate.

Born into a cultural legacy of slavery, Black American women have interpreted defiance as something that is not inherently bad. Harriet Tubman was defiant. So too was Sojourner Truth and countless other enslaved women who dared to reject oppression. Early constructs of power, both racialized and gendered, dictated who could look where and who could speak when. Enslaved Black women in the eighteenth and nineteenth centuries were plagued by dehumanization and a sexual victimization that Angela Y. Davis has described as "barbarous mistreatment that could only be inflicted upon women."[2] As children are routinely told to "speak only when spoken to" in many cultures, so too were those who occupied the *status* of minors. To be a "minority," a colored person, or a woman in this context was to bear the mark of subjugation and relative insignificance. Over time, this wound has deepened through invisibility, violence, and objectification, and for Black girls who have lived in ways that align with and result from a castigated identity, the struggle to be a "good girl," especially in the ghetto, is connected to performances of power.[3]

For Black girls, to be "ghetto" represents a certain resilience to how poverty has shaped racial and gender oppression. To be "loud" is a demand to be heard. To have an "attitude" is to reject a doctrine of invisibility and mistreatment. To be flamboyant—or "fabulous"—is to revise the idea that socioeconomic isolation is equated with not having access to materially desirable things. To be a ghetto Black girl, then, is to reinvent what it means to be Black, poor, and female. Under these conditions, volume and force are powerful tools, but so too are love and loyalty. The "attitude" often attributed to Black girls casts as undesirable the skills of being astute at reading their location—where they sit along the social hierarchy—and overcoming the attendant obstacles. These were lessons learned through generations of struggle, and these lessons sit at the apex of what provides Black women and girls the audacity to demand being treated with dignity. However, when the way of the world includes a general lack of cultural

competence and an aversion to valuing the unique considerations
of gender, these survival characteristics are degraded and punished
rather than recognized as tools of resilience. Under these circumstances, girls fighting for their humanity end up being pushed out
of schools, jobs, homes, houses of worship, and other places where
they might otherwise feel whole.

According to Nikki Jones,

> ["good girls"] do not look or act like men or boys. Good girls do
> not run wild in the streets; instead, they spend the majority of
> their time in controlled settings: family, school, home, or church.
> Good girls are appropriately deferential to the men in their
> lives. Good girls are not sexually promiscuous, nor are they any-
> thing other than heterosexual. Good girls grow up to be ladies and
> once they have achieved this special-status position, they become
> committed to putting the needs of their family first.[4]

Good Black girls are supposed to be all of these things, even while
the males around them are not held to the same standard. When
Black girls rebel against these expectations, they risk being labeled
a "bad" girl, a "ghetto" girl, or, in more recent vernacular, "ratchet."

Bad Black girls are those who are eager for sexual exploits—with
men or women. They may curse, drink, smoke, fight, steal, and/
or lie. All of these characteristics built the mythical "bad" Black
woman who, according to Fannie Barrier Williams in 1904, made
the Black woman "the only woman in America for whom virtue
was not an ornament and a necessity."[5] Black girls who have challenged authority or attempted to negotiate poverty and racial isolation by participating in underground economies have been sent
away to group homes, training schools, detention centers, and
other institutions that attempt to transform "bad girls" into "good
girls."

Who these girls are and why it is so hard for them to simply
survive are questions tied to the larger forces that create and sus-

tain the politics of survival in America, particularly those prevalent in high-poverty areas. These are questions that beg an examination of the laws, practices, and consciousness that facilitate our understanding of who struggles and how that struggle manifests. Being "sick and tired of being sick and tired"—words made famous by civil rights activist Fannie Lou Hamer—is a concept that is immediately understood by Black women.

Twenty-five percent of Black women live in poverty.[6] The unemployment rate for Black women age twenty and over at the end of 2014 was 8.2 percent, compared to 4.4 percent for White women and 5 percent for all women.[7] In 2012, Black women earned 89 percent of what Black men earn, and only 64 percent of what White men earn.[8] Black women are also disproportionately employed in low-wage occupations—jobs that pay them less than $21,412 per year. And while they do not constitute the majority of women on public assistance, Black women are disproportionately represented among those who receive what are collectively known as welfare benefits (e.g., SNAP or food stamps, Section 8 housing vouchers, etc.). Black women are about three times more likely to be imprisoned than White women, and one in nineteen Black women will be incarcerated at some point in her lifetime.[9]

These are struggles that many Black women have felt since their girlhood. Forty percent of Black children live in poverty, compared with 23 percent of all children nationwide.[10] For Black girls under the age of eighteen, the poverty rate is 35 percent.[11] Black girls drop out of school at a rate of 7 percent, compared to 3.8 percent of White girls.[12] At 18.9 percent, Black girls have the highest case rate of "person offenses" (e.g., assault, robbery, etc.).[13] And they have a higher rate (21.4 percent) of being assigned to residential placement than Latinas (8.3 percent) and White girls (6.8 percent) combined.[14]

Sometimes their struggles are matters of life and death. Homicide is the second-leading cause of death for Black girls and women ages fifteen to twenty-four.[15] The rate of domestic or intimate partner violence is highest among Black women and girls ages twelve and older (7.8 percent), compared to their White (6.2 percent), Latina (4.1 percent), and other (3.8 percent) counterparts.[16] The struggle is real. Yet when girls strike back against this fatigue, society casts them as deviant—as disruptive to the order of a (supposedly race- and gender-neutral) social structure without consideration of what might be fueling their agitation.

These circumstances did not emerge through osmosis. The contemporary social conditions that Black girls experience are an extension of long-standing, judgmental popular perceptions about Black girl responses to injustice. Take, for example, Claudette Colvin. Nine months before Rosa Parks made a similar decision that would launch the Montgomery bus boycott, fifteen-year-old Claudette Colvin protested the segregation of Montgomery buses by refusing to give up her seat to a White passenger. But most people do not know her name. Why is that? Well, she didn't fit the profile of a "perfect" protestor. Though Colvin was a member of the Youth Council of the National Association for the Advancement of Colored People (NAACP), she was so incensed by the demand to give up her seat that she shouted. She resisted with her body. And she was arrested.

In the days and weeks that followed, she was viewed as belligerent and "unreliable."[17] Then it was discovered that she was pregnant and soon to become an unwed teen mother. Colvin was cast as a troublemaker and pushed out of one of the country's most vivid civil rights memories, as well as public and private discourses on the role of poor Black girls in the shaping of American democracy.[18]

Colvin herself has also acknowledged the role of colorism—a socially constructed hierarchy where lighter-skinned people are perceived as more socially acceptable than darker-skinned people—in shaping the negative reaction to her as a spokesperson for integration. Colvin's skin was dark and did not "fit the profile" of a middle-class woman who might be viewed as more strategically appealing to the civil rights movement.[19]

This is a scenario all too familiar to many brown-skinned girls who respond to injustice the way that Colvin did—by daring to get loud, daring to challenge their place.

Black and . . . Female and . . .

In *The Souls of Black Folk* (1903), W.E.B. Du Bois articulated the presence of a "double consciousness" among Black Americans—a "twoness" that he described as "an American, a Negro; two souls, two thoughts, two unreconciled strivings."[20] For Black women, their unreconciled strivings and stirred consciousness are also informed by their other identities, including gender, sexuality, and class, among others. In fact, most people walk through life consciously unaware of their multiple identities (no one is *just* Black, *just* a woman, *just* a parent, *just* a student, etc.). The interdigitation of sex and race create barriers to continued economic and intellectual advancement for Black girls and young women under eighteen years old. In modern ghettos, Black girls are routinely expected to seamlessly reconcile their status as Black *and* female *and* poor, a status that has left them with a mark of double jeopardy that fuels intense discrimination and personal vulnerability.

Still, despite the intersection between these identities that shapes how people see themselves as much as how others see them, Black women and girls are often challenged to pick an allegiance. Many Black girls—whether in California, Georgia, or New York— pretend that they can isolate and prioritize their "competing" identities. "I'm Black first, female second," I've heard many times over the years.

Indeed, a failure to acknowledge one's *whole* self silences a more sophisticated analysis about how race, gender, class, sexual identity, ability, and other identities interact. Acknowledging the complexity of social identity has been termed "intersectionality," a

concept coined by legal scholar Kimberlé Crenshaw.[21] Her scholarship advances the work of Anna Julia Cooper, Angela Davis,
Audre Lorde, and other Black feminist scholars who argued that
there is no hierarchy of oppressions.[22] Each identity intersects with
the other to generate a more complex worldview than the one that
would exist if any of us were ever truly able to walk through life
with a singular identity. Oppressed identities further complicate
this experience. This assertion—that no single form of oppression
is more important or dominant than another—is key to understanding and combating the harmful and dehumanizing experiences faced by all manner of human beings, including all too many
Black girls. Actively engaging this framework in daily life creates
places to expose, confront, and address questions of privilege. In
this practice and in those open places, freedom lives.

But the process of getting free is not easy. It demands a close
look at the current public construct of Black femininity and how
that translates—or doesn't—into opportunity for Black girls and
women. Feminist scholar bell hooks writes and talks of an "oppositional gaze," a way to examine the presentations of Black feminine identities and confront the paralyzing stereotypes that
undermine the well-being of Black women and girls.[23] She's one of
many critical minds whose work offers guidance for confronting
such images, interrogating them, dismantling them, and rebuilding new images in a more perfect and complex representation of
Black female identity. Yet one-dimensional stereotypes, images,
and debilitating narratives persist, creating a pressing need to
explore why the struggle for survival is a universally accepted rite of
passage for Black girls. Most importantly, individuals, communities, and all sorts of institutions have an obligation to understand
why the pushout of Black girls—the collection of policies, practices, and consciousness that fosters their invisibility, marginalizes
their pain and opportunities, and facilitates their criminalization—
goes unchallenged.

Culture, Conforming, and Context

The drive to cast contemporary America as a "colorblind" society impairs our ability to recognize two important phenomena: the persistence of segregation and how it shapes the identities of Black girls, and the impacts of systems that reproduce and reinforce unequal access to educational opportunity. No institution is immune to these forces. But our schools are the places where most of our young people spend their days; they are places that have just as much (arguably more) influence as any other social factor on how children understand themselves personally and in relation to the world around them. Schools are, not surprisingly, one of the largest influences on the life trajectory of Black girls.[24]

As institutions with a mission to educate children, public schools are overtly shaping the minds of future leaders, architects of opportunity, and civilians of all types. Explicitly, schools teach curricula that are meant to provide children with the skills to be functional in contemporary society. Educational leaders who ostensibly have an expertise in child cognition, learning, and/or the relevant subject matter (algebra, American history, etc.) design these curricula. High-quality instruction is also an important component of student learning. While the exact definition of high quality is the subject of many heated debates, Stanford professor Linda Darling-Hammond offers a well-rounded description. She contends that quality teaching includes engaging students in active learning, creating intellectually ambitious tasks, using multiple teaching modalities, assessing student learning and adapting to the learning needs of the students, creating supports, providing clear standards, reflection, and opportunities for revision, and developing a collaborative classroom in which all students have membership.[25] This collaborative atmosphere is strengthened by a strong student-teacher relationship.

Jan Hughes and Oi-man Kwok have noted that "African American children are less conforming and more active than are

Caucasian children" when they first begin school and that this
may inform teachers' interactions with Black students, which may
be "characterized by more criticism and less support."[26] Gloria
Ladson-Billings described this culturally competent educational
practice as "the ability of students to grow in understanding and
respect for their culture of origin. Rather than experiencing the
alienating effects of education where school-based learning
detaches students from their home culture, cultural competence is
a way for students to be bicultural and facile in the ability to move
between school and home cultures."[27] There are in fact culturally
relevant curricula, gender-responsive curricula, and trauma-sensitive
practices being used in schools across the nation, but not uniformly or prevalently.

Few curricula taught in elementary and secondary schools were
designed with Black girls in mind, especially those who are living
in racially isolated, high-poverty areas. If the curriculum being
taught does not even consider the unique needs and experiences of
Black girls seeking to climb out of poverty and the ghetto, as is
most often the case, do they *really* have equal access to education?
If schools are teaching curricula that have erased the presence of
Black females from the heroic narrative of American exceptional-
ism (save for a few references during Black History Month in
February), are they not implicitly constructing a narrative of exclusion? In a world of normalized exclusion, how and where, then,
do Black girls situate themselves as Americans and as global
citizens?

Caroline Hodges Persell described a "structure of dominance"
as an institution in which societal biases are reinforced.[28] Sadly,
many schools are dominant structures, sustaining our society's
racial and gender hierarchy. Educational institutions that are not
intentionally "learning organizations," ones that evolve through a
quest for knowledge and social change, end up playing a reproductive role.[29] They churn out individuals who will adeptly maintain

the status quo. In upholding compulsory education, we trust, or at least hope, that schools are teaching our children basic reading, writing, and mathematical skills as well as the critical thinking and social skills that are needed for socioeconomic advancement—their own and that of their communities. But if ghetto spaces are, by definition, inferior in quality and rife with socioeconomic and political oppression, what it means to operate schools in these spaces takes on new meaning and challenges our widely accepted assumptions and presumptions about schooling. The impact of a "ghetto school" on Black girls, their safety, and education in these spaces warrants interrogation.

Bad Girls Do Cry

Seventeen-year-old Portia grew up in the Bay Area foster care system. She was a larger girl in height and girth, and felt that her physical stature made her both a target and perpetrator of bullying. Though playful—I found her dancing in the classroom just before we sat down to talk—she felt that for most of her life, she'd been dodging the label of "bully." Some of the earliest school memories she shared were of teachers accusing her of bullying smaller girls, but to her, she was always standing up for herself. Portia talked about an incident in eighth grade that changed her experiences with bullying.

"I had on white shorts and a white shirt. We was at the park and it was muddy. We were playing by the creek, but I wouldn't go near [the water], so I was standing at the edge. And the teacher came behind me and pushed me . . . and I was the only Black kid in that class. And she didn't like me . . . She tried to make it seem like I tripped off the slope into the water and stuff."

"Why do you think she pushed you?" I asked.

" 'Cause I was Black," Portia responded.

Portia felt that her teacher had bullied her by forcing her into water that she didn't want to go into, but at that point there was a power dynamic that prevented Portia from doing something about it. Instead of fighting back, Portia cried—but no one responded to those tears.

"I got up and cried," Portia said. "When I was younger, before I turned fourteen or thirteen, I never stood up for myself. But now . . . I cry to myself. Or sometimes I have breakdowns and stuff, but other than that, I stand up for myself."

At this time in her life, Portia identified as female, but the enforcement of a gender binary added to her alienation from the very programs meant to help her. She made it her practice to stand up for herself, but she was not interested in being paired with other women who might not understand her. One day, while we were talking about the school programs that she most connected with, she found an opportunity to challenge the idea that because she was a girl, she had to be paired with women educators and professionals.

"I don't never [seek to] have mom figures," she said. "It's always either a male teacher or something. I don't know what it is . . . like ever since I was little, I always wanted to play with the boys. You know, stuff like that, but it's not like being attracted to male teachers . . . But it's always a male, never a female." She had to choose where she was going to go, where she would fit. Portia always felt like she preferred going with the boys, but she wasn't a "boy." So her question to me was, "What do I do if I am not responding to these female teachers that they keep putting me with?"

Portia was not a "good" girl, nor was she a good "girl." She did not fit neatly into the characteristics of what these girls do. She sagged her pants; she presented as masculine. As part of her "rehabilitation," well-meaning probation officers had asked her to put on a dress for a formal program. All of the adults around were celebrating her, telling her how pretty she looked, but she didn't want to wear the dress. She wasn't necessarily interested in being whatever they meant by "pretty." Inside, she was melting. She shared a picture of herself in the dress with a staff member in confidence, stating that she felt "terrible" and that she wanted to destroy the pictures because she felt ruined.

Remember, there is no hierarchy of oppressions.

What was intended to interrupt Portia's contact with the criminal legal system—an approach supposedly shaped with her gender in mind—failed to consider the gender continuum that includes not only "girls" and "boys," but also those who identify in between or outside of polarized notions of gender. Teachers, counselors, advocates, and many others often misunderstand or ignore this complexity, particularly among Black youth.

Paris, who transitioned* in New Orleans during her high school years seemed to understand this completely.

"My transition wasn't easy," she said. "As far as physical altercations, yes, it was with the students, but mostly, my problems didn't come from the students. It came from the staff and the faculty of the school. And it was ridiculous because . . . some of the teachers that were complaining, I didn't have their class . . . at the end of the day, [they would say] I was a 'distraction' to the students. I was 'disruptive' because how could a student focus knowing there's a person like [me] in the room?"

Paris wondered why her gender identity and expression would matter. I saw it as an illustration of how gender has become the third primary "consciousness" informing the experiences of Black women and girls.

Triple Consciousness in the Ghetto

Black racial identity in America has been a function of many things: a pseudo-scientific racial hierarchy that rendered Black people inhuman, violent political forces that enslaved and further dehumanized people of African descent, a sociocultural order that enabled an economic and intellectual hierarchy to take

---

* In this context, to "transition" refers to the process of changing one's gender identity.

root, and spatial dynamics that structured a physical environment and opportunities for movement around the aforementioned hierarchies.

The ghetto is among the spatial dynamics that greatly influence a common, collective interpretation of Black feminine identity in the United States. In *American Apartheid*, Douglas Massey and Nancy Denton described the ghetto as "a set of neighborhoods that are exclusively inhabited by members of one group, within which virtually all members of that group live."[30] Massey and Denton went on to state that "the emergence of the black ghetto did not happen as a chance by-product of other socioeconomic processes . . . [it was] a series of deliberate decisions to deny black access to urban housing markets and to reinforce their spatial segregation."[31] Other scholars have parsed the ghetto into tiers, defining the slum ghetto as a "zone of minority-group residential dominance denoted by inadequate housing, high morbidity and infant mortality rates, and related social pathologies."[32]

However, the isolation and neglect that facilitated ghetto or slumlike conditions for poor Black people in the United States has been present since Black bodies were enslaved, commodified, and traded for public and private use. American plantations established crude manifestations of racial ghettoization: the living spaces for Black field hands were separate, markedly inferior to those of White slave owners, and locations for random but persistent surveillance.[33]

Though haunted by slavery's despicable trauma and legacy of exclusion, Black spaces were simultaneously "home" and "public." In other words, the public nature of Black living spaces was marked by its absence of controlled privacy, reinforcing the idea that Black people were available to the public gaze at all times. This dynamic continues today in streets, buses, schools, and elsewhere. Indeed, this ethos has been extended to many of the learning spaces where the majority of Black children are educated. The public school is constantly subject to a judgmental gaze, externally and from within.

This is doubly true given the ever-expanding surveillance of Black and Brown children.

Ghettoized Opportunity

In principle, access to a quality public education is not a gendered right. While the privileges of all women and girls are up against entrenched patriarchy, the selection of *which* girls are privy to a formal education has always been informed by race and class. Globally, education is by and large recognized as a key pathway out of poverty. However, not every type of education opens up that path, and the quality of education has everything to do with being prepared to thrive as an adult. School resources, the quality of teaching and curriculum, the quality of relationships with parents, and the community network to support all these elements shape the character of formal education. It should be no surprise that low-performing schools are also high-poverty schools that produce higher rates of dropout (as it is traditionally understood) and underperformance among its students, and that high performing schools are often low-poverty ones.*

High-poverty schools are often churning out—or tacitly ignoring—children who are expected to remain poor. Nationwide, about sixteen hundred "dropout factories" are responsible for nearly half of all students who leave high school before earning a diploma and about two-thirds of the students of color who do so.[34] About 58 percent of Black students and 50 percent of Latino students who made the decision to leave school were being educated in one of our nation's high-poverty, low-performing schools.[35] This suggests that a higher percentage of Black girls who dropped out of school—and who were likely struggling in school—were

---

* A dropout is traditionally understood as a person who has made the decision to leave school. While in this book I am challenging how we understand this decision in the context of other conditions, data and other reports cited here refer to "dropouts."

also likely to have been attending a low-performing school. Such a path has grave implications for the economic opportunity for these girls.

Destiny, a Black and Latina girl from California, noticed that in many of these low-poverty schools, girls were searching for pathways out of poverty that were not made clear by their educational community.

"I noticed that girls who get caught up in prostitution, they feel like *working* is more important than anything else," Destiny said. "So, like, the girls that I know who are prostitutes, I hardly ever see them because they are, like, working all the time . . . It's better to go to school and get a career, but it's like, if you can get money, like right then and there, then why would I want to go to school for however many years?"

What is often lost on girls is that the more education a person (of any race) has, the more likely she or he is to be employed in higher-paying jobs.[36] The unemployment rate of Black women with less than a high school diploma is 20 percent, while the rate for Black women with a bachelor's degree or higher is 6 percent.[37] Quality education matters.

Since the time when Linda Brown, Daisy Bates, and other Black women and girls stood on the frontlines of the battle to end racial segregation in schools, the educational story of Black girls has become more convoluted—largely *because* education plays such an important role in the economic opportunity for women and girls. When girls get access to a quality education, they tend to do well. But that is only part of the story.

The educational history of Black girls and how it is understood to this very day reflects an inconsistent and dichotomous narrative. In 1970, only 33 percent of Black women had graduated from high school. Today that proportion of Black women with a high school diploma or higher is 90.5 percent.[38] Black women and girls have made tremendous gains in educational attainment—a fact that has been and should continue to be widely celebrated. However, this statistical narrative of progress obscures other narratives that reveal a continued struggle for both academic achievement and anything resembling equality.

The No Child Left Behind Act, the 2001 legislation that reauthorized the Elementary and Secondary Education Act (ESEA), ushered in an era that prioritized high-stakes testing and established an educational climate that linked assessment of student achievement to the single measure of performance on these tests. According to the National Center for Fair and Open Testing, which has voiced an open critique of the growing reliance on standardized tests, youth of color are disproportionately affected by grade retention (being held back) as a result of this practice.[39] Though largely ignored in national discussions about state-level high-stakes standardized testing, Black girls have struggled to perform well on such tests, which inform advancement in school or graduation.[40] Performance on national standardized tests also reveals racial disparities among girls.[41] These controversial, single measures of knowledge may deter Black girls from continuing on with their education or lead them to internalize that they are not worthy of completing school. They say things like "School's not for me" or "I was never good at school," when their performance may actually be impaired by many other factors, including socioeconomic conditions, differential learning styles, the quality of instruction at their schools, the orientation and presentation of questions on the test, their own mental and physical health, and disparities in access to early childhood education.

For those who do make it to college, the story is encouraging but still incomplete. We know that the benefits of an education have grown more for women than for men across all racial groups since 1994.[42] Among White Americans, Black Americans, and Hispanic/Latino Americans, there is a gender gap in college enrollment.[43] However, when we examine the trends among only *women*, we find that while college graduation rates have increased among first-time, full-time White, Asian and Latina women, there has been no such increase among Black women.[44]

So what's the real story? Are Black girls performing at an unprecedented high level, or are they failing and being marginalized? The answer is: both. And the reason for these competing narratives is complex.

Caricatures of Black femininity are often deposited into distinct chambers of our public consciousness, narrowly defining Black female identity and movement according to the stereotypes described by Pauli Murray as "'female dominance' on the one hand and loose morals on the other hand, both growing out of the roles forced upon them during the slavery experience and its aftermath."[45] As such, in the public's collective consciousness, latent ideas about Black females as hypersexual, conniving, loud, and sassy predominate, even if they make it to college and beyond. Public presentations of these caricatures—via popular memes on social media, in advertising, or in entertainment—prescribe these traits to Black women. However, age compression renders Black *girls* just as vulnerable to these aspersive representations.

As children or as adults, Black girls are treated as if they are supposed to "know better," or at least "act like" they know. The assignment of more adultlike characteristics to the expressions of young Black girls is a form of age compression.[46] Along this truncated age continuum, Black girls are likened more to adults than to children and are treated as if they are willfully engaging in behaviors typically expected of Black women—sexual involvement, parenting or primary caregiving, workforce participation, and other adult behaviors and responsibilities. This compression is both a reflection of deeply entrenched biases that have stripped Black girls of their childhood freedoms and a function of an opportunity-starved social landscape that makes Black girlhood interchangeable with Black womanhood. It gives credence to a widely held perception and a message that there is little difference between the two.

Thirteen-year-old Mia from California echoed this when she described her own experiences avoiding truancy arrest.

"Half of us look older than our age," she said nonchalantly. By whose standards?

The legacy of slavery and segregated opportunity socialized punishment and discipline (as opposed to, say, love and opportunity) as an appropriate response to "bad" Black girls who rebelled against normative ideas about proper feminine behavior. The current practices and prevailing consciousness—in homes, neighborhoods, schools, and other places young people occupy—regularly respond to Black girls as if they are fully developed adults. And in turn, the responses to their mistakes follow a similar pattern. Society treats them this way, and our girls believe the hype. And when they do, adults ignore the power dynamics that affect youthful decision making. They also miss the specific ways in which Black girls learn adaptive behaviors—ways of responding to oppressive conditions defined by race, sexuality, class, and gender. Any or all of these may come into play as girls confront growing pains within structures where (their) age is ultimately nothing but a number.

Black women and girls in America are subjected to dormant assumptions about their sexuality, their "anger," or their "attitude." They have long understood that their way of engaging with the world—how they talk, how they walk, how they wear their hair, or how they hold their bodies—is subject to scrutiny, especially by those in positions of relative power. They feel the gaze. They intuit its presence. They live with this knowledge in their bodies and subconsciously wrestle with every personal critique of how they navigate their environments.

Poverty matters, too. The idea that Black girls in ghettos behave in ways that cast them as "low-class" places a glass ceiling on their opportunity—a stained glass that obscures their vision of what is possible. The interactions between race, gender, and poverty may block a young woman's ability to even see her success, particularly if she has been conditioned to respond to her poverty by selling "fruit cocktail." If Black girls do manage to locate their dream and partner it with an opportunity, the lack of Black female role models in certain professions and the active way in which Black girls are discouraged from pursuing certain professions (e.g., those in the STEM fields) make visioning their futures difficult.

A poor or low-income Black girl might be enrolled in school, but she may not be encouraged to demonstrate her leadership skills on a school sports team or in other areas of school leadership. She may be the first face that greets you in the office or the voice you hear when you call to make an appointment, but her opportunities to break through to the next level or to become a leader are all too often limited or nonexistent. Her senses might even intuit that upward mobility is possible, but if she manages to crack through the ceiling, her mobility will likely be impaired. And, impaired or not, she will still have to navigate the misinformed gaze of Black femininity. She will still feel the pressure to work twice as hard to be respected for her contributions.

Sixty years after *Brown v. Board of Education*, our nation remains in the throes of defining what a quality, desegregated education looks like for all children. But one thing is certain—the civil rights movement was not about our girls (or our boys) being assigned to racially integrated yet structurally unequal high-poverty and low-performing schools. That struggle was about expanding opportunity, not limiting it.

The real and perceived experience of being a Black female student is informed not only by historical ideas about girls attempting to navigate spaces that have underserved their educational needs but also by how well Black girls have performed against the odds. When asked to describe public school in their own words, girls routinely say that their schools are filled with classrooms and hallways where people "fight" and are disciplined, where security personnel roam the halls, and where they learn about a democracy they don't experience in school.

Many of the Black girls that I have spoken with perceived their district or community schools as chaotic and disruptive learning spaces in which fighting and arguments were the norm and where adolescents were vying for attention and social status. These conditions led some—like Mia, who was in middle school—to consider going to school a waste of time.

"All the schools . . . like, they're hecka bad. Like . . . people be smoking up in the gym, and it's always a fight every single day," she said.

"They gotta have like four cops in the school building," she continued. "Like, every single day, all day, 'cause somebody tried to bring a gun, and somebody tried to do something stupid. I don't know . . . Sometimes, if you're already like that, and you're already raised up to be around people like that, like, you just get used to it and you don't really care, you know? And then you start doing bad."

We know children mimic behaviors. We also can understand why someone might not want to stay in an environment they consider dangerous.

"I'd just be out," Mia said. "I wouldn't be at school. . . . You can't even really learn. . . . So it ain't no point in getting up, it ain't no point in going to school, because you cannot learn—not when everybody's yelling, not when everybody's fighting and screaming, throwing erasers and shit at the teacher."

Fifteen-year-old Shanice, also from California, observed a similar dynamic in her classroom. She said that her classrooms were filled with "loud kids . . . A teacher pass out the work and sit back down. . . . The whole school's just loud. . . . The kids, they loud. And it's like, sometimes the teachers don't care, they ignore it and keep going."

Only Shanice didn't see the benefit of playing by the rules if they were going to be broken by everyone around her.

"Say it's a whole classroom," she continued. "Say 75 percent of the classroom's loud, they just talking and on their phones and stuff like that, but the other 25 percent, they quiet, they just sittin' there like, you know, they not doing nothing. They just sittin' there quiet . . . Like, they ain't going to get a higher grade just 'cause they sittin' there quiet, you know?"

Girls like Mia and Shanice draw important connections between their desire to learn and their inability to do so in chaotic learning environments. Across the country, Black girls have repeatedly described "rowdy" classroom environments that prevent them from being able to focus on learning. They also described how the chaotic learning environment has, in some cases, led to their avoidance of school or to reduced engagement in school. In other situations, girls described contentious and negative interactions between teachers and students as the norm. In today's climate of zero tolerance, where there are few alternatives to punishing problematic student behavior, the prevailing school discipline strategy, with its heavy reliance on exclusionary practices—dismissal, suspension, or expulsion—becomes a predictable, cyclical, and ghettoizing response.

Believing the Hype

The extent to which family traditions and values mirror school expectations is important to the relationship between schools and families, as well as to the external motivation of the student.[47] However, Black students' academic performance is more directly linked to their relationships with teachers, which may be problematic given that Black children are often labeled as "less conforming and more active" than their white counterparts, resulting in interactions with teachers that are "characterized by more criticism and less support."[48] A Seattle study found that even a Black student who "tries to please her teacher, tries to get good grades, and is willing to put up with things she doesn't like about school may not be rewarded (in terms of higher GPA) in the same way her [European American] classmate would be rewarded."[49] Personal attitudes and biases still inform how a student-teacher relationship develops.

In a conversation with Destiny, who attended a high-achieving large public school in a Bay Area suburb, she shared that in her experience race influences the way teachers respond to students and their learning needs. Her school had a small Black student population, and an even smaller representation among the advanced courses that she was taking.

"I feel like . . . because there are so [few] Black people on campus . . . I've noticed that other races get more, like, special attention in class," Destiny said. "Like, if they're struggling or like, if they want to see the teacher after class, I noticed that the teacher will be more willing to help them after class."

"What do they say to the Black girls?" I asked.

"Usually they'll say something like, 'Well, you can stop by for ten or fifteen minutes, but you know, I'm not going to wait after school for an hour or something.' You know, and it's like . . . shoot . . . they just did that for the Asian girl . . . There's a lot of, like, Indian people there, and they'll stay after school till like five [o'clock], doing extra work or working on an extra project that the teacher gave them to do, and then everybody else will be there for ten or fifteen minutes just to talk. And I tried to talk to my geometry teacher after school and she really rushed me . . . and she didn't even have anywhere to go. She just wanted to rush me to hurry up and get me out of the classroom. And I was like, 'Well, never mind, I'll just see you in class.' "

I asked how that made her feel.

"I don't know . . . I didn't like that. I should be able to go to you for help if you're a good teacher."

To be ignored is traumatic. Without speaking to this teacher, I do not know whether or not it was her intention to rush Destiny from her classroom. However, for Destiny, this signaled that she does not have the same opportunities as other students in her class—at least not at *that* school. At sixteen, she was already taking advanced placement courses and had expressed an interest in robotics, engineering, and art. She was an articulate communicator and mentioned that she had been taking trigonometry—before she found herself in juvenile hall, for what was (at the time of our discussion) the fifth time in six months. Once she was labeled as a "juvenile delinquent," the quality and rigor of her education greatly declined, a function of the curriculum and instruction offered at the facility where she was confined. I asked if the teachers in her juvenile detention school responded to her differently, knowing that her learning skills were more developed than those of the other girls in her classes.

"Yeah, they know," she said.

"Have you ever received any different assignments?" I asked.

"I'll finish my work before everyone else because I know what I'm doing. [Then the teacher] gives me something completely different to work on—like a poster to put up in her class. Like, it gives me something to do in class, but it's not furthering anything."

It was busy work. And Destiny knew it.

"I really don't like being in school [in juvenile hall]. I don't like the teacher-student relationships," Destiny offered. "[One of the] teachers . . . she's like, really stubborn and so it's hard . . . Sometimes I'll ask a question . . . if I have a question, she's like, 'You already know that, you're just trying to get attention.' And I'm like, 'No, I'm really asking.' I've gotten kicked out of class like three times for that . . . and she's like, 'You're being really annoying.'"

"For asking a question?" I clarified.

"Yeah, and I'm like . . ." Destiny shook her head slowly back and forth.

You're being really annoying. Calling a student "annoying" for asking questions is not only a demonstration of lowered expectations, it is also not effective in fostering student achievement. Later, I spoke with this teacher about her philosophy of discipline, specifically asking how she understood and managed classroom disruptions in the controlled environment of juvenile hall.

"Well, I have to say that [the teachers] enjoy a really good relationship with our particular sets of [institutional] staff—and we've worked on that and tried to cultivate that, so that I think its kind of a seamless experience in terms of what the girls understand as expectations for behavior in the classroom, as well as on the unit," she said. "We have established a positive reward system with our students for not only academic behavior but [also] personal behavior in the classroom, and as a result, the [institutional] staff has created an offset of that. Kids are motivated, not just because of our reward system, but because of their reward system. That's number one. Number two, I've made my expectations—and I think [the other teachers] have made their expectations—really clear, not only to the kids but to the staff. And our staff agrees with that, and so they support us, wholeheartedly . . . And we have high standards in our classroom—there's not a lot of acting out. And if there is acting out, it is dealt with immediately."

"Who typically takes responsibility for dealing with the girls who act out?" I asked.

"In the classroom? It's me. On the other hand, I can make recommendations as to whether a student needs to be kept in the room or lose privileges on the unit . . . or whatever. And I even have a system—there are small infractions, where there's no loss of privileges, [and] there's not-so-small infractions, where they're gonna get a little bit of a write-up to go into the file."

"So what would you consider a small infraction and a not-so-small infraction?" I asked.

"A small infraction is like talking when they're not supposed to be talking or taking other people off task . . . the slip of [a] curse word when they know better. A not-so-small infraction is when a kid deliberately is being disruptive . . . continually being disruptive, being oppositional, you cannot be in my classroom and intentionally take up air and space. You can be bewildered; I get that. But you can't sit there and decide that you're not going to do something. You have to be participatory even on the most fundamental level. So if I have a child who is in some kind of anguish, I don't expect them to do their work. If they're in a surly mood and they've been so for a week, they're not going to be tolerated, actually, for very long. And I will tell them, and warn them, and then if they start escalating, or trying to take other people off work or being totally disrespectful, then I'll do a write-up for the file. And then if they *really* get bad . . . I've had two girls at the same time who were violent and throwing things around and destroying property . . . that's when I get the school suspension in place. They're taken out of the classroom for a couple of days, and they're either isolated [here] or sent down to another unit for isolation for a couple of days until they're ready to conform."

While she had developed her own rubric for mediating the behavior of troubled girls, her interpretation of what was acceptable was largely absent a rigorous analysis of how she came to determine whether someone was "intentionally taking up air and space" (e.g., sitting quietly and not participating in class) or why she had a adopted a punishment-or-reward system that presented young women in this classroom with a narrow set of options regarding their supposed rehabilitation. I noticed the specific emphasis this teacher placed on the issue of tolerance—primarily the behavior that she would *not* tolerate. She was not the only one reflecting on this concept.

"It's really weird," Destiny continued. "I don't have a lot of tolerance [in my juvenile detention classroom] because it's like I'm not learning anything in the class and when I am trying to ask a question, I'm being 'annoying' and 'trying to get attention,' and . . . I don't know, I don't like that."

Who would?

"I feel like it's just the relationship between the teacher and the student," Destiny said. "Because, like, the teachers [in detention] know that we're just going to be here temporarily, so I feel like

they don't make sure that we're really learning. Like me, personally, [I'm not] really learning anything, and so I think, like, people
aren't going to take school seriously here if we're not getting paid
attention to, like our learning."

It seemed to me that Destiny and her teacher were affected by
the "hype" of inferior ability, which facilitated a learning environment marred by low expectations.

Jazzy, a sixteen-year-old girl whom I met in the psychiatric
"special needs" unit of a juvenile detention center, had a critique of
her primary school's dress code, but her assessment of the policy
was cloaked in rhetoric—the kind that reflected negative perceptions and judgments of the norms in her community, rather than
a simple critique of the policy itself.

"I think the Black girls, they just dress more ratchet," she said.
"Not trying to say it like that, but they be dressing in all those
wild colors and just trying to be seen. I'm a more conservative girl,
like I don't gotta wear all that to be cute, but they don't care what
they got on. They just want to be [in] ghetto fashion, and that
affects them. . . . But they grew up with that mentality, so it's like,
we don't know what make them think like that."

Internalized racial oppression is "the process by which Black
people internalize and accept, not always consciously, the dominant White culture's oppressive actions and beliefs toward Black
people (e.g., negative stereotypes, discrimination, hatred, falsifica-
tion of historical facts, racist doctrines, White supremacists ideology), while at the same time rejecting the African worldview and
cultural motifs."[50] For Black women and girls, internalized racial
oppression is also gendered.

Black women and girls, especially those in fragile circumstances, absorb widely accepted distortions of Black American
feminine identity (that they are less intelligent, hypersexual, loud,
sassy, "ghetto," or domestic), and it undermines their healthy
development and performance in school.[51] In combination with
oppressive patriarchal ideologies, internalized *gendered* racial

oppression acknowledges that Black women and girls may appropriate behaviors and ideologies that reflect self-loathing or degradation, reinforcing the very notions of Black feminine inferiority that deny their full humanity.[52] Black girls are quickly cast as undisciplined deviants who reflect the most negative stereotypes of Black femininity. The punitive and marginalizing responses from teachers and others with Black girls under their charge go unchallenged as justified or even necessary. The ways that internal and external oppression play out in intimate spaces—in families, friendships, and relationships—is a book unto itself. This book focuses primarily on how learning institutions and the people working in them don't recognize this dynamic, how this results from a widespread lack of awareness, and how all of us might reimagine and construct different paths for Black girls by listening to them and learning from their experiences.

For Jazzy, while school was "easy," she carried a belief that her teachers did not have a vested interest in her success. This made her feel that she needed to pursue other options. She described her "normal school" as a rowdy place where children regularly fought, teachers were distracted, and she and her friends were tempted to do harmful things to themselves and to others for money.

That year, the school Jazzy had attended before being sent to the juvenile detention center had a student population that was 29 percent African American, 55 percent Latino, 8 percent Asian, and less than 2 percent White. The school's physical condition, according to its School Accountability Report Card, was "poor," with gas leaks and mechanical and sewer conditions that required repair. More than 85 percent of the students in this school were classified as socioeconomically disadvantaged. Only 62 percent of Black students in the senior class completed their high school graduation requirements. The school's suspension rate was more than twice that of the district, and its expulsion rate was three times higher than that of the district or the state.

"I don't know, all my friends . . . we're all addicted to fighting," she said. "We got to rob somebody so we can have money in our pockets, 'cause it's not a lot of opportunities out there for us. Like, we could get jobs at [the youth outreach programs] and stuff, but it's only going to last so long, and it takes so long to get that job. What we going to do in the meantime?"

Jazzy's statement "it's not a lot of opportunities for us" brings to life the experience behind the numbers. Nationwide, in 2013 the unemployment rate for Black youth was the highest of all groups, and it remained so through 2014.[53] In California, Black youth had the lowest high school graduation rate (59 percent), which seemed to have an overall negative impact on their employment opportunities: The unemployment rate for Black Californians in 2014 was 14.6 percent, much higher than rates for White (8.3 percent) and Latino (9.9 percent) Californians.[54] Notwithstanding her illegal grind for money, Jazzy wanted to lead a productive life, and she knew that education was an important element of that journey.

"I honestly can say that when I was on the run from the system, I really wanted to go to school," she said.* "It was upsetting me that I couldn't go to school 'cause I cut my [electronic ankle monitor] off."

Jazzy admitted that when she wasn't in school, there were greater temptations that would occupy her time.

"All I did was go rob or fight somebody, and [it took] up so much time to do all that," she said. "You gotta go meet up with the person you fighting, you gotta call your friends . . . that takes all day!"

Violence produces violence. If she was fighting, it was likely in response to not feeling safe herself.

So I asked her, "Did you feel safe in school?"

"Well, my [art] school was different," she said in reference to a school she'd attended previously. "It wasn't like all the other

---

* Being "on the run" is a reference to turning off her court-ordered electronic monitoring device.

schools. Like, they wasn't so much focused on disciplining you, because they wanted you to express your creativity, like, they wanted you to teach them the way that you wanted to learn . . . We used Khan Academy on our computers . . . we had those computers and stuff [and] it brought us up to the level we on . . . so the teacher knew what level we was on. The other school, they be cussing at the teacher, throwing stuff around in the class. Like, really, I was the only girl that was doing my work in class. Everybody else was arguing [and] about . . . to fight. I'm like, 'Oh my God. I gotta be *here*?' "

"Like, in class?" I asked.

"In class, yeah," she replied.

It's not uncommon for educators, parents, and community stakeholders to argue that girls (of any racial or ethnic affiliation) who get into trouble in school and end up leaving "bring it on themselves." For example, they may say that these girls are "unruly," "talk back" to teachers and principals, fight each other, show up to school "half dressed," and display an overall lack of self-respect or respect for others. These are the "bad girls." "These girls are out of control," adults say.

Control is an operative word that carries great meaning and consequences for the girls who are deemed to lack it. Girls who challenge authority are often told that they are "wild" or problematic—sometimes to the point that they will internalize these ideas and echo them as if they were born of their own consciousness. Like Jazzy, who struggled to "other" herself out of "ratchetness," or Destiny, who tried to make sense of being called annoying for wanting to learn.

What does it mean to suggest that Black girls dress more "ratchet" or that they ascribe to an aesthetic that negatively impacts how they are received when they go to school? What is the mentality (e.g., taking on an oppositional gaze or posture) that makes being seen so important to them? Listening to Jazzy and

Destiny with a deeper awareness of the historical and social factors at work, school leaders just might conclude that policies that fail to interrogate what is "disruptive" behavior in class, overtly marginalize so-called ghetto fashion, or mandate other punitive actions in response to Black girls' expression of cultural norms are harmful. They might begin to ponder what would happen if parents and schools worked together to construct a set of norms that wouldn't confuse or mislead girls, but would instead elevate everyone's consciousness.

Mia explained that in her experience, sometimes schools don't reach out to parents or address the learned behavior of students because they're afraid to do so.

"A lot of times, the teachers are scared to send you to the principal's office," she said. "It's not like back in the day. [Kids will] throw a chair at you. They'll come and punch you if they really feel like it. One girl spit on a lady 'cause she was like, 'Go to the principal's office' and whoop-tee-whoop. She didn't, like, spit in her face, but she spit on her. That's just hella nasty, but . . . other times, they'll be like, 'Sit out until you're calm, and then you can just come back in' because they're just too scared of you."

"Why do you think the teachers are scared?" I asked her.

"Because sometimes . . . I mean, our parents is like us, you know? Our parents get down just like us. This is how we're raised. So if we see them come after school, we could easily just beat her up. Somebody could just jump her, even shoot her if it got that serious, you know? Like anybody could see her in her car, see where she live, and follow her home. I mean, it ain't that hard, you know?"

Again, Mia was harking back to a familiar concept. Children emulate the behavior of parents, who somewhere along the way made an observation that this behavior yields results, or at least the one they might be looking for at the moment: perceived respect that is in fact fear, whether provoked or latent. Black students' academic achievement differs on the whole, a result of institutions and curricula that have historically reinforced unequal opportunity, racism, and oppression, as well as a result of peer pressure and other factors.[55] Parental expectations regarding the academic successes of their children are also important to a student's high performance.[56] While there is little consensus on how to define or measure "parental involvement," those who have researched the topic agree that parental impact can be felt in the school as well as at home.[57]

Most parents, regardless of racial or ethnic affiliation or economic status, want their children to succeed in school. Black parents have expectations for their children's academic achievement that are similar to those of White parents.[58] Structural inequalities (underfunded schools, fewer resources to support positive educational outcomes, less access to quality early education), past negative school experiences, and their children's current experiences may negatively impact their confidence in their child's ability to be a high performer.[59] Black parents who actively talk about school at home may have children who perform better in schools, as opposed to those who just engage directly in the school or simply place a high value on academic achievement, but parental involvement *by itself* is not a predictor of positive student outcomes.[60] While it has been found that Black parents who are more involved in their children's education have children who perform better in school, Black student achievement is largely a function of the expectations and interactions they share with teachers.[61]

This had not yet been explored with Mia. Her family prioritized respect over most other things, which led to performances of power that got her into trouble.

"My family is a certain way," Mia shared. "They always be like, if some girl call me a bitch, I have to beat her ass, or else they're going to beat my ass. But then, if I skip school, I'ma get my ass beat. So I'm like, okay, I got to go to school, but if somebody call me something, like a bitch or something, then I got to beat they ass too."

This was Mia struggling to make sense of her family's confounding expectations for her as a student—and as a girl. To be called a "bitch" was an insult because its roots are derogatory. There are certainly better ways to handle the situation than to fight, but I could understand why she was expected to stand up for herself. In her own way, she was asserting her humanity. Mia couldn't understand why teachers were so unforgiving, but she later admitted that these kinds of power struggles had become so commonplace that some of the students felt that they *had* to assert their own independence everywhere they went, even if it broke the rules, to prove that they could actually hold some aspect of power—*some* amount of control—in school.

Mia continued, "But sometimes I feel like we giving ourselves a bad rep. Like everybody say that White people think that Black girls is ratchet. You know, stuff like that . . . but most of the time, we are doing things that [put] us in that category. You know what I'm sayin'?"

Mia described behavior in the classroom, such as playing music in class and cursing at the teacher, that would be unacceptable to me and to most educators. But I could not help reflecting upon her words: "We are doing things that [put] us in that category [ratchet]." Her willingness to embrace personal accountability ("we give ourselves a bad rep") can be read as an asset, but I considered the other factors that lead teenagers to push limits. Mia's understanding didn't consider the way in which Black girls' actions are particularly subject to scrutiny and public judgment. When Mia said, "Everybody say that White people think that Black girls is ratchet," she was accepting society's marginalization of Black girls as valid—but she was obviously conflicted about it. Her conflict seemed nestled in the idea that she and her peers *had* to accept as truth this automatic characterization of them as "ratchet"—that they had to behave in ways that provided evidence for this claim just because "everybody" said or believed it was true.

Absent a lens that factors in the forces constructing and reinforcing a "ratchet" identity, the adults charged to care for and educate Black girls may only see them as "self-harmers" who bring drama upon themselves.[62] And as a function of their own internalized, gendered racial oppressions, Black girls who are rarely offered any alternative conception may also believe this of themselves.

Permission to Fail

The ghetto's impact on the student identity of Black girls also plays out in the classroom as neglect, or what Gloria Ladson-Billings has referred to as granting Black children "permission to fail."[63] In writing about Shannon, a young Black girl in the first grade, Ladson-Billings reflected on seeing Shannon routinely and intentionally refuse to complete a writing assignment.

"I ain't writin' nuttin'!" Shannon had declared, to which her teacher responded, "That's okay. Maybe you'll feel like writing tomorrow."

But it was not okay. To this point, Ladson-Billings wrote, "Although most students were encouraged to write each day, Shannon was regularly permitted to fail. Her refusal to write was not just stubbornness but a ploy to cover up her inability to read, or more specifically, her lack of phonetic awareness."[64]

Black girls in classrooms across the country have been granted permission to fail by the implicit biases of teachers that lower expectations for them. I doubt this teacher intended to lower her expectations for Shannon or treat her differently than her peers. It is safe to assume that this teacher likely believed that she was responding to Shannon with patience and respect. Indeed, teachers, like the one leading Shannon's class, are likely committed to supporting the education of all of their students, but their unconscious associations between Black girls and underperformance might lead them to assume that these girls are not capable of performing. This is speculative; there is a dearth of research that actually explores the implicit bias and attributional stereotyping affecting Black girls in schools. Still, it is important to remember that implicit bias is often inconsistent with a person's stated values, so a teacher may believe that he or she treats all students the same even while aspects of their engagement are reflecting latent biases. The belief that it was "okay" for Shannon not to participate in the activities was facially just a decision to allow her to engage when she was "ready." However, the determination of her readiness was a function of how the educator read her behavior and interpreted her attitude toward learning. Once again, the external is compounded by reflex: internalized, gendered racial oppressions give Black girls permission to lower expectations for themselves.

Today, Black girls across the country are struggling to make meaning of their status as Black, female, and disproportionately represented in high-poverty, low-performing schools. They use terms like "ghetto" or "ratchet" to describe their condition and are actively engaged in the creation of counternarratives that allow them to move through life with dignity—but it's not easy.

Pierre Bourdieu and Jean-Claude Passeron note in *Reproduction in Society, Education and Culture*, "Every power which manages to impose meanings and to impose them as legitimate by concealing the power relations which are the basis of its force, adds its own specifically symbolic force to those power relations."[65] Schools serve a greater social function than simply developing the rote skills of children and adolescents. As Black girls become adolescents, the influence of schools is critical to their socialization. This is especially important given that schools often serve as surrogates for influences that might otherwise be lacking in the lives of economically and socially marginalized children. Coupled with increasingly rampant suspensions and expulsions and a minimal emphasis (in both curriculum and school climate) on cultural competency, trauma sensitivity, or gender responsiveness, too many of our schools—both those in the community and those operating in penal environments—marginalize Black girls, especially if their curiosity and critical thinking are misconstrued as a challenge to authority.

Asking the Tough Questions

By the time I met fifteen-year-old Faith in a juvenile detention school classroom, I was already aware of how educational and juvenile justice systems routinely fail our girls (a subject explored further in Chapter 4). We were talking about the types of programs that she would like to see implemented in her community when she slumped in her chair and let her fingers trace the perimeter of the desk. Then she asked me an important question.

"You know how they say this is a man's world?" she asked.

I nodded and replied, "Yep."

"I don't like that," she said, staring into my eyes.

"Neither do I," I said softly.

We shared a nervous laugh, but then I asked, "I know why it bothers *me*," I said. "But why does it bother *you*?"

"Because I feel like . . . it shouldn't be just one person's world. Like, what you mean, it's a man's world? Like, what does a strong girl get out of that? Like, how is this a *man's* world? I just don't get it. I feel like it should be equal, and I don't feel like that's equal. I feel like boys . . . men got more rights than girls, and that shouldn't be right."

In Faith's eyes—and her words—was a rejection of patriarchy and the idea that she was inferior just because she had been born a Black girl. All around her were signs that she was supposed to adhere to an imposed hierarchy reinforcing that she was less important than adults, less important than boys, less important than kids who came from families with money, and—because of her sexual identity, which she described as gay—less important than heterosexual girls. Faith was fighting not just for her right to voice her opinions but also to be seen and respected. All while being a Black girl and a ward of the court.

As we talked, I noticed the posters in the classroom. My eyes roved over the letters and posters above the whiteboard until they settled on one in particular, a photograph of President Obama and his family. In that picture, the Obamas look "official"—clustered together, well dressed, and smiling directly into the camera. There they were, a Black family of the highest privilege. Most Black Americans looked upon that photo with great pride, particularly in 2012, when Obama was beginning his second term as president. But at that moment, all I could see was their juxtaposition to Faith and other girls like her who had suffered from a lifetime of neglect and harm—so much so that they had learned to do harmful things to other people. The Obamas' smiles felt inappropriate in an institution that provided so little response to girls with such significant needs. In that juvenile hall, the image and the privilege it represented felt unreal, out of touch, and unfair.

For Faith, whose prominent tattoos displayed a nickname given to her by a deceased loved one, prospects for employment would be complicated and radically different than the young women who smiled down at her from the photograph hanging in that detention center classroom. Even their manifestation of "family" was different from the reality for the girl sitting with me and describing her experience of being expelled from eighth grade for trying to create a family by "making a gang."

Faith vehemently opposed being treated like she was an inferior human being, and she rejected structures that supported this treatment as legitimate. In her, I recognized a spark that could initiate a vision for making conditions equitable for girls, but it was hidden behind a lot of pain.

I asked her what she felt would improve her experiences in juvenile hall. "They should make this a learning environment to make you understand that [juvenile hall] ain't the place. And I feel like, they say they making this seem like it ain't the place by making it harder. That just make it *hard*. It don't make it that I don't want to come back here, 'cause half the time, people still come back. . . . I just feel like, you should make it helpful. . . . They don't make it helpful by making it hard on people, 'cause you got it hard out [in the community], too."

Faith felt that the institutions with which she was most familiar—schools, juvenile detention centers, group homes, and social service agencies—were, individually and collectively, intentionally disruptive to her ability to establish self-worth and to her ability to challenge those whose actions she felt were oppressive.

"If it's a student and teacher, the student's automatically in trouble, 'cause it's the teacher. Like jail, if it's an argument with me and staff, I feel like, I'm going to lose, period. 'Cause I damn near don't have rights no more 'cause I'm in jail. So I feel like, in school, if you get in an argument with a teacher, you damn near lost, 'cause that's her job. You know? I see if the teacher was like beating on you or being like racist or something like that, or homophobic or something like that. But most of the time, over an argument, you out. It's his class. Like, get out! They won automatic. Like I feel like they go off the teacher first, before they go off the child. 'Cause, like, you a child! I don't give a damn about being no child. You still not going to talk to me that way. I feel like, I don't go off 'cause you an adult. I'm a child? I shut up? No. I feel like, I'm human, you human, so I talk just like you talk. If you disrespectful, I'm going to be disrespectful too. . . .

"I'm human. Just a human being, like this whole world . . . and then, I feel like, when you question somebody, it's wrong 'cause [they're] an adult. I feel like, why I can't ask a question? 'cause you an adult? What do 'adult' mean? Like, that don't mean nothing to me. That's just a word to me. That don't mean nothing to me . . . I'm supposed to shut up and not ask questions? I can ask questions if I want to. That's why I got a mouth. My auntie and my god-mama said, if you don't get it, or you don't understand, you ask a question. And that's what I do, I ask the question. And I always do that. I always question. And then sometimes, teachers get mad off of that. Questioning them about why they doing this in they classroom or why they doing that . . . I don't understand how you get frustrated off of a question if I'm not being disrespectful . . . why you get mad?"

Faith's curiosity was infectious. Why do adults get mad when strong girls ask questions?

"They say I'm disrespectful. That's my label, *disrespectful,* 'cause I always got something to say. . . . [They keep] telling me, 'Sometimes you got to bite your tongue.' . . . I don't know how to do that, though."

2

A BLUES FOR BLACK GIRLS WHEN THE "ATTITUDE" IS ENUF

Little Sally Walker, sitting in a saucer.
Rise, Sally, Rise! Wipe your weeping eyes,
Put your hands on your hips, and let your backbone slip . . .

In 2007, six-year-old Desre'e Watson was placed in handcuffs by the Avon Park Police Department for having a bad tantrum in her Florida classroom. According to the police, Desre'e was kicking and scratching, which presented a threat to the safety of others in the school, specifically her classmates and her teacher. According to police chief Frank Mercurio, "When there is an outburst of violence, we have a duty to protect and make that school a safe environment for the students, staff and faculty. That's why, at this point, the person was arrested regardless what [*sic*] the age."[1]

When Desre'e was arrested, she became a symbol of all that was wrong with zero-tolerance policies in the United States. Despite her petite, six-year-old frame, Desre'e was perceived as a threat to public safety. Many were outraged, but most seemed to dismiss it as an isolated incident. Then other incidents began to reach the media.

In 2012, six-year-old Salecia Johnson was arrested in Georgia for throwing books, toys, and wall hangings, amounting to a "tantrum" that was again determined by the school authorities to be an incident worthy of police intervention.[2] Not only was Salecia handcuffed during this "horrifying" incident, she was actually hauled to the police station, an experience that left the kindergartner—according to her mother, Constance Ruff—waking at night screaming, "They're coming to get me!"[3] This episode was followed by one in 2013 involving eight-year-old Jmiyha Rickman, an autistic child who suffered from depression and separation anxiety.[4] Her hands, feet, and waist were restrained when she was arrested in her Illinois elementary school after throwing a "bad tantrum" and allegedly trying to hit a school resource officer.[5] Following her removal from campus, Jmiyha—despite her special needs—was held in the police car for almost two hours. And there were others—most of which did not make the nightly news.

Today, Black children are 18 percent of preschool enrollment, but 42 percent of preschool-age children who have had one out-of-school suspension, and 48 percent of preschool-age children who have experienced more than one out-of-school suspension.[6] Between 2002 and 2006, per-district suspension rates of Black girls increased by 5.3 percent compared to a 1.7 percent increase for Black boys.[7] Among the nation's ten highest-suspending school districts, Black girls with one or more disability experienced the highest suspension rate of all girls.[8]

The experiences of Desre'e, Salecia, and Jmiyha represent the worst and most egregious applications of punitive school disciplinary practices. However, from coast to coast, Black girls tell stories of being pushed out of school and criminalized for falling asleep, standing up for themselves, asking questions, wearing natural hair, wearing revealing clothing, and in some cases engaging in unruly (although not criminal or delinquent) acts in school—mostly because what constitutes a threat to safety is dangerously subjective when Black children are involved.

What's happening is about more than whether or not girls are sitting in the back of a police car because of a tantrum. This chapter explores the discipline disparities that affect Black girls, and the gaps that are generally fueled by three core issues: the perceived "bad attitude" of Black girls, zero-tolerance policies and other highly punitive school practices relying on instruments of surveillance that conflate student conflict with criminal activity, and the criminalization of Black girls' appearance, absent any actions or behaviors that threaten the safety of students or teachers on campus.

"They're Not Docile"

I once asked a classroom of college students how they would describe the Black girl "attitude."

"Neck rolling," one student yelled out.

"Eye-rolling, finger snapping," said another student.

"Just ghetto," said another.

It's infamous, that attitude. Even as you read this—no matter your race, background, or ethnicity—your mind is likely floating toward an image of a brown-skinned young woman with her arms folded, lips pursed, and head poised to swivel as she gives a thorough "eye-reading" and then settles into either an eye roll or a teeth-sucking dismissal. Or maybe you imagined her head tilted, her eyebrows raised, and her hands on her hips (one or two, depending on the circumstance). Or possibly you envisioned her face with a scowl, her lips slightly turned up to show just a few teeth.

Across the country, the student identity of Black girls is often filtered, assessed, and understood through how much "attitude" she gives to others around her. Discussed as if it were as concrete as eye or hair color, the Black girl "attitude" cannot be defined by some set of static traits or actions. For the purposes of this book, the "attitude" is an open inquiry, one that informs not only how adults engage with Black girls but also how these girls identify themselves as young people and as students.

bell hooks explored the attitude as a complicated component of Black femininity, characterized in the public domain as Sapphire, a character on *The Amos 'n' Andy Show* from the 1940s and 1950s.[9] In these broadcasts, Sapphire was nagging and combative with her husband, Kingfish. Their relationship reinforced a narrative about Black femininity as dominant, overbearing, and unreasonably demanding of Black men—an idea that stands directly in opposition to the norms of what White femininity is supposed to be, which is passive, frail, and deferential to men. Both notions are incorrect and harmful exaggerations.

The angry Black woman meme—a neck-rolling, finger-in-your-face, hands-on-hips posturing—is at the center of the public misunderstanding of what it means to be Black and female in America. In schools, this misunderstanding sometimes manifests when girls speak their opinion, especially when it is unsolicited, or if they stand up for themselves when they feel that they have been disrespected by peers or by adults. When relationships between students and teachers are poor, Black girls may exhibit any number of behaviors that openly signal their dissatisfaction, including yelling at or using profanity with the teacher. Marcus, an administrator at a California high school, commented on a scenario in which girls could and do receive a disciplinary referral.

"I get referrals for the simplest reasons," he said. "For a girl yelling, 'I don't understand!' a teacher replying, 'Did you come to school to learn?' earning the retort, 'You come to school to teach?' . . . You know, our babies can be kind of snappy, so the way [they] say it, you know, it might have an expletive in there somewhere. And I mean, just overall, it's just that . . . The sisters bring a lot of attention to themselves. . . . They're not docile."

Our babies can be kind of snappy. By itself, this statement reflects the assumption that Black girls communicate in a way that is biting and provocative. The suggestion that girls' tones must be mediated and their questions made less incisive in order to be tolerated in the classroom is both problematic and sexist. That the comment was made by a well-meaning African American administrator reflects the pervasive and internalized nature of the "angry Black woman" cliché, which serves no one particularly well. Most often in this type of exchange, we're left with a stand-off that leaves both the student and teacher harmed. It usually ends with the removal of the student from the classroom, thus beginning or continuing a negative school experience that can have lasting effects on her relationship with teachers, her faith in her ability to perform well academically, and her commitment to school. In this case, the young woman was removed from the classroom, but should her learning really be interrupted because of her sarcasm? Because of her "attitude"? Because she is not docile?

Students participate in constructing the school climate from the moment they walk through the door. How they see themselves reflected (or not) in the material and how they experience (or don't) a welcoming reception into their learning environment, both the classroom and the school in general, all influence whether a young woman responds to others in a way that she believes is respectful. Because children co-create their learning environments— they either choose to abide by stated rules or work in ways to circumvent them, discreetly or overtly—they are active players in their own socialization, and in the socialization of teachers. Toss that dynamic in with interpretation and effective communication, and it means teaching is hard work. So is learning.

When the teacher asked, "Did you come here to learn?" it may have been heard as a challenge to the girl's willingness to participate in reproducing that school's social norms, or worse, a challenge to her perceived interest in learning as measured by whatever characteristics that teacher may have been using (the student's chattiness, for example). Her reaction, "Did you come here to teach?" called into question the teacher's effectiveness and commitment to her education. The implications of "Did you come here to learn?" might have triggered a feeling of inadequacy in the girl from her previous experiences in the classroom. Instead of saying, "Did you come here to learn?" the teacher could have phrased it as "Listen, your education is important. How can I help you focus on what we're learning so that you can have your best chance to succeed?" This could have been followed by intervention and accountability processes that do not include a referral to the dean but rather elevate the collective responsibility in the classroom and the unconditional belief that all students possess an ability to succeed. Of course, that's a reimagining of this incident—but it's not as utopian as it may seem. Schools are modeling this kind of love every day, when they believe that the children they teach are worth it.

At another alternative school in California—let's call it Small Alternative High—a new Black girl was being introduced to the classroom. She had been waiting to be shown to her desk for at least twenty minutes and was growing impatient with the entire process. I quietly watched as she grew more and more upset that staff members at the school were mispronouncing her name. Finally, after another mispronunciation, she became visibly agitated—folding her arms, sucking her teeth, and rolling her eyes. In other words, she was developing what some would perceive as an attitude.

"Y'all wanna call me every name under the sun!" she said, raising her voice.

Two teachers instantly responded to her. One quickly apologized for mispronouncing her name, explaining that her family was from a town in the South with a similarly spelled name, and that her inclination was to pronounce the name as it is pronounced in her hometown. "I'm sorry," she said after completing her explanation.

Meanwhile, the other teacher repeated, "It's okay . . . we're all human."

The girl's shoulders began to relax until she finally lowered her arms, nodded, and continued to work toward getting acclimated to her new learning environment. In this instance, teachers demonstrated compassion and effective communication, and were able to defuse a situation that could have become hostile. They saw her agitation and recognized her need to feel respected. She, in turn, responded by accepting their apology.

In some instances, the expressive nature of Black girls appears to fuel student-teacher conflict—particularly an almost instinctual need to get back at someone when they feel disrespected. Mia talked about this in the context of her own experiences in class.

"Us Black girls, like, if we don't get it, we're going to tell you," Mia said. "If we don't feel that it's right, we're going to tell you. Where everybody else want to be quiet, it's like, no . . . we're going to speak up, we're going to speak what's on our mind."

On the other hand, teachers who felt successful with their students attribute their success to connecting with students beyond the classroom. At Small Alternative High, more than sixty students were collected in a large classroom, sitting in front of computers, while three teachers roamed to answer questions and work in small groups as necessary. The school's walls were covered with inspirational quotes from prominent African American historical figures such as Malcolm X and Rosa Parks. Small Alternative High was, in many ways, a laboratory for educating students who have been marginalized by a traditional educational experience, combining individual instruction in an independent-study atmosphere with small-group activities. Students attended school for either a morning session or an afternoon session, depending on their schedules. Such flexibility supported student retention and completion of credits, particularly for students who may have a history of truancy, incarceration, pregnancy, or addiction. Nancy, a lead teacher from this school, observed that given the plethora of issues that affect a student's performance, "the teacher has to teach more than just the curriculum." She offered, "In my experience, the young ladies that are having trouble and going through the justice system because they've been in trouble, a lot of it is because they didn't feel success in school." Indeed, education is a critical protective factor in the lives of girls.

"If they had something . . . if their self-esteem was better because they were feeling success, I don't think they would have made those choices that they made," Nancy continued. "Their biggest academic hurdle is self-esteem . . . [I teach] high school. I've got to talk about what I see as a teacher. Ninth-grade boys are exuberant. They're full of energy. They're dominating the conversation. They're just 'out there.' Girls in the ninth grade have a lot more insecurities about puberty and [are preoccupied with the question] 'Do the boys like me?' You know, there's a whole lot of social things that are happening with boys and girls that are different but that certainly impact each other in the classroom. . . . The boys get most of the attention. The girls are marginalized, which I think affects their self-esteem. . . . To feel more confident, sometimes they'll act out to try to get more attention, but a lot of times it goes in a negative way."

The pattern Nancy describes is even more evident in those cases where a girl feels disrespected. To put Mia's point in a different way, sometimes these girls are triggered by adults "talking down" to them, or speaking to them as if they are not worthy of respect.

The student-teacher relationship is a critical component of whether a girl's comments will be seen as part of her expression and learning, or as a deliberate and willful affront to the teacher's authority. Neither of these is against the law, by the way. Yet many schools punish girls who speak out of turn or challenge what they feel is injustice as if it were a violation of law rather than an interrogation of fairness. Punishment often involves removal from class, which facilitates young people feeling disconnected from the material their classmates are learning, exacerbates underperformance on tests or other assignments, or leads to other situations that can and often do escalate to contact with law enforcement and the criminal legal system. Black children, who tend to display fewer "conforming" behaviors in the classroom than their White counterparts, are often subjected to less support and more criticism by their teachers.[10] Black girls feel this and intuit the differential treatment. While teacher-parent relationships are also of tremendous importance, studies show that Black student performance and motivation are often a function of the students' social relatedness with teachers, especially in the early grades.[11] So when teachers feel physically threatened by a six-year-old or when "bad tantrums" are cause for handcuffs, there is a larger problem.

Anecdotally, when I have asked Black students why they underperform on tests or in other measures of school-based understanding, they often respond with "My teacher doesn't like me" or "I don't like that teacher." This is the case even among high-performing Black girls, who recognize when they are being treated differently and can't understand why.

For Sheila, who was a graduating senior at a university in California at the time of our conversation, this was a particularly confounding experience, because she couldn't understand why someone like her—generally quiet and a good student—would be stereotyped into being a problem. Sheila went to a large public high school in an affluent community in Southern California, where the percentage of Black students was very low. She struggled to establish her own student identity, even when it appeared that teachers had different expectations of her.

"I was in AP European History my sophomore year," she said, "and during that time, my uncle passed away and also with that, I was getting my contacts fitted. I had passed out and hit my head on the floor, so I was having migraines galore for about a good year, and they weren't able to actually figure out what was going on because my brain scan was normal [and] everything else was normal. They couldn't figure out why I was having these migraines. In that class in particular, I wasn't doing all the notes at the same time that everyone was doing their notes, and she noticed that. She would constantly get on me, like, 'Why don't you have your notes?' Even though I explained all of this to her, she wasn't very sincere about it. I wanted to talk to her about it, like, 'Hey, there was a death in the family, and [I'm] dealing with these things.' She had none of it. It was like, 'Why aren't you doing this?' 'Why aren't you keeping up in class?' [Meanwhile], I was going to school every day and I had a really good understanding of European history . . . and it showed when I was in class and participating. . . . She was always doing little check-ins, but they always felt more invasive. . . . I noticed that she showed more preferential treatment toward my classmates. One week, [a white student] just didn't want to do her notes, and the teacher was like, 'Oh, that's okay . . .' Well, that didn't happen with me! Why does she get to skip out on this, and I don't? . . . The first semester, I ended up getting a B, and ended the second semester with an A. I remember [the teacher] coming up to me and saying, 'I didn't think you were going to finish.' Like, *no*. This is really important to me."

Before the end of the semester, the teacher suggested several times that Sheila take a less advanced course. Perhaps it was because of the initial interruptions, but to Sheila, it didn't feel that way.

"Even after I was turning in all assignments and my test scores were really high, she continued to suggest it. That wasn't the problem. I was like, 'Why do you keep suggesting this to me?' I really didn't understand why she kept doing that."

Sheila responded to her teacher's differential treatment by trying harder, but for some girls the bias they experience is too upsetting for them to ignore. Some may have parents who taught them the mantra of having to work "twice as hard to get half as far," but for others, that burden is so fundamentally unequal they refuse to play along. Instead, they find other ways to assert their dignity and to gain respect. Even if those ways get them in trouble.

In a society so shaped by race and gender, we all live with implicit biases that inform our ideas, stereotypes, and norms of Black femininity. Our perceptions of difference can sometimes fuel unconscious biases that inform our subconscious reactions to individuals based upon latent, involuntary ideas about race, gender, sexuality, or other aspects of identity.[12] This is important because, well, educators are people. It's unreasonable to think that they are not impacted by the barrage of negative images associated with Black female identity in the popular consciousness.

Certain individual interactions offer evidence of bias—as is the case with many of the stories offered by the girls and young women in this book—but we also see it at a structural level. The greater a school's proportion of students of color, the higher the likelihood that punitive exclusionary discipline will be used in response to student behaviors deemed disruptive and problematic.[13] It's unlikely that administrators of these schools are intentionally of the mind to punish youth of color more than their White counterparts. But punitive responses to student behaviors are especially prevalent in schools where principals and other school leaders believe that "frequent punishments helped to improve behavior."[14] And these leaders are disproportionately found in schools with high numbers of students of color. Their presence there is not an accident.

Standing Their Ground: Zero Tolerance, Willful Defiance, and Surveillance

For two decades, the nation has been enthralled in a punitive whirlwind that has reshaped how educators respond to students, how administrators understand and interpret adolescent misbehavior, and how institutions respond to the learning needs of children in high-poverty schools. For their part, women and girls experience multiple ways of knowing.[15] They gather information not only from what people (adults and peers) tell them but also from experiences, symbols, and metaphors that are woven into the tapestry of their environments.[16] Black girls notice the verbal and nonverbal cues that signal what they are supposed to do and be in life, and they are astute enough to realize when the learning environment is producing something other than its stated goal of educating children. What is often being produced creates a climate so hostile that it pushes girls out of school, and so toxic that it is giving us all an attitude.

Zero-tolerance policies are rules and practices that emerged from the "broken windows" policing theory, first developed by criminologists George L. Kelling and James W. Wilson.[17] It suggests that small criminal acts are indicative of more severe, negative behavior that may later manifest. In the 1990s, law enforcement, particularly police forces in many of the nation's large urban centers, turned toward arresting individuals for minor infractions or incidents of misbehavior. The idea is that by not tolerating any infractions, they are mitigating future, possibly worse offenses. This preventative "tough love" has ushered in a climate and culture of harsh punishment in communities already strained by economic and social exclusion.

In 1994, at the height of a hyperpunitive approach to criminal justice policy and rhetoric in the United States, President Clinton signed into law the Gun Free Schools Act (GFSA), which required schools to expel for at least one year any student who brought a weapon to campus.[18] The policy was in response to a series of school shootings—more than fifty across the country—that together garnered the attention of the American people, as well as national policy makers.[19] Then, on April 20, 1999, two boys opened fire on the campus of Columbine High School in Colorado, killing twelve students and one teacher and injuring more than twenty other students before committing suicide.[20] Columbine spurred a heightened awareness of gun violence on school campuses, and precipitated the implementation of instruments of surveillance that were said to provide the highest degree of "safety" for students.

While structural inequalities preceded the incident in Columbine, zero-tolerance policies that were first intended to protect students from guns and weapons on school grounds have greatly expanded to include automatic suspension for students who bring drugs onto school campuses, fight with one another on campus or within a certain radius of the school, or are perceived as threatening other students or teachers with physical violence. Marked by the wide latitude of their interpretation, these policies vary across schools and districts but remain in many ways a justification for overzealous, punitive reactions to student misbehavior. The ones mentioned here are common guidelines in places where zero tolerance is enforced.

Nationwide, the number of girls (of any racial and ethnic affiliation) who experienced one or more out-of-school suspensions decreased between 2000 and 2009 from 871,176 to 849,447.[21] Still, the racial disparities remain. While Black girls are 16 percent of girls enrolled in school, a figure that has declined only slightly in the last decade, their rate of discipline has remained elevated. In 2000, Black girls were 34 percent of girls experiencing an out-of-school suspension. In 2006, Black girls represented 43 percent of out-of-school suspensions among girls. By the 2009 academic year, Black girls without a disability were 52 percent of all girls with multiple out-of-school suspensions.[22] In the 2011–12 school year, there were eighteen states with out-of-school suspension rates for Black girls higher than the national average (12 percent).[23] Across southern states, Black girls are particularly vulnerable to the use of exclusionary discipline, representing 56 percent of girls suspended and 45 percent of girls expelled in this region. In ten southern states, Black girls were the most suspended among all students—an unusual and noteworthy problem.[24] Over the course of this decade, there was an important shift in the public and policy interpretation of how to secure school campuses, and it's had a largely negative impact on Black girls. In the 2009–10 school year, Black girls without a disability were 31 percent of girls referred to law enforcement and 43 percent of girls with school-based arrests; in the 2011–12 school year, Black girls remained 31 percent of girls referred to law enforcement and were 34 percent of school-related arrests.[25] Since 2000, the rate at which Black girls are harshly disciplined has remained disturbingly and disproportionately high.[26]

In Wisconsin, which produced the highest suspension rate for Black girls in 2011–12, no Black girls were referred to law enforcement directly.[27] However, digging a little deeper into the numbers reveals a dire situation. During that time, the truancy rate for the Milwaukee Public Schools (MPS)—the metropolitan area with the highest incidence of African American poverty in the United States—was 81 percent.[28] In 2013–14, Black students were 56 percent of students enrolled in MPS, and 83 percent of students considered habitually truant.[29] The truancy rate for female students in MPS was nearly 53 percent and for Black female students, it was 68 percent—the highest rate among all students.[30] In Madison, where more than 74 percent of Black children live in poverty, where Black females are almost six times more likely to be unemployed than their White counterparts, and where Black youth are more than nine times more likely to be habitually truant than their White counterparts, the arrest rate for Black youth is six times the rate for White youth.[31]

In the twenty years that followed the implementation of the GFSA, Black girls have become the fastest-growing population to experience school suspensions and expulsions, establishing them as clear targets of punitive school discipline. The National Women's Law Center and NAACP Legal Defense Fund released *Unlocking Opportunity for African American Girls: A Call to Action for Educational Equity*, a 2014 report that explored not only the disparities in school discipline but also the extent to which other obstacles undermine Black girls' ability to fully engage as learners in schools. According to that report, "Decades after legal battles were fought to dismantle legalized racial segregation in education, African American students are still disproportionately enrolled in schools without access to quality resources, credentialed teachers, rigorous course offerings, and extracurricular activities.[32] In *Black Girls Matter: Pushed-Out, Overpoliced and Underprotected*, a report by the African American Policy Forum, it was noted that Black girls are expelled from New York schools at fifty-three times the rate for White girls and resort to acting out (using profanity, fighting, having tantrums, etc.) when their counseling needs are ignored.[33] Why?

In her book *Sugar in the Raw* (1997), Rebecca Carroll shared the narratives of Black girls, including some who foreshadowed how zero-tolerance policies would treat them in the years to come. Fourteen-year-old Latisha from Portland, Oregon, said, "A lot of people say I got an attitude, but I don't really see it. The only reason people be saying I have attitude is because I stand my own ground."

In an era when "stand your ground" laws are associated with judgments of justifiable homicide in the shooting deaths of unarmed Black men and boys (for example, George Zimmerman's killing of seventeen-year-old Trayvon Martin in Florida), "standing one's ground" now has other connotations. But for too many Black girls in schools, it has become associated with being perceived as "willfully defiant"—a relatively nebulous term that harks back to how others view their disposition or so-called attitude.

"Willful defiance" is a widely used, subjective, and arbitrary category for student misbehavior that can include everything from a student having a verbal altercation with a teacher to refusing to remove a hat in school or complete an assignment. It is essentially a formalized way for a school to reprimand students for failing to follow orders. As an undefined catchall category for student misbehavior, willful defiance has been scrutinized for how often it is used to suspend children of color. In 2014, when California discovered that 43 percent of its suspensions in the 2012–13 academic year were for willful defiance, the state became the nation's first to limit suspensions tied to this offense.[34] However, this arbitrary category remains a fixture in many other states and educational systems nationwide.

At the time the GFSA was being implemented, little research centered adolescent Black girls in discussions about school safety. In fact, there were only a few narratives that explored the experiences of Black girls, particularly in schools that were experiencing higher levels of violence. Zero-tolerance discipline policies, specifically the controversial category of willful defiance, have become a routine way by which to punish and marginalize Black girls in learning spaces when they directly confront adults or indirectly complicate the teacher's ability to manage the classroom—not necessarily actions that pose a threat to the physical safety of anyone on campus.

Zero-tolerance policies ignited a consciousness and school discipline ethos that supported the removal of students from the classroom if their actions were perceived as defiant in any way. In many cases, this quashed student voices and limited the ability of teachers and administrators to use discretion and respond to the unique events that led to a conflict. Consequently, the new culture also thwarts their ability to develop responses that might heal or repair the relationships between those involved in the conflict—students and teachers alike. Zero tolerance results in choices and decisions based on fear and punishment, not personal accountability.

To describe the complicated and nuanced impact of zero-tolerance policies and the greater school culture of punishment on Black girls, it's instructive to examine one of the most notorious and complicated school districts in the nation—Chicago Public Schools.

Chicago, Then and Now

Chicago Public Schools is the third-largest school district in the United States, with more than six hundred schools serving about four hundred thousand children.[35] With a student population that is 39 percent African American, 46 percent Hispanic, and 9 percent White, Chicago Public Schools is composed primarily of youth of color.[36] Chicago is now in the arduous process of dismantling zero-tolerance policies; however, it will take decades to unravel the legacy of punishment and reduce the Black student marginalization produced by years of relying on exclusionary discipline. Black students in the Windy City represent 80 percent of Chicago's multiple out-of-school suspensions, 66 percent of school-related arrests and nearly 62 percent of referrals to law enforcement.[37] According to the Consortium on Chicago School Research, the overwhelming majority of these were for offenses that did not pose a "serious threat" to student safety.[38]

Although Black boys have been drastically and disproportionately affected by conditions that lead to punishment and
criminalization in schools, Black girls are also affected by these
conditions—a reality frequently obscured by biases in how harm
is defined, what information is gathered, and who is deemed
worthy of study and understanding. In Chicago, 23 percent of
Black high school girls received out-of-school suspensions in the
2013–14 school year, compared to 6 percent of Latina girls
and 2 percent of White and Asian girls. For Black girls in middle
school, the rate was 14 percent.[39] Similar trends have been found
for in-school suspensions, where the rates for Black girls in high
school doubled from 10 percent to 20 percent between the
2008–9 and 2013–14 academic years.[40]

Chicago has long served as a case study of ghettoized learning
spaces. In 1922, Charles S. Johnson published "The Negro in
Chicago: The Study of Race Relations and a Race Riot," in which
he examined the living conditions of Black people in Chicago
following a 1919 race riot that resulted in more than five hundred
injuries and the death of fifteen White and twenty-three Black
Americans.[41] More than a thousand Black families lost their homes
to vandalism by White rioters, which had a significant impact on
the landscape of residential segregation and educational opportunity on the South Side of Chicago for decades following the riot.[42]
Johnson, a sociologist, conducted a study that documented not
only the general physical and social conditions that exacerbated
the tensions between Black and White Chicagoans but also the
specific ways that Black communities in the city, including its
girls, were affected by educational disparities. On the topic of
school discipline, Johnson found that differential discipline was
used when teachers themselves appeared to harbor racial bias.

There was considerable variety of opinion among the teachers as
to whether Negro children presented any special problems of discipline. The principal of a school 20 percent Negro (Felsenthal),

for example, said that discipline was more difficult in this school than in the branch where 90 percent were Negroes (Fuller). This principal is an advocate of separate schools. She was contradicted by a teacher in her school who said she had never used different discipline for the Negroes. In schools where the principals were sympathetic and the interracial spirit good the teachers reported that Negro children were much like other children and could be disciplined in the same way. One of two teachers reported that Negro children could not be scolded but must be "jollied along" and the work presented as play. This is interesting in view of the frequent complaint of the children from the South that the teachers in Chicago played with them all the time and did not teach them anything.[43]

Strained racial relations are endemic to the learning climate for Black girls in Chicago, and they are part and parcel of the girls' own internalization of where they belong—or don't belong. Black girls have always struggled to learn alongside other children and been forced to explore their "otherness" in ways that set them apart from their Black male counterparts and their female counterparts of other racial and ethnic groups. Their struggle to be seen occurs even in learning spaces that have since become less "integrated" than they were in the early 1920s. Today, Black girls—particularly those who did not self-identify as high performers—interpret their teachers' actions to suggest that their learning and involvement in school are marginal to the overall success of the courses being taught.

In the summer of 2014, I met with young women in Chicago, high school age or just above, to talk about their experiences in school. Each of the young women I spoke with had been born and raised in Chicago and was intimately familiar with the public schools in her communities. I asked them to tell me what school was like for them, and in a manner consistent with that of most girls and young women to whom I have posed this question, they began to describe a hyperpunitive, chaotic learning space that was preoccupied with discipline.

"First of all," twenty-one-year-old Michelle said, "they all look like mini-prisons."

Other girls in the group nodded in agreement and said, "Yes . . . yes . . ."

"I graduated in 2010," Michelle continued. "It felt like you were always being watched, like, as if we were going to do something, and I felt like it was favoritism with people in the schools— especially coming from security guards. . . . The same actions would take place, but different people would get different consequences. . . . And the whole police station in the school, and everything . . . it wasn't the space for that, and I just didn't understand why they would put something like that in place."

"I went to [that school] too," said eighteen-year-old Leila. "The crazy thing for me is, school [in a more affluent neighborhood] was *not* like jail. I could walk the halls. I was going outside. I was cool with all the police. When the counselor took me in, I was making good grades, so she was just like, 'Just go to class.' I went to [another school]—an all-Black school as well, but it's in [a high-poverty neighborhood] and they had stricter security. Everybody was in class because we couldn't just roam the halls. . . . At [the high-poverty school], they had metal detectors. At this [more affluent] school, we didn't. I could have more freedom."

Metal detectors, security guards checking bags, and police patrolling the hallways of high schools might have become the norm for the young women who were in conversation with me that summer, but it wasn't always this way. Since the mid-1990s, police officers have been increasingly assigned to schools, expanding the role of school resource officers (SROs) into a part of the educational climate. Seen as a "new type of public servant; a hybrid educational, correctional, and law enforcement officer," SROs were defined as "law enforcement officers who engage in community-oriented policing activities and who are assigned to work in collaboration with schools and community-based organizations."[44] Under the best circumstances, says a Congressional Research Service report, SROs help develop community justice initiatives for students and train them in conflict resolution, restorative justice, awareness of crime, and problem-solving with regard to criminal activity. Over time, the number of SROs has grown tremendously—in 2007, there were about 6,700 more SROs than in 1997.[45]

According to the FBI's Uniform Crime Reporting Program, White males between the ages of thirteen and eighteen are the most likely to initiate a school-based shooting.[46] However, schools in which the student population is largely composed of youth of color have the highest degree of implementing metal detectors, security officers, SROs, and other police forces.[47] While only 1 percent of schools in 1975 had police that were stationed in schools, the latest Crime Victimization Survey (2014) shows that 43 percent of students reported the presence of one or more police officers and/or security guards in their schools.[48] Additionally, 88 percent of U.S. public schools in the 2011–12 academic year "reported that they controlled access to school buildings by locking or monitoring doors during school hours."[49]

Though the implementation of zero-tolerance policies was largely a response to a moral panic surrounding male aggression (particularly that which involved gun violence), girls were targeted under the new policies as well, principally because they were attending schools that emphasized punishment and removal from school, rather than the repair of relationships or addressing the root causes associated with the violence.

Research on the impact of SROs has found that the presence of SROs in schools has contributed to the formal processing of youth into the justice system. A 2011 study by criminologists Chongmin Na and Denise Gottfredson found that schools with SROs record more crimes that involve weapon and drugs, but they also report more nonserious crimes to law enforcement—thereby expanding the reach of the criminal justice system, a practice that is referred to as "net-widening": "For no crime type was an increase in the presence of police significantly related to decreased crime rates. The preponderance of evidence suggests that, to the contrary, more crimes involving weapons possession and drugs are recorded in schools that add police officers than in similar schools that do not. The analyses also showed that as schools increase their use of police officers, the percentage of crimes involving non-serious violent offenses that are reported to law enforcement increases."[50]

Police in schools may not be responsible for an increase in the use of exclusionary discipline, but they nevertheless reinforce the idea that youth of color need surveillance. Where law enforcement is present on the school campus, they are sometimes challenged to shift their own punitive thinking—a transition that takes time. For example, Victor, a dean of students for a school in California, spoke with me about having to work with officers on his campus to get them to understand that the school was trying to operate as a family. Victor described how one officer would routinely tell students who misbehaved, "It's time"—a phrase that was intended to communicate with students, for whom enrollment at this alternative school was one of their last chances to salvage a high school experience, that it was time to drop out of school. Victor made several efforts to remind this officer that on their campus, his role was to secure the location and ensure that students were not presenting a physical threat—not to advise them of when to drop out. Still, this officer, according to the dean, resorted to the use of verbal threats that reflected his desire to remove certain students from the school for good.

The presence of law enforcement (including school resource officers, school-based probation officers, security officers, and others) has been cited as one of the largest contributing factors to the increased rates of student citations in schools.[51] The increased surveillance of Black youth in particular has led to increased contact with law enforcement, and in some cases, the juvenile court, for actions that would not otherwise be viewed as criminal, even if they violate school rules—such as refusing to present identification, using profanity with a school administrator, or "misbehaving."[52] The presence of law enforcement in schools has instead blurred lines between education and criminal justice, as daily exchanges and interactions with law enforcement expand the surveillance of youth of color and normalize prison terminology (and culture) in school settings.[53] Approximately 76 percent of students in middle and high schools nationwide attended a school with a locked entrance or exit door during the school day in 2013, an increase from 65 percent in 2011 and 38 percent in 1999.[54] In this context, even asking a question can be seen as misbehavior, depending on the tone.

"What was it like to have metal detectors in your schools?" I asked.

"Annoying as hell," Michelle said.

"You was getting checked every day," said nineteen-year-old Nala.

"Okay, so how did that make you feel?" I asked.

"I felt like I was visiting somebody in jail," Nala replied.

"For real," Michelle agreed. "It's a downer for your morning to have to walk through a metal detector, you know?"

"They search through your bags and stuff," Nala chimed in. "Especially for girls...like we have personal things inside of there."

"Yeah, and they have men checking it sometimes," Michelle noted.

Nala was referring to personal items like feminine hygiene products, extra underwear, and/or sports bras. Imagine a young girl's embarrassment to have to look at a man, or any SRO, after such an inspection—especially if she has a history of sexual victimization.

"For me that was the norm," said Leila. "I just thought that's how school was. I actually like low-key did feel halfway protected because a girl had got sliced in the throat with a blade. And we did have a lot of fights and stuff. And so for me, I used to just walk in, put my book bag on, and boom . . . I didn't really link it to jail or nothing like that; I just thought it was the norm, it was a lot smoother, and I still wasn't scared. I thought I'd be a lot more nervous, but [I wasn't]. . . . I just thought that's how school was, like 'Ain't this how it's supposed to be?' Then you go to *another* school and be like, 'Dang . . . that's how *y'all* learn.' True . . ."

Leila paused to mimic looking around the room in awe, with her eyes and mouth open as if in shock at the new environment. The young women laughed, but there was something more to be said about the different—separate and unequal—learning spaces that were provided for concentrations of poor Black and Brown children, as compared to their more affluent counterparts. Her mention of feeling "low-key . . . halfway protected" by security in school because of the threat of physical violence was part of her inability to envision an alternative. For her, surveillance was a typical strategy used to provide safety in school, as opposed to building a collective culture that elevates safety through equity and respect. This is the principle that was most elevated in her comparison between what she observed in her original school and what she observed in another school.

In describing her learning environments, Michelle mentioned that she felt teachers responded best to students who were already high performers, at the expense of other students who may have needed more attention. She linked this practice to the school-to-prison pipeline and noted it was a way of intentionally giving certain children permission not to perform well in school. She reflected on feeling "lost" in class at times, as if she was supposed to already know what was being taught.

"They'll focus on the ones that have it already, whereas if you don't, they'll just leave you be," Michelle said. "When they come at you like you should know it already, it's like, mmm . . . should I know it already? You know, you shy away from even opening your mouth."

"That's true," Leila agreed. "Me being one of the people that grasps knowledge real easy, I'm one of the ones that talk too much, right? Yeah . . . I'm asking every question. I'm thirsty. I'm like, 'Did you remember the homework assignment you were supposed to get?' . . . When I do be quiet, couldn't nobody speak up. The teacher didn't encourage them to speak up. Instead, he took me in the hallway and asked if I was okay, even though he just asked me to be quiet the day before!"

"I was the kid who was quiet, who was paying attention, but not necessarily asking questions. It was like, talk when you're spoken to . . . or be seen and not heard," Michelle chimed in.

When girls spoke out of turn, they were often seen as disruptive.

"I was the type that asked questions," Leila said. "Because I understood that the class didn't get it. You can feel it. So I'm one of those students that's like, 'So you subtract the four from both sides, right?' And he'll say yes, and you can hear people be like, 'Oh.'"

"That's what's up," Nala said.

That's what's up among the students, because they were searching for understanding but not always getting it from their teacher. To some, Leila's willingness to speak up might be misinterpreted as being disruptive, though she saw herself as being helpful to the other students. The audacity to stand up and be heard in the face of fierce patriarchy and racial oppression is not always celebrated; instead, adults with authority have misinterpreted it as being angry and combative. Michelle's and Nala's experiences in the classroom reflect the dichotomous narrative about Black girls in schools—one loud, one quiet. Michelle's interpretation of her disconnect from the material as a pathway to confinement was largely about how the school's "permission to fail" has produced consequences that could extend well beyond unemployment. Failing out of school leads girls to the dangers of street life, so to Michelle, doing well in school was an important strategy for staying out of prison. For Nala, who was outspoken and "thirsty" as a student, conflicting messages about her student identity complicated her relationship with her teachers, which also put her at risk of under-performance in the classroom.

Compounding these classroom dynamics were broader social conditions inside schools that led Black girls to have conflict—or an "attitude"—with others. I asked the girls in Chicago what issues or actions have set them off in the past. In response, they identified several triggers: "a look," "the way you look at [us]," "boys," "talking behind each other's back."

"That's the main thing. 'I heard you was talking about me,'" Nala said loudly.

"People hyping the situation up," Michelle offered.

"Especially the boys . . . but the security guards and the teachers get in it too," said Nala.

I wasn't expecting that one.

"Yeah, the security guards are the worst, though," Michelle said. "Because the security guards will get cool with the students, and then they'll get to talking to them about the situation and then go back and tell."

"And that's how the fight starts," Nala said.

"So what happens when there's a fight?" I asked.

"Then the security guard will break it up and get them suspended," Michelle said. "After they done hyped this all up . . . they live for fights, so they can have a job to do."

"They break it up when they feel like breaking it up, though," Leila said. "They'll sit there and watch the fight for a little while and then they'll do their job . . . so they can have something to talk about."

For girls who attend a zero-tolerance school, the consequences of fighting are severe.

"Zero tolerance," Michele said. "You fight, you're gone . . . I was at [an alternative school]. It was your last chance."

"You can go to another alternative school," Nala offered.

"Yeah, but they won't give you a reference. If you want to go to another school, they're not going to help you," Michelle said.

"If somebody fights in a [traditional school], that's ten days automatic suspension," Leila said. "That's two weeks of school that you already missed, and so now you're playing catch-up. So that's already unfair. But when you get into a fight, they don't solve the situation. They just say, '*You* go home for ten days, and *you* go home for ten days' . . . instead of trying to really figure out why did y'all fight and what's going on."

Indeed, that was true when Leila was in school. Revisions to the Chicago Public School Student Code of Conduct now require that out-of-school suspensions be a last resort, and that schools follow specific measures to ensure that students are suspended from school for the minimum number of days.[55] Also, the code requires that school employees "guide students in developing new skills in social competency, learning personal boundaries and peaceably resolving conflict, and to model appropriate social interactions."[56] To Leila, suspension is a heavy penalty that should never be taken lightly and should always be accompanied by work so that the student doesn't fall behind. But suspensions in Chicago—like suspensions in other school districts around the country—seem rarely to be coupled with an automatic learning activity or assignment.

"You can ask for your work," Leila said. "And hope that they'll give it you."

"Some teachers . . . if they don't like you already, they're not going to help you," Nala said.

Throughout the country, school suspension policies differ regarding the assignment of homework, classroom activities, and/or testing. According to the Chicago Public School Student Code of Conduct, "The principal must ensure that a student serving suspension is able to obtain homework, and upon the student's return, provided with the opportunity to make up any quizzes, tests, special projects, or final exams given during the period of suspension."[57] Though most of the young women had graduated from high school by the time we spoke, the teacher discretion that they observed may have been a violation of district policy.

Schools are supposed to be safe havens for our children and a place where their intellectualism grows and their skill sets—academic, emotional, and social—sharpen. This is achieved through academic coursework, but also through play. For children in younger grades especially, recess not only supports the academic achievement but also provides children with health benefits. Children are known to perform better on literacy tests and to be more likely to raise their hands in class after they've had a recess break.[58] The benefits of recess to children with hyperactivity is even greater, as offering children a break strengthens their ability to stay on task for assignments.[59] What happens when our schools remove these important opportunities for learning and recreational play and instead focus primarily on discipline?

Chicago Public Schools eliminated recess for its elementary and middle school students in 1991.[60] In 1998, the district implemented a policy that granted school administrators the discretion to choose whether or not to allow recess. This resulted in two-thirds of Chicago schools opting for a "closed campus," which means that for nearly twenty-five years, there have been children attending Chicago public schools who have never experienced school recess. This practice was condemned by the American Academy of Pediatrics, the National Association of Early Childhood Specialists in State Departments of Education, the Alliance for Children, and many others.[61] Still, the decision has been left to the discretion of the schools in the country's third-largest school district, and many administrators have opted out, perceiving recess as a "waste of time."[62]

For the students, this meant they had limited time to take a break, release, and reset.

"It went from learning all day, going to your prep, and then you leave," said Michelle.

"With no breaks?" I asked.

"You get a lunch break . . . a bathroom break," the young women said in unison.

"That's when people usually get riled up, because it's like [you've been] in school so long," said Michelle.

"Now that's when you talk the most . . . they want you to sit at a table," Leila said. "I been wanting to tell her something since nine o'clock! . . . It's not just 'cause they're Black. If you're born poverty-stricken, you ain't got no recess. The only time to talk is during lunch or after school. Y'all ain't got no sports. Y'all ain't got no activities. You don't have nothin' to be proud of at your school. You ain't paint nothing on the walls, or participate in nothing. You just coming from nine [o'clock] . . . to four or three-thirty."

For these girls, the ways in which the learning spaces of children were designed to prepare students for a lifetime of institutionalization was shamelessly transparent. However, even in the context of incarceration, people get a "recess"—recreational time, usually outdoors, to take a break. In the absence of a break from the monotony of the day, girls may be less able to pay attention, more irritable and disruptive in class, and less inclined to feel connected to their schoolwork and their classmates.[63] These are conditions that facilitate agitation and aggression, undermine student performance in class, and lead students to question why they are coming to school at all. Chicago has since extended its school day to provide more opportunity for recess, but there are still many young adults whose cognitive, physical, and emotional development have been harmed by the absence of recess.

Smart Mouths and Fighting Words

As discussed in Chapter 1, without intentional efforts to combat old ways and norms, schools routinely function as institutions that reproduce dominant social ideas, hierarchies, and systems of oppression. Schools that approach learning as an exercise in classroom management are often preoccupied with discipline—exclusionary discipline, to be exact. Black girls are more likely to be punished for talking back to a teacher, cursing, or being "loud" in ways that are interpreted as disruptive to the classroom.[64] Black girls are also on the receiving end of school-based sanctions associated with who they are as Black girls—whether or not they have behaved "badly."

In 2005, Hurricanes Katrina and Rita raged through the Gulf Coast, exposing one of the nation's blind spots regarding inequality. Prior to these devastating hurricanes, New Orleans was home to 124 public schools that were part of three distinct school systems. Of these schools, 117 operated under the governance of the Orleans Parish School Board, 5 were under the governance of the Louisiana Recovery School District (a special statewide district created to take over "failing," schools), and 2 were independent charter schools.[65] The hurricanes not only devastated the personal property of many New Orleans residents but also severely damaged schools—at least forty-five schools suffered sewage and flood damage.[66] Affected by displacement and ongoing efforts to rebuild after the hurricane, New Orleans reorganized its entire education scheme. As of August 2014, there were eighty-three schools, seventy-six of which were charter schools, most of which were under a new school system: the Recovery School District.[67]

In the Crescent City, these monumental shifts have come with new rules, but old attitudes about how to treat Black girls. This was of particular concern to eighteen-year-old Gina in New Orleans, who felt that adults in her school were inclined to "talk to you any ol' kind of way"—which triggered her own "bad behavior."

"One time I was in the computer lab," she said. "So I raised my hand, and I'm like . . . 'Can I go to the restroom?' He said, 'Yeah, go 'head. You're gonna get your education in the hallway anyway.' So I'm like, 'What?' Like, I clicked out . . . I clicked out."

Suggesting to Gina that her education was "in the hallway" elicited the same reaction that it did for the girl in the Bay Area who was asked if she had come to school to learn. Gina's teacher's suggestion that she was not equipped to learn in the classroom and would be better served in the hallway was insulting; she responded using the tools she had available to her at that moment.

"Did you curse at him?" I asked.

She laughed and said, "Yeah . . . I said I was going to call my mama. He said, 'Call your mama, 'cause we can get it on too. I don't care! I don't care!' So I called my mama. My mama came up there and then it was, 'See, 'cause I ain't even say it like that . . .' You know, the whole script done flipped once my mama came up there."

"I feel like teachers try to be on the same level with teenagers sometimes," fifteen-year-old Francine said. "Sometimes you need to just understand that you're the adult. Like, let them say what they have to say, and you handle it like an adult. That's why I don't like certain teachers like that. That's why they get attitude, because they try to come back at you. Like, you're not going to seem cool, you're just going to seem immature and childish, and I'm not going to want to learn from you because you're trying to be on the same level as me and I don't want that. And then they want to be, 'Oh, I'm the teacher, you got to listen to me' . . . If you're going to be a teacher, be a *teacher.*"

Gina and Francine were not the only girls to express feeling triggered by their instructors. In discussions in New Orleans, Chicago, New York, Boston, Northern and Southern California, and other places where I have spoken with girls about "bad" behavior, Black girls have shared that their "attitude" is often a reaction to feeling disrespected. At times that reaction is verbal, and at other times the reaction is physical. However, it is important to understand these reactions in context.

People who have been harmed are the ones who harm others. When Black girls are perceived to be lashing out against others and themselves, what's happening can't be understood without an illumination of what brought them to that place. While teacher-student relationships are paramount and teachers taking time to know their students as whole people can make all the difference, not every teacher or school official can possibly be expected to be familiar with the particular journeys and backgrounds of each student. What can (and should) be developed and nurtured in educational settings, but almost never is, is a deeper awareness of the numerous social factors—related to race, gender, sexuality, disability status, or other identities—that have the power to trigger Black girls and shape their interactions with people in schools. Every girl is unique, but understanding widely shared experiences connected to structural forces bigger than us all would go a long way toward supporting the success and education of Black girls.

In my conversations with girls and young women across the country, it became clear Black girls interpreted their attitude not as a stagnant expression of anger and dissatisfaction. Rather, it lived along a continuum of responses to disrespectful or degrading triggers in their lives—many of which were present in their learning environments. From the hundreds of scenarios that were collected as part of this exploration, specific themes emerged about what was triggering an "attitude" among Black girls. Most common was the notion that an "attitude" was provoked by incidents of disrespect. In other words, these girls saw the "attitude" as a response to suggestions (overt or implicit) that their identity was an inferior one. This was shared with me in different cities, by very different young women between the ages of fifteen and twenty-three, but the theme was consistent.

"She's Slow. What's Wrong with Her?"
For Shai in Chicago, it was the suggestion that she was not smart.

"[My school is] predominantly White," she said. "Okay, I'm terrible in math. So when little Suzie gets the question wrong, it's like, "Aww . . . you got the question wrong." It's funny. When I get a question wrong, it's like, "Oh, she's slow. What's wrong with her?" I get so angry, number one, because I already told them I'm bad at math. Number two, because I'm not slow. Like, don't call me slow at all. I take my education seriously. Do not call me slow.

That's why I'm at school, to learn. . . . That triggers it. It does not only make me want to fight them, it makes me want to . . . it makes me want to ask them, why would they say something like that? The fact that I'm the only Black kid in the school, it's like, 'Oh, are we back in the 1950s now?' "

Shai's identity as "the only Black kid in the school" produced a degree of anxiety that she would be received as embodying a lower status than her White counterparts. To her, being called "slow" was a euphemism for "inferior." Her admitted insecurity about not being good at math could be a true admission of weakness or a reflection of dominant social ideas (which she might have internalized over time) that generally position girls, especially Black girls, as not being good at math. Still, Shai's negative reaction is more than just a response to the teasing of her peers. It is also in response to the *absence* of teasing when her White counterpart gets the problem wrong. Suzie is allowed to make mistakes without being labeled as "slow," but Shai is not. It is the unfairness that triggers Shai, not just her personal frustration about the difficulty of math.

"She Tried to Put Me in the Corner . . . I'm Just Outspoken"

For Malaika in the Bay Area, it was the suggestion that she should be quiet in the face of perceived injustice.

"I always get suspended . . . [ever since] the first grade," she said. "I told my teacher, 'Don't yell at me,' but she kept talking. I was like, 'Can you call my mom? You're yelling at me and I don't want you yelling at me.' . . . After they got off the phone with my mom, I still had an attitude. She [tried] to put me out of the class, so I got mad.

"I just kept talking," Malaika continued. "Told her to shut up . . . and then she [tried] to put me in the corner. I'm not going in nobody corner. . . . She tried to put me in the corner. I'm not going in no corner! [Then my mom came up to the school] and had a talk with the teacher. . . . I ended up in the principal's office,

doing my work for three days. . . . I just got a smart mouth. I don't
be meaning for it to come out like that, but if there's something on
my mind and my heart, I just say it. Even if it don't got nothing to
do with me, if one student's getting treated unfair from the next
student, I'ma raise my hand and put my input in. You know, like,
'Why'd you do that?' They'll be like, 'You is not the teacher, why
are you talking?' . . .

"I'm just outspoken. . . . They're always telling us to voice our
opinions, but then when we voice our opinion, we're going to get
in trouble. So that's irritating. And I think they're just mad 'cause
I'm telling the truth, you know?"

Malaika's narrative reflects the complicated nature of speaking
one's truth as a Black girl in the United States. The messages that
she received regarding her duty to speak up and the reactions to
her resistance to an oppressive silence or humiliation were confusing. They would be for any of us! As with Shai, the absence of
fairness underscores Malaika's desire to speak up, but it was her
resistance to being marginalized, to being physically placed in the
corner, that set her off. Malaika was aware of how being placed in
a corner is both a punishment for individual behavior and also a
warning to other children about what might happen to them if
they engage in similar behavior. Malaika was fundamentally trying not to become the symbol of "bad behavior"—particularly
since she felt that she was speaking her truth. It is the idea that her
truth has no place in the classroom that triggers Malaika.

"The Moment You Call Me a Bitch, I Will Lose It"
For Dee in Chicago, it was being teased about her physical disability, laughed at, or called a "bitch."

"There are several things that trigger me," she said. "If I get
something wrong in class and people laugh at me or ask me if I'm
dumb or say, 'Oh, you have a disability so you're not supposed to
be in this class, you're not smart . . . blah blah blah,' well, the next
day I might get something right. You might see me get an A or a B

on a test and now you want to talk to me to ask me to help you. No, I'm not helping you. . . .

"Another thing is if someone calls me a 'bitch' instead of Dee. You either call me Dee or by my nickname, or you don't call me anything. Because the moment you call me a 'bitch,' seriously or prank, I will lose it. I will get very quiet at first and then I can feel my face turning red, like seriously turning red. My eyes will get bigger and I'll have tightness in my arms and both of my legs and then I'll start yelling. I'll scream [and] do anything. People will say, 'Oh, she's crazy, so get away from her.' It's like, 'Okay, you can call me crazy, but don't mess with me. Don't trigger me because I will curse back at you even though it's immature and inappropriate. I'll just keep going and going. I'll never shut up. That's just how I am.'"

Dee was aware of her vulnerability and the stigma that followed her as a Black female student with a physical disability. Her trigger was ridicule—whether it was being laughed at, called by something other than her name, or regarded as less intelligent than her peers. No child wants to be teased in this way. Her hostile reaction to the teasing from her peers is a predictable reaction from someone who may have been conditioned to make it clear that she will command respect. It's the assault on her dignity, the disrespect, that triggers Dee.

"I Got a Smart Mouth"

For Stacy in the Bay Area, it was the suggestion that she was weak.

"I'm a fighter," she said. "When I was in elementary, this girl said I couldn't play double-dutch with her. So I got mad at her and I pulled her rope, like if I can't jump here, nobody else going to jump here. So, so, um . . . she started chasing me. I'm thinking she playing with me. Then I said, 'Hold on, let me stop,' 'cause I'm not scared of her. So I stopped. She [was] tryin' to, like, run up on me, feel me? I just took off on her. Afterward, 'cause her hair was ugly, I just pulled her hair . . . and all of her hair came out. Like, all of it. But, I didn't really do it that hard. I mean, all her hair came out. I was, like, in the third grade or the fourth—and everybody was like, 'You going to have to go to the office. You 'bout to get in trouble.' I [was] like, 'I don't care.'

"But they should have let me come back to school, 'cause I was hecka young. Why would they expel me? And then I got expelled out of [another] middle school 'cause . . . like I'm a problem child, so every school I go to, I have problems. . . . Also, see, I know how to dress hecka good. . . . Like, I have fresh shoes on. And then, like some drunk, they'll step on my shoes or whatever. I get hecka mad, like . . . and they don't be sayin' excuse me. Like somebody bump me. That's hecka rude. I'll be hecka mad, like, 'You ain't going to say excuse me?' So then I'm like, 'You can say excuse yourself' . . .'cause I got a smart mouth. So I'm like, 'You can say excuse yourself,' but if they [don't] want to say it, I just take off on them 'cause I'm hecka mad."

Stacy took pride in her fighting ability. A competitive spirit, she enjoyed a challenge, but she—like so many other girls—was conflating her fear of being perceived as weak or a "punk" with her identity as a "problem child." That any child would refer to him- or herself as a problem is heartbreaking. Our most basic hope for children should be that they see themselves as sacred and loved, not problematic. She drew her "respect" from outward manifestations of prestige—looking "cute" or fighting—but she was also responding to her fear of not being seen or highly regarded in some way. Stacy framed her behavior as a tendency to get in trouble, but I see her trigger as anything (or anyone) that might interfere with her own visibility politics. Stacy was triggered by a fear of being ignored.

"I Had to Defend Myself"

For Paris in New Orleans, it was the assault on her human dignity.

"I didn't have physical altercations up until probably my freshman year in high school," she said. "That's when I learned that the playground was a lot different and I was dealing with people with different mentalities and stuff. I never did mostly have a problem, but my thing was different because I transitioned through school. So I started my transition at sixteen, and I went all the way through graduation year still transitioning . . . but of course, further along my transition than I was at sixteen. So it was a lot different because once you became a junior and a senior—of course I was at the school all four years, so a lot of people had got to know who I was . . . so it wasn't nothing new to those particular students. But I did always have problems with the freshmen that were coming into the school because now they're new to the school, they're new to me as well, and now when I assume that everyone had gotten used to Paris, here come these new individuals that are just coming out of middle school, fresh out of middle school, and don't know how high school operates and stuff like that. So I had to punch a few people down within school. I always had to make an example out of one or two people. Eventually, the rest of the freshman class realized, 'Well, maybe Paris is not the one to play with' . . .

"It was mostly because, again, mostly feeling like I had to defend myself," Paris continued. "Because my mama always told me, like, people do to you what you *allow* them to do to you. So maybe I mix-messaged what my mama was telling me, but you know . . . well, then I'm not going to *allow* them to do *anything.* That's the mentality I grew up [with]. Don't get me wrong, my mama is very wise. She taught me a lot, but me as Paris, I took the message a little too far. I put my own little twist on it. . . . I just thought I had to fight. My mama gave me the freedom to go and fight and that's what I did. My mama gave me a green light, like, 'You better fight . . . don't you let nobody do this or that to you.' So I kinda, like, waited . . . I wasn't the type to go start mess, even though my mama gave the permission that it was okay to fight. I never did went looking for it, but God, did it come knocking at my front door!"

The permission to fight—granted by both Paris and her mother—was a matter of personal safety. It's important to note that Paris was responding to bullying. That her physical safety was in danger is a statement both about the prevailing culture of oppression around her gender identity and about the absence of protection in schools for students who are transitioning their gender during these adolescent years. Paris was triggered by her inability to discover and live in her own body without judgment.

Disciplining Appearance

In September 2013, seven-year-old Tiana Parker was sent home from school in Tulsa, Oklahoma, for wearing dreadlocks. Her small charter school had a dress code, which stated, "Hairstyles such as dreadlocks, afros, mohawks, and other faddish hairstyles are unacceptable."[68] A few months later that year, twelve-year-old Vanessa VanDyke in Orlando, Florida, faced expulsion from her parochial school for wearing her hair in a large Afro.[69] Together, these cases raised a collective eyebrow among girls whose hair is no stranger to being the object of discussion, regulation, and, too often, ridicule. While neither of these girls was ultimately expelled for her hairstyle, because of decisions made either by the parents or by the school, these cases elevated the importance of protecting Black girls from policies that threaten to undermine their ability to learn in good schools simply because of *who they are*—not for something they have done.

The politicization (and vilification) of thick, curly, and kinky hair is an old one. Characterizations of kinky hair as unmanageable, wild, and ultimately "bad hair" are all signals (spoken and unspoken) that Black girls are inferior and unkempt when left in their natural state. Dress codes in the United States are arbitrary, and in general they are sexist and reinforce the practice of slut shaming. They can also reinforce internalized oppression about the quality of natural hairstyles on people of African descent.

While personal taste may lead many of us away from wearing leggings or dreadlocks at school, any school policy that is designed to keep girls from being "too distracting" for boys or presenting in ways that are deemed too ethnic is at minimum sexist and inappropriate.

Though often used to further objectify Black girls or police their sexuality, which I discuss in Chapter 3, school dress codes have also become tools for disciplining Black girls. Rules about how they wear their hair and clothes become grounds for punishment, rather than tools to establish a uniform student presentation. Young women in New Orleans attested to this.

"I was in the eleventh [grade]," said Gina. "They made you leave school because you didn't have on the right shoes, you didn't have on a belt . . . for real, you're going to stop my education because I don't have this stuff?"

"Tattoos," Nicole, who was also educated in New Orleans schools, chimed in.

"Because it's a distraction," Gina said, mimicking the voice of an adult. "It's a *distraction*."

I asked the group to describe what they had observed as schools' responses when girls arrived in clothes that did not adhere to the dress code.

"They turn you around," Gina said.

"It's like no other way you can get in class," Nicole agreed.

Dress codes do more than slut-shame Black girls. They marginalize and criminalize them. They cast them as deviant and reinforce social ideas about Black girls' identity in a way that can be very destructive. Getting turned away from school for not wearing the "proper" clothing—however that is defined—feels unconscionable in a society that, at least on the surface, declares that education is a priority. This practice is primarily about maintaining a social order that renders girls subject to the approving or disapproving gaze of adults. It is grounded in respectability politics that have very little to do with education and more to do with socialization. So when Black girls respond to this treatment with cries of discrimination, it's important to see them as disruptors of oppression, not as defiant, willfully or otherwise.

The culture of zero tolerance has seeped into nearly every corner of school discipline, creating rigid, unforgiving policies aimed at a demographic—kids—whose existence is defined by growth, development, and change. Recall that Black girls were not at the center of the debate on public safety when zero-tolerance policies were being passed, so little thought went into how these new policies might uniquely affect them. Black girls' "attitudes" and "defiant" behaviors were often in response to feeling disrespected—by institutions that constructed conditions that facilitate failure (e.g., increased surveillance, no recess, and punitive discipline policies) and by individuals who triggered them with words and/or actions.

While observing at Small Alternative High in California, I watched teachers skillfully engage girls who might have otherwise been dismissed as "throwing shade" or as having an "attitude problem" under other circumstances.

In one instance, a girl let out a few sighs and then settled her head comfortably into her folded arms on the table, resting there for approximately five minutes. Finally a teacher walked past her and asked what was wrong. She lifted her head and shared details about being "tired and hungry." The exchange between the student and her teacher was neither contentious nor judgmental.

The teacher, a Black woman, simply stated that the young woman's expressed fatigue was "all in [her] mind," to which the student replied, "Really? I thought it was my body."

I watched as the teacher pursed her lips, put a hand on her hip, and stared at the girl. In return, the girl raised her eyebrows and shrugged. On the surface, it appeared to be an "attitude" for an "attitude"—but it was more than the stereotypical, negative perceptions associated with the expressions of Black girls and women. This was a slightly comical exchange of information, and from what I observed, it was based on a preestablished relationship in which the student trusted this teacher. A less attuned, empathic teacher could have easily caused the interaction to devolve into conflict and perhaps result in dismissal from the classroom. Yet the exchange, while playful, resulted in the young woman getting a snack, voicing her frustrations about being required to focus on her work, and then returning to her desk. No harm, no foul.

Across the country, Black girls have shared narratives that reflect their own understanding of the rules that push them from school and the behaviors that have rendered them increasingly vulnerable to the expanded use of exclusionary discipline. The examples in this chapter also show how Black girls often interpret responses to their perceived attitude and have normalized a disregard of Black femininity. The experiences related in this chapter have mostly focused on attitudes and violent behaviors as expressions of how girls adapt to this disregard. Just as common, perhaps even more so, is adapting to a disregard associated with the sexual and gender expression of Black girls.

3

JEZEBEL IN THE CLASSROOM

Tra-la-la boom-di-yay
I met a boy today
He gave me 50 cents
To go behind the fence
He knocked me on the ground
And pulled my panties down
He counted 1-2-3
And stuck it into me
My mother was surprised
To see my belly rise
My father jumped for joy
Because it was a boy

See, my boyfriend, he's older than me," said fourteen-year-old Diamond. "He's twenty-five. He's very older than me."

On most evenings—and even during some days—Diamond could be seen strolling the streets for sex work or spending time with a much older man, the man she referred to as her "boyfriend." For Diamond, the time that she was spending out of school was important to her ability to maintain her relationship with this man, and a critical part of her participation in the sex industry.

"When you're a prostitute, 'cause I have been one for a couple of months now, like, when you're a prostitute, you *gotta* stop going to school because it's something that you have to do all day. And if you don't do it all day, you gotta hang out with your boyfriend all day, or like your pimp all day. You have to. You have to. All day. And if you don't . . . you could still go to school for like, a couple of months, you could still get your education . . . that's if he lets you. But usually, the girls that's in the sex industry stop going to school."

If he lets you.

Diamond was aware of the power dynamic between her and her pimp. For Diamond, who floated between cities in California, there was often no personal choice regarding whether or not to attend school. Under the duress of this older man, she followed orders. Though she was in contact with the juvenile justice system as a result of "prostitution," there is no such thing as a child prostitute (more on this point later). In this relationship, only he had the ability to determine whether or not she attended school—and most of the time, according to Diamond, she had to stay with him.

One day, after feeling alienated and tired of constantly being challenged to fight, Diamond wrote in bold letters on the wall: "I hate the bitches at this school." Administrators and teachers at Diamond's school had missed that she was being trafficked and that, consequently, the decision whether or not to attend school was often not her own. They had also missed that other girls were teasing her after one of them had spotted Diamond "on the track." According to Diamond, the writing on the wall resulted in her immediate expulsion.

Diamond, who had previously been in contact with the criminal legal system, had been ordered by the juvenile court to attend school. The expulsion rendered her without a permanent learning community. Without a school to attend, Diamond was in violation of this order. She resorted to being with her "boyfriend" all day, every day.

"Girls are ride or die for their boyfriend," Diamond said. "So [the police] try to get her too. . . . Usually, Black girls, they have older boyfriends . . . 'cause their boyfriends have a car and they hanging out all day and driving around and stuff like that."

Diamond's eyes were wide and flanked with cascading false eyelashes. Combined with her long hair weave, they might suggest that she was a little older than she actually was. But when she smiled, there was a youthful quality. Her skin, her teeth, her mannerisms—they belonged to a child, one who had been through too much, too soon. After a few months of truancy and being "on the run," law enforcement finally found her. She was arrested and confined to a secure detention facility.

"The pimp or 'boyfriend' that is keeping you from going to school, does he have an education?" I asked.

"Mm-hmm," Diamond said, nodding. "My boyfriend, he graduated from college." She looked proud.

"So why wouldn't he support that for you?" I asked.

"Well, he tried to . . . like tell me, go back . . . go back home. But I stayed with him because I love him . . . Now look at me," she said, looking around the juvenile detention classroom where we were seated. Then she collected her thoughts, raised her head, and said, "My boyfriend's different."

Different, I thought. *Really?*

Her eyes really tried to convince me—and herself—until they started to well up.

"Well, okay," I said, in an admittedly halfhearted tone. "But in general, if you see a dude who's got his education, but he's like, 'No, you can't have yours,' how does that make you feel?"

"I don't know," she said, lowering her eyes to the table.

"Do you think that's fair?" I asked.

"Well, not really. But like, I've known girls who still go to school and do the sex industry. In the beginning, she'll probably still go to school for a couple of months, but when the students start find-

ing out she's doing it . . . 'cause people find out. . . . They're on the
bus. They see you on the track."

"Like people from your school can see you?"

"Yeah," she said. "After [kids] find out, [girls] just stop going to
school 'cause they feel like, 'Oh, nobody needs to know.' . . . They
see your face. They know you."

What Diamond had to say about what keeps girls like her out
of school was insightful. Her own experience with bullying certainly informed her reaction to school—and why she might think
that it was necessary to avoid seeing other students who may have
spotted her "working." My conversations with other girls who were
victims of sex trafficking revealed that the primary motivating
factor for being in the sex industry was the need for money. For
many girls who were actively "on the street," school stopped being
a priority, especially if they had an older man reinforcing the idea
that her greatest attribute was her sexuality. If a girl attends school,
there is another influence in her life. In general, it's a game of control, and only one person can have it: the pimp. Diamond's use of
the phrase "if he lets you" was evidence of that. She, like other
girls I'd spoken with, was relatively clear that in addition to not
having full control over her time when she's on the street, there
was a financial incentive—something school doesn't immediately
provide.

"It's the money," Diamond said. " 'Cause we think like, 'Oh . . .
if I go out to work today, I can get this, this, and this. If I go out to
work today, I can get my nails and stuff done.' . . . It's usually about
clothes and hair done and stuff."

Diamond, like other girls who come from poverty, understood
that education is a tool for economic success, but she was also feeling pressured to find a way out of poverty sooner rather than later,
one of many outcomes associated with being prematurely cast as
an adult. Along with "working" came an immediate gratification
of material goods that otherwise seemed far out of reach—hair

and nails done, new shoes or clothes, and in some cases a much better living environment. Staying in school, even if it could produce these things later in life, required a longer investment of time in order to reap these sorts of benefits. Children from middle-class or higher-income families often take for granted the social and material investments (manicures, new shoes, new clothes, extra-curricular activities) that reflect the inherent commercialism of a capitalist society. These are influences that reach all children. Choosing a life on the street is ultimately about survival—and that's what schools are up against. When girls in the sex trade are removed from school or sent the signal that their presence in school is problematic, they are being handed over to predators. Essentially, schools are throwing them away.

In New Orleans, where girls are trafficked in strip clubs, commercial-front brothels, truck stops, hotels, and over the Internet, Black girls are at increased risk of sexual exploitation.[1] The first-ever report on human trafficking in Louisiana revealed there was a significant increase in the reported number of sex trafficking incidents between 2012 and 2013.[2] In New Orleans, a city that is 59 percent Black, Paris understood Diamond's plight and the similar dangers of being trafficked for sex in Louisiana versus California.[3]

"I was out in California and they have this one [area]," Paris said. "That's where a lot of the girls that perform sex work hang out at, and I tell you, it was just so mind-blowing to me to see that not only were they out there like damn near twenty-four hours around the clock, but how *young* a lot of those girls were that were trafficked. Because one thing that California does have is pimps. That is real. Houston, Texas, has pimps. They are real. In New Orleans, most girls that are trafficked are trafficked *through* our town . . . the girls that work here in New Orleans are [mostly] independent workers. But for the most part, those girls in California, I have witnessed it, I have outreached to a lot of those girls on the stroll, and they are nervous to even talk to you, because their [pimps] watch other [pimps'] girls while he's out. Just like the prostitutes hang together, the [pimps] hang together. They know whose girl belongs to who, how many they have out there working, so it ranges from the ages of ten, eleven, twelve all the way up to fortysomething years old. . . . Even girls that's twenty-three or thirty . . . 'if he lets me,' that is the thing."

There it was again: *if he lets me.*

A recent report, *The Sexual Abuse to Prison Pipeline*, highlighted the way in which girls, particularly girls of color, are criminalized as a result of their sexual and physical abuse. Nationwide, girls who are victims of sex trafficking are routinely in contact with the criminal legal system for truancy and placed in detention and/or child welfare facilities.[4] This report was an important contribution to the public narrative on pathways to confinement and incarceration and broadened the lens on what has otherwise been a narrow critique of discipline practices. It has become commonplace to talk about truancy, discipline, and bullying as ways that children are pushed out of school, but quite often ignored is how sexual violence can also become a pathway to confinement. We flag chronic absenteeism as an indicator of underperformance and alienation from school, but not necessarily as a pathway to (and symptom of) exploitation, delinquency, and incarceration. Under these circumstances, it's not a stretch for a girl to see only what her pimp or much older "boyfriend" sees. Diamond may have bragged about her boyfriend's college degree, but just like sex traffickers, she perceives limited options for herself. The lucrative nature of the commercial sex industry provides a perverse and immediate financial incentive for sex traffickers, regardless of their educational attainment, to keep a girl or young woman out of school. This manipulated worldview often furthers her exploitation and facilitates a dynamic in which she is neither a dropout nor a pushout but instead a pullout—not of her own volition, but rather by someone who is already "out" himself or herself.

The Pullout: Sexually Exploited Children

Prostitution is the trade or sale of sex for money. For as long as our memory will carry us, terms such as "prostitute," "whore" or "ho," "hooker," "streetwalker," "harlot," and "lady of the night" have been used to describe women who participate in the sale of sex. But here's the thing: children cannot be prostitutes. Children cannot legally consent to sex, which means that when they participate in the sale of sex they are being sexually trafficked and exploited, usually by much older men—and sometimes by women, teenagers, and even society at large (the use of women's and girls' bodies to sell other products such as apparel, alcohol, or chewing gum). Any and all of these may coerce girls into selling their bodies.

Girls who are commercially sexually exploited or victims of sex trafficking are children under the age of eighteen who are coerced into selling their bodies in exchange for money. In the United States, racial disparities in trafficking are pronounced. In terms of what's reported, 40 percent of sex trafficking victims in the United States are Black.[5] In New Orleans, the Bay Area, and Chicago, the reported number of Black girls being sexually trafficked is much higher. For example, the Los Angeles County Probation Department reported in 2015 that 92 percent of commercially sexually exploited girls in the county are Black. Despite ongoing legislative and legal interventions, there are inadequate (to put it lightly) educational interventions and partnerships to interrupt the pushout—and pullout—of girls in these areas who are being sexually exploited, or who are at high risk of being trafficked.

In the Bay Area, where Black girls are disproportionately represented among juvenile court cases involving commercially sexually exploited children, there are a host of services and programs that are designed to interrupt the likelihood that they will return to the sex industry. In Alameda County, particularly Oakland— which is considered the epicenter of a child sex trafficking triangle between San Francisco and West Contra Costa counties—the majority of girls who are trafficked are between the ages of thirteen and fifteen, though some are younger.[6] The Bay Area has a sophisticated and growing network of service providers who continue to develop responses to the needs of trafficked girls. Still, the voices and influence of educators, who quite often are uniquely positioned to prevent the start or repetition of harmful cycles, are underdeveloped or completely nonexistent.

Sixteen-year-old Jennifer in the Bay Area was among the forgotten.

She had not been to school in three years when we spoke in 2013 and had failed out of the seventh grade. She claimed that she was so busy "running the streets" and bouncing to and from multiple foster homes that she never found a rhythm in school. In fact, her pattern of school attendance had become so irregular that she had developed a dislike for school and decided to avoid it altogether.

"I didn't know anything," Jennifer said. "I was in foster care and I went to hecka foster homes. They put me out of sixth grade, and the next school, they put me in seventh grade. That's what messed me up. So then I had to flunk seventh grade."

As a child in foster care, she had been sent to live with a family in the San Joaquin Valley. Though we did not discuss the conditions within her birth family that led to the decision to place her with a foster family, she did mention that she had other "family" influences—none of which were positive—that ultimately impacted her decision not to go to school.

Jennifer was a "runner," which meant that she often ran away from her foster care placements and other locations that she considered threatening. When asked why she was running, she just shrugged and replied that she "didn't like it." On the surface, that might look like she was running away out of defiance, but experience had taught me better. For years, I had heard justice system workers describe the conditions that led girls to run from their court-assigned residential placements in detention centers, group

homes, shelters, or private homes.* Sometimes these girls were described as "incorrigible," "manipulative," or simply drug-addicted,
without explanation. Anecdotes from Black girls revealed a different perspective. They had run away from these places because of
experiences like being forced to wash their hair every day and/or
use hair products that were not designed for Black girls' natural
hair texture. While these conditions may seem minor, especially if
brought up in legal proceedings, to the Black girls who told these
stories they were "deal breakers," not only because these hygienic
mandates were inconsistent with cultural norms for Black hair
care (and certainly off-limits for girls who wore protective hairstyles like braids or artificial hair) but also, and mostly, because it
was a trigger for them—a signal that they were not truly welcomed
in these alternative living spaces. Some girls ran away from their
placement after being triggered by the actions of other girls in
these spaces.

In the course of a group discussion in a juvenile hall, one girl
offered that she had run away from her group home because she
was the only Black girl there and was being bullied by the other
girls. Still other girls I've spoken with over the years offered their
own explanations for why they ran.

"Why'd you run from *your* foster home?" I asked Jennifer.

"Because, like, they wasn't treating me right . . . I had a foster
dad and . . . he knew I was a prostitute . . . and he was like, if he

* The Department of Justice defines residential placement as "secure and
nonsecure residential placement facilities that house juvenile offenders, defined as persons younger than 21 who are held in a residential setting as a result
of some contact with the justice system (they are charged with or adjudicated
for an offense). This encompasses both status offenders and delinquent offenders, including those who are either temporarily detained by the court or committed after adjudication for an offense." Statistics on residential placement do
not include data for prisons, jails, federal facilities, or those exclusively for drug
or mental health treatment or for abused/neglected youth.

was a pimp, he'd recruit me. If he was a john, he would date me . . . and I don't know . . . they just didn't treat me right."

They didn't treat me right.

"So did you feel safe?" I asked.

"I didn't like it . . . and they, like, talked about me. Told me I'm stupid and never going to be anything. And I believed it, and so that's when I went back to prostitution."

Jennifer agreed that education was important—even if she had missed years of school while simply trying to survive.

"I think education is important, because nobody can take that from you," she said. "Even if I'm in jail, nobody can take it from me, so I want to be somebody in jail. That's why I'm going to work hard. . . . I got kicked out of foster care. My family . . . I don't really know my family like that."

"How'd you get kicked out of foster care?" I asked.

"'Cause I kept running from my group homes. I kept going back to prostitution. I kept doing hecka stuff, so like, once I got back [in juvenile hall], they kicked me out of foster care."

I wondered if anyone had ever come looking for her. Jennifer had been out of school for three years, hustling to survive in a world that saw her as expendable. How could her extended absence from school pass under the radar for so long?

"When you were enrolled in school, did the school or district come looking for you?"

"No, my foster mom didn't even know," Jennifer said. "My school never called her."

I looked at her face. She had a persistent furrow in her brow, which made it appear that she was frowning or squinting even when she was not. A youthful innocence remained in her spirit, even though her eyes knew a lot more than her age suggested.

"What was it like trying to manage your foster care and go to school?" I asked.

"I didn't feel supported at all. It was hard," she said. "Plus, the foster kids . . . Like, I fought a lot and my foster mom didn't do anything. So I had a lot of fights. . . . It was just hard."

Managing school and life was difficult for Jennifer, who mentioned that she often felt that the only person she could rely on was herself. Her independence is what also led to her conflict with other girls, and in some instances her suspension from school for skipping class or fighting.

"What are some of the things that would start the fights?" I asked.

"Uh . . . a lot of people didn't like me because . . . you know how some kids don't like you because of the way that you dress? And I used to dress raggedy because I didn't have anything. Like, my foster parents would buy me shoes from [a budget store]. So I would fight them because they would talk about me."

Then she mentioned that she had once been in a gang.

"It's just . . . it's a squad, not a gang, really," she said.

"Okay," I said. "Did they ever encourage you to go to school?"

"Mm-mm," she said, shaking her head.

I understood that the "squad" had not encouraged her to go to school, but wondered if that was really at the heart of what prolonged her sexual exploitation.

"No," she said. "I got into prostitution because the guy that raped me, he forced me on the track. Basically, I didn't go willingly at first, but ever since he did that to me, my whole life just changed, and that was at twelve years old. Ever since then, my life's been off-track."

She spoke the words with such direct honesty that I suspected she had told this story before. Her youth was obscured by a very painful and complicated past. Her large wide eyes continued to squint as she discussed her struggle to learn and to acquire skills that could help her earn a living without having sex.

"Has anyone worked with you to try to help you get what you need to get back in school or talked to you about how you can make the transition off of the street?" I asked.

"No. Nobody really helped me. Honestly, it took me about four years to get back on track. I'm just now getting back on track. So all this stuff I go through, I go through myself. I encourage myself."

Jennifer sighed as she retold her story of personal pain and struggle for redemption. The persistence of her frown when she spoke was a subtle cue that she did not like what she was saying or that she was at least aware of how it might sound to someone meeting her for the first time. I held no judgment against her, and I let her know that. The safety of our space mattered, and I really wanted to better understand how her story might inform ways to rebuild a path from confinement to school for her and for other girls in similar situations. We talked about how being sexually exploited was a significant factor both in her school failure and in her attempt to recover from other traumatic experiences in her life.

"I did it 'cause I didn't have nobody. I did it because I hated myself. I did it because I didn't love myself. I did it because I never had anything. So when I was hustling, I would hustle hard to get what I need and want . . . to make myself look good and feel better. So I started selling my body."

"Was there anything about that that kept you out of school, though?"

"Yeah . . . money. It's just great. When I hustle, I ho by myself. Like, it's . . . better. Like, you know some of these young girls when they hustle, they hustle with they friends or hang out with their friends. Like, I don't know. I felt like a businesswoman. You know?"

When Jennifer detached from the man who raped her, she began working for herself. She needed money not only for herself but also for her child, who was a toddler when I met Jennifer. In fact, she credited pregnancy as her best educational experience.

"Being a mother is a blessing," she said. "And it taught me how to have patience, 'cause I really don't have patience."

Parenting teens often face tremendous obstacles to completing a high school education, but more often than not, girls interpret their parental responsibilities as an incentive to perform better. While these girls are plagued by social narratives that warn of an end to their lives if they have a child as a teenager, they also understand their heightened responsibility and make great attempts to rise to the occasion.

Notwithstanding their resilient attitudes, earning a diploma can be a difficult process for girls who have become pregnant during their high school years, particularly given the hurdles associated with it. Some schools unlawfully bar pregnant girls from attending school or discriminate against them in other ways, including penalizing their success or ridiculing them.[7] When girls are able to attend school, they often face the additional hurdle of finding child care or recuperating credits that were missed.

When I spoke with Terri, another girl from the Bay Area, about her experiences as a teen parent, she offered that school remained a priority for her, even if it was difficult to go every day.

"I missed some days [at school] because I have a baby, and I had to find a babysitter. Sometimes I can, sometimes I can't . . . People [at my school] help you. . . . Like, they was helping me find a day care to where I could take [my daughter], and stuff like that. It was people there that were helping me. . . . So I just try to get my work and then go home, but sometimes I'd rather be at school. It seems like you can't do anything without school. You can't get out of this mess that we in unless you go to school."

Terri was also coming to terms with school attendance as a condition of her probation. The juvenile court, understanding the value of education, had prioritized school attendance in her district, which meant that truancy was no longer just a decision not to go to school—it was also a violation of her agreement with the court.

"That's the main thing that they look at," Terri said. "If you go to school or not. That's one of the first things that they look at . . . they want to know, what are you doing besides . . . you know . . . doing the stuff that you're already in trouble for. They want to know if you're going to school. Are you there? Are you on time? That's one of the main things that they do push here. Go to school. If you don't, then you're just going to be right back [in juvenile hall]."

Contact with the criminal legal system might be the first time a girl has access to medical screening. For some, this experience may reveal a host of health conditions that affect their ability to return to school, including pregnancy. However, being in juvenile hall or other forms of detention is about more than gaining access to health care. Just as there are relationships that make girls vulnerable to contact with the criminal legal system, there are also a number of relationships within the justice system that keep girls from reconnecting with school and performing well when they are there.

Going Back to School

School administrators are often unsure how to play an effective role in interrupting the pullout of sexually exploited girls from schools. Though many teachers and school leaders understand what a challenge it is to compete with the lure of money and the adult influences that place children at risk of harm, they have also largely been absent from the public discourse on how to keep our girls from becoming throwaway children. For many educators, classroom deportment drives much of their approach toward these girls. Julio, the principal of a California high school, shared his perspective on the matter.

"A lot of it is behavior," he said. "But the behavior comes from first and foremost a lack of success in school, a lack of socialization for one thing. They are not socialized properly. They never had that experience."

Julio continued to describe how a particular girl, a Black girl who was being introduced to a class as a new student, displayed behavioral issues that complicated the school's ability to respond to her needs.

"We had a girl who would just act out with one of our teachers," he said. "As soon as she got there, and we couldn't figure it out, and so the teacher asked for her file and started reading over it, and she had a long case of issues in school and there have been issues of abuse, and one of the triggers for whatever reason was older white women. The teacher was an older white woman, and it set her off."

"So what was your approach?" I asked.

"Because she has special ed, because she has an IEP, I'm going to bring in somebody to work with her one-on-one, and so I did do that. We will work with her one-on-one in a special class, and [the specialist] worked with her a couple of periods and tried to transition her. So what we have seen is a big improvement, actually work is getting done, and then the acting out in the other classroom is not there anymore. So we are not where she can be in a classroom with a teacher yet, and you know logistically I can't replace the teacher, but what I can do is provide some outside support for her."

Still, this principal lamented, external supports and specialists require funding. "If a child isn't in school enough, then that child may get misdiagnosed," he continued. "That process takes time, but if the child is not there, it won't happen, so year after year it's compounded. . . . And then in the school sense too—when funding gets cut, then the kids ultimately suffer. Kids are resilient, and those that are on the college track are going to stay on the college track. It's the average kids that are going to suffer because of [a lack of] funding."

Public education remains one of the nation's most ripe environments for inequality. From Julio's perspective as a principal, chronic absenteeism made it difficult for the school to reach out to students who might have special learning needs. The structure of the learning environment made it difficult to develop innovative approaches for girls in trouble with the law, many of whom are also being trafficked. Indeed, though many of the girls in his school had a history of sex trafficking, he felt that there was little he could do to intervene. He did, however, feel that the school could be an important partner.

According to Jennifer, a special education student who was never able to fully develop her relationship with school, educators and other key stakeholders have to take a more proactive role in explaining to girls why education is so important to their development.

"Make them care more about their education," she said. "'Cause a lot of these girls don't think education is important, or why, like, 'What is education going to do for me?' It's going to do a lot for you. You have to go through a process to get what you want. Just like you have to hustle for a lot of money to get what you want, like the new Jordans or whatever, you got to go through that process of getting your money. Just like education."

In a separate conversation, Diamond agreed. When I asked her what might keep her in school, she replied, "Like, probably, more attention. More attention and providing of what I ask. Like, if I ask that I need something, it's not that I'm trying to annoy you. I'm trying to ask you for things that I really actually need."

"When you think about the other needs you have in your life," I said, "how can the school help you so that you don't have to do anything illegal to get it? What do you need to stay focused in school and doing what you've got to do?"

"I don't know about the other girls that's in the sex industry, but for me, like, I like to talk about it and get it out of my system. . . . I don't know, cry about it and stuff. I think that would help me better because, I don't know, I like to share."

Narrative is a powerful tool for learning and for rehabilitation. In Diamond's response and in Jennifer's call for a space that would allow her to talk through the importance of education were requests to rebuild a relationship—not just with individuals but with school as an institution.

I asked Diamond if there were things that could happen in the school environment or with teachers that might help her transition back into school smoothly. We talked about the potential for school-to-career programs that might help her understand the connections between her education and work. Like Jennifer, she felt making this connection was necessary, and particularly appealing to girls who have been trafficked.

"I think that would help. . . . I can't speak for nobody else. But like, I think that would help because, for some reason, for some kids, coming [to juvenile hall] won't help them . . . I probably need counseling. Like, I'm trying to get stronger, but my boyfriend . . . he's like, I don't know . . . it takes a while . . . I think I'm processing faster since I been here. I should have never done that. I'm not making that mistake again. That person wasn't right for me. I'm not taking that chance again. It's going to hurt *me* in the long run. It's not hurting him. He's free right now . . . while I'm sitting here locked up twenty-four hours."

Then, Diamond started to cry as she came to terms with having been abandoned by a man she depended on to care for her—a man who sold her body and who did not come to visit her while she was in detention. A man who she suspected had moved on. I consoled her but also let her sit with the realization that this man might not be what she expected.

"What kind of people do you need in your life, at school, to be successful?" I asked. "Like, what would your ideal counselor look like?"

"I just need somebody that is not there just to *listen*, but who actually *feels* me . . . who knows where I'm coming from and really understands. . . . Like, 'Oh, you been a prostitute, I feel you' . . . somebody like that. . . . Somebody that's going to be there when I need them, like . . . three times a week, four times a week. Like when I feel bad and stuff."

Regularly available counselors and therapists in school are critical to providing the type of emotional support that formerly trafficked girls need to heal from the pain and trauma that they have experienced. Otherwise, schools risk becoming a location where girls continue to experience harm. Diamond and I talked some more about how to avoid that.

"So, aside from a counselor who would be there, how do you think schools in general could better respond to Black girls in crisis?" I asked.

"Usually the teachers, like, will only connect with certain students that think they deserve more because they get straight A's. There's a reason why they're getting straight A's—because they're faster learners. Y'all [are] teaching them more, and they study more and they're getting more attention than the other kids. Like Black kids at home, we don't get that much attention. Our mother and dad are working. Our sister is taking care of us. Our auntie, grandma . . . is taking care of us. We don't have that attention that we want from our parents, that makes us disrespectful in class and make us be like, [to the teacher] 'Bitch, I don't care . . . I see my mama . . . I don't see you. You're not my mama.'"

Though nationwide the numbers tell us that Black parents are involved in their children's education—checking homework, talking about the importance of education with their children[8]—that was not Diamond's experience. For many of the girls on the margins, their parents are also suffering from debilitating conditions of poverty, addiction, and their own tumultuous relationships with people and with schools. Diamond was calling for a different reality, at least when she walks into school. In other words, for girls who have a history of sexual exploitation and abuse, school cannot ignore them or what they experience outside school walls. Even though institutions are prone to reinforcing or replicating the norms of society, Diamond's path reveals why schools should actively work to generate a different culture, one that doesn't prioritize high performers over everyone else. Our public schools—especially for these girls—need to be a place of stability and consistency, a place where new norms can emerge. For too many kids, school is the only place they can learn how *not* to play the circumscribed role the rest of the world casts them in.

"So, basically, what I hear you saying is that you want somebody who *cares* about you," I said.

"Yeah! Exactly. Like, somebody that I can trust. Not somebody that I can be like, we're cool one day and not cool the next day. How can I talk to this person? How can I ask them questions? Why would I raise my hand . . . [when the response is] 'Why are you talking to me? Oh, do your work'? Okay, I just wanted to ask you a question. Okay, I won't bother you. Okay, I'm not going to do the work. F——it. You know? [Then we] get careless because we don't feel like it's worth it if we don't connect with that person."

Going Back in Time

The steering of girls into sex work is a global culture, not just a decision point in the criminal legal system in the United States. Girls of all backgrounds are up against the sexist and dismissive notions that they are choosing a life of prostitution rather than being trafficked into it, though this characterization is significantly more common when it comes to Black girls. As Paris explained, Black girls are often trafficked by more than just a single individual. Latent in our willingness to cast them as "choosers" of this underground economy are racialized gender stereotypes about the hypersexualization of Black girls—a myth that was historically used to justify the rape of enslaved Black females, and which has since morphed into a stereotype about "fast" Black girls that renders them vulnerable to multiple forms of abuse.

The myth of the "bad" Black woman is rooted in the historical assumption that Black women possess an elevated level of sexuality beyond other women, that they are eager for sexual exploits, or that they are "loose in their morals." Therefore they are perceived, as they have been historically, as deserving "none of the considerations and respect granted to White women."[9] The sexual terrorism to which Black women were subjected as enslaved women was justified by casting them as immoral and sexually insatiable.

This sentiment was memorialized by an anonymous article written in 1902 for *The Independent*, in which the author, a self-described "colored woman, wife and mother," wrote, "There is a feeling of unrest, insecurity, almost panic among the best class of negroes in the South. . . . A colored woman, however respectable, is lower than the white prostitute. . . . We are neither 'ladies' nor 'gents,' but 'colored.' "[10] Two years later, Fannie Barrier Williams, a northern Black educator and activist, advocated for a fully integrated women's rights movement. This, she argued, would include the need to address the myth of innate Black female promiscuity— which in turn affected social and policy responses to the victimization of Black women. In an article published by *The Independent* in 1904, Williams wrote the following:

> I think it but just to say that we must look to American slavery as the source of every imperfection that mars the character of the colored American. It ought not to be necessary to remind a Southern woman that less than 50 years ago the ill-starred mothers of this ransomed race were not allowed to be modest . . . and there was no living man to whom they could cry for protection against the men who not only owned them, body and soul, but also the souls of their husbands, their brothers, and alas, their

sons. Slavery made her the only woman in America for whom virtue was not an ornament and a necessity.[11]

Such long-held, deeply ingrained stereotypes have had a lasting imprint on society's understanding of Black feminine sexuality. Iterations of the "jezebel" remain a part of our contemporary narrative about Black femininity.[12] We see her not only in the presentation of hypersexualized "vixens" in hip-hop videos but also in social discourses that produce public policy responses to child welfare, health, and criminalization or incarceration.

The educational domain today is infused with the prevailing stigma of "jezebel"—primarily in the form of concerns among school officials about the moral decency of girls. The regulation of this so-called decency often happens through dress codes and other comments and behaviors that sexualize Black girls in schools. But it is most apparent in school responses to girls who have been sexually exploited. Teen girls who wear tight or revealing clothing, who are parenting, who are "slut-shamed" and bullied, who express gender along a continuum, and/or who are sexually assaulted are all living under the cloak of jezebel.

The Real

"I was involved in sex work for a very long time," Paris, who is now a community organizer in her early twenties, admitted. "And was forced into sex work, not by a [pimp] . . . We talk about trafficking, but we don't talk about it in terms of how *society* traffics individuals. Because society could traffic you, especially transwomen. And what I mean by society, I'm talking about not having any job opportunities, not having any housing opportunities, not having so many different opportunities that y'all may have that we don't. So I had to get it how I did . . . but one thing I did do was go to school. I didn't care how long I was on that corner for, or how long I was up the next night, I made it to school. I graduated. That's one thing I did not play with, was my schooling. To each his own, though . . .

again, I didn't have a [pimp], I didn't have anybody making me stay home, and a lot of these girls that are trafficked deal with not only the abuse, but they deal with being raped.

"Those men have to train those girls to be scared of them, to make them not want to leave," Paris continued. "We be like, 'Girl, child, we'll leave, we'll go on the block one night and we'll disappear.' But a lot of them men store fear into those women, to where they feel like wherever [they] go, [they'll] always have somebody watching . . . so they keep tabs on you and stuff like that. Some of those girls . . . before they are actually put out on the streets, they're held hostage in houses for months at a time getting raped, getting drugs injected into their veins, and coke forced up their nose, just to get them hooked on these addictions just to drag them through the mud. Basically, beat them down, then put them on the stroll because now you're dealing with addiction, you're dealing with so much other stuff. 'If you want your drugs, I'm going to supply them to you, but you have to bring me the money first.' So, those girls . . . I know for sure have to meet a quota. Those girls have to go out. . . . If he got twelve girls out there working for him, he expects at the end of the night to have all twelve of those girls to bring in $100. You know that's $1,200 he just made at the end of the day. . . . If you don't meet that quota, he will either have one of the other girls assault you, or he will assault you himself. So, I mean, it's a whole lot. This is real. School-to-prison pipeline or school pushouts . . . all these things are real and sex work has a big part to play in it.

"A lot of girls are performing sex work and don't even know that they are performing sex work," Paris pointed out. "[He might say], 'Give me a little head or give me a little tail and I'll buy you something.' Hell, what you think you doing? Sex work. You are providing services for materialistic stuff."

In my conversations with other young women who were involved in sex work, many did not identify as "sexually exploited" or "sex-trafficked" girls, nor did they believe themselves to be "prostitutes."

Like Diamond, they might say instead that they have an older "boyfriend" (rather than a pimp) or "bust dates" to indicate a casual participation in the sex trade without fully committing to the idea that they were or are selling sex. These girls are vulnerable— very vulnerable—because they are often clawing their way out of some intense situations, without the supports of advocates or trained professionals who know how to respond to the needs of sexually exploited children. The men in their lives know that. These girls, who are often in foster care or come from unstable homes, become invisible in efforts to dismantle school-to-confinement pathways. With little understanding of how they're being pulled out, we call them dropouts. We—educators, neighbors, and other community members—fail to include their stories and experiences in our understanding of how and why girls may not be attending school, or how the jezebel stigma affects their ability to go to school.

"If you haven't eaten in a week because there's no food in your house," Bobbie in New Orleans said to a group of us discussing life in trafficking, "and someone pulls up to you on the street and says, 'If you do this for me, I will feed you' . . . you're going to do it."

"And if someone feeds you and they do have sex with you," I continued, "they may make you feel like the most special person in the world."

"Or the most nastiest person," Paris said. "Because at the end of the day, like again, as a person who was involved in sex work, those types of men have the mentality of like, 'I can do whatever I want to you because I'm paying to do this to you.' So . . . you have some men who want the GF experience, and by that I mean that 'girlfriend' experience. They not going to treat you like, you know, any type of way. They'll treat you like it's some type of relationship there. Then you have those men that want to talk to you crazy, want to talk to you reckless. . . . 'Put this in your mouth, put that in your mouth, touch this, grab that . . . and then at the end of the day, it makes you feel like, so degraded, like so low. . . . That was my problem with sex work. Although I was doing it for survival. . . . At the end of the day, I had a roof to provide. I had to put food in my stomach. Not only that, but I had a transition I had to keep up with, so it was a lot. . . . For those that are forced to deal with each and every man they come into contact with . . . these men auction them off. They will sit there and be like, the younger you are, the better, because you're young. You know, you haven't really been tampered with. So, a lot of men will pay a lot more for a younger girl."

Child exploitation isn't free, and the girls who survive these experiences pay the highest price. Despite U.S. law that requires courts to order convicted traffickers to pay trafficking victims lost wages, they are much less likely than those who are labor-exploited to receive a monetary award for their suffering.[13] This payment, which rarely if ever comes, could never compensate for the deep damage and losses that have little do with finances.

Nola Brantley is co-founder and former executive director of Motivating, Inspiring, Supporting and Serving Sexually Exploited Youth (MISSSEY), an organization that predominantly serves African American young women who have been sex-trafficked in the Bay Area. She says that the public's failure to embrace Black girls as trafficked may also be a function of how Black girls present to the public when they are still under the watchful eye of their predator, pimp, and/or gang. Brantley argues that sexually exploited Black girls are not choosing to participate in the sex trade; they are in the traumatic throes of a "domino effect" of choices made for them. "Did they choose to grow up in poverty?" she asks. "Did they choose sexual abuse? Did they choose to get raped, some of them before they could walk? Did they choose to grow up in a world where women and girls are not safe? . . . As women and girls become more sexualized in the world, the more they are seen as property."[14]

Black girls have been our forgotten daughters in responses to the global convergence of racial and gender inequality. Black girls are fully human—they are more than "hos" or a "thing" to break and/or take.[15] For many girls, unwanted sexual attention in their early years sometimes leads to premature sexual behaviors. When a little girl who has been sexually assaulted is told and taught through children's rhymes passed through generations to "shake it to the East, shake it to the West, shake it to the one that she loves the best" and is routinely singing lyrics from songs that objectify Black girls' and women's bodies, her spirit is further fed with ideas that affect her understanding of relationships and her perception of herself. For many girls who have survived sexual victimization, these revelations may not come right away in part because of the ways their social world reinforces the idea that they *are* their sexuality—rather than the idea that they *own* and control their sexuality. Their personal acknowledgment of their true potential is further obscured when sexual victimization goes unchallenged, or worse, is embedded in schools.

Too Sexy for School

From fourth through sixth grade my friends and I, like many others our age, played a game during recess called Hide and Go Get It. It was a variation of hide-and-seek in which boys would chase the girls and then "go get it."

"Go get what?" I remember asking a classmate one day during recess.

"You know what," she said to me with a smirk.

I remember feeling helpless. In this game, in which girls had to literally hide to avoid sexual encounters with the boys, I felt a complete lack of control. There were some girls who were rumored to "like" being "caught" by the boys. Why would a girl "like" that attention at such a young age? What was this attention providing for her? For me, as a survivor of sexual abuse, the idea was terrifying. I ran fast to avoid being caught in those games. Some days I wondered why I was even playing, but I had learned that this was the game that the "popular" girls played. In this case, "popularity" came with being subjected to ridicule and speculation by boys, other girls, and the many ways all children mimic the adult policing of girls' sexuality. Experiences like this, which are seen as nothing more than normal and harmless child's play, leave very young girls with the impossible task of trying to negotiate their own sexuality within ever-present gender and racial stereotypes. It's the tip of the iceberg when it comes to understanding the dynamics of more tangible victimization.

At nearly 19 percent, the rate of sexual victimization for Black girls and young women is among the highest for any group in the nation.[16] Girls experience sexual assault, objectification, or being seen as hypersexual in many places—including their homes, in the street, on buses and subway systems, in their places of worship, and in schools. It's a web that not only entangles Black girls' bodies but can also ensnare their minds. In the hallways, in the classrooms, on the yard, and in the bathrooms, Black girls describe conditions in which their bodies are scrutinized, touched (often without permission), and objectified in ways that make them feel self-conscious and constantly defensive.

In Chicago, a national hub for sex trafficking, young women were keenly aware of the ways in which assumptions about their sexuality and sexual behaviors were influencing their interactions with others: with other girls, but particularly with the men and boys in their schools and communities.[17] Discussing this sexualization of Black femininity with a group of Chicago girls, Leila explained how she sees the role of mentorship.

"That's why we have so many THOTy bodies," she said. "Do you know what a THOTy body is? A THOT is someone who is promiscuous.* And to me, someone who is promiscuous is when you have multiple partners in a short amount of time . . . so I feel like the fathers being absent connects to the mother and it also

* Urban Dictionary and other pop culture sources define "THOT" as a slang acronym meaning "that ho over there."

connects to the daughter. . . . These mamas [are] THOTy bodies, too, so I'm trying to figure out where it started. . . . My mama is very promiscuous and [she's] like forty-plus . . . yeah, it's hard for today's females.

"Like, I was trying to talk to this guy, and he was like, 'You want to kick it?' I was like, 'I don't kick it. I don't go in people's crib or whatever.' Why leave my crib to go to his? He was like, 'So what you want to do?' I was like, 'I like to go to the movies, and I like to go on dates.' He was like, 'You a goofy.' That's what I feel like we have to deal with."

In other words, this boy wanted Leila to come over to his place to have sex, but he thought it was ridiculous that she might actually be interested in going on a date.

"So if my self-esteem wasn't high enough," Leila continued, shaking her head, "if anybody steady getting [told] 'You a goofy' for respecting themselves or 'You don't look as pretty 'cause your titties not out' . . . you got a group of females at school that's not even focused on school, but more focused on being accepted. . . . You could act proud of yourself, but every time you try to display that, you're getting knocked down. You doing something wrong. He told me that I was crazy! But luckily I know that I'm not crazy. . . . To me, that's a big struggle for females, and it has to do with sexuality."

"TV plays a role, too," Michelle chimed in. "And I seen something on Facebook yesterday."

"I'm not going to lie," Nala said. "I do engage that VH-1 *Love and Hip-Hop* or whatever. . . ."

The group laughed. For many in the group, watching reality television was a guilty pleasure.

"But," Nala said. "I don't have the same mindset. I've gotten to the point where I'm okay doing things for me. Like, I don't have to do extra for other people's attention. If I get it, I get it. If I don't, I wasn't supposed to, you know? But it has gone from like, *The Cosby Show*, *Family Matters*, [and shows] that actually had like . . .

families and everything to 'Oh, this chick is just trying to have a baby by me and take my money.' We have that to look forward to on television."

"I know a lot of people," Leila chimed in, "girls [who] pop mollies.* And people don't know the effects of mollies yet. Now, think about what that's going to do to your education. You don't even know the effects of it . . . and a lot of them are getting into gangs as well because it's becoming so hard out here. There's no jobs. There's no structure. There's no role models. When you get that, you got young people ruling the world, and without structure, young people can't rule the world because life is what gives you that experience. They learning . . . and a female is going to be a THOT to get a guy's attention or be a gang banger to get a guy's attention. It's hard to just be a lady and get a guy's attention nowadays."

Black girls, like other girls, want to be appreciated for who they are, not solely what they look like. In the summer of 2014, I observed girls in a media program write signs that read "I am not my booty" and other signs that declared their desire to be seen for more than their bodies. Throughout years of talking with girls, they have consistently, in both quiet and robust ways, inquired about why their bodies are objectified and their minds dismissed.

Across the country, nearly half of public schools (49 percent) have implemented a formal uniform policy or dress code designed to regulate the presentation of clothing in school or establish norms for student dress as a part of the school culture.[18] Uniforms provide a structure to the way students arrive in school and are associated with having a positive impact on classroom discipline, image in the community, student safety, and pride.[19] There is less peer scrutiny, critique of a young person's socioeconomic status, and emphasis on the "fashion show" because everyone is wearing the same

---

* The National Institute on Drug Abuse defines molly as ecstasy, a synthetic psychoactive drug that has similarities to both the stimulant amphetamine and the hallucinogen mescaline.

thing. However, there are two sides to this coin. As discussed in Chapter 2, enforcement of uniform or dress code rules can lead to different battles, ones that result in girls being asked to leave the school. Dress codes, for all of their benefits, have become a tool of oppression.

School structures often fail to recognize their role in facilitating the punishment—and policing—of Black girls' sexuality. Marcus, the same high school dean who noted that Black girls were "not docile," felt that dress codes are an important part of establishing the school climate.

"We have a dress code," he said. "Every school in our district has a dress code. And I believe that it has to be in place. So if a girl really doesn't want to be in school that day, they're going to test the limits with how revealing they're going to come to school. That's one way that they check out."

From Marcus's vantage point, girls may intentionally come to school in clothes that violate the dress code and use it as an excuse not to stay for the day. Yet the girls who spoke with me never turned clothes into an excuse not to go to school. To the contrary, dress codes actively turned them away from school. They repeated several stories of showing up to school only to be turned away for something minor—like a belt missing, or the wrong color shoes—rather than a blatant affront to the dress code. For some of these students, the shoes they wore were the only shoes in their closets, and the absence of a belt was an oversight. And when it was deemed a more serious violation of the code, such as wearing tight-fitting garb or clothing that revealed cleavage, thighs, or other parts of their bodies, girls tended to perceive its implementation as subjective and arbitrary.

For some of the young women in Chicago, for example, dress codes were seen as playing a role in furthering the objectification of Black girls, rather than curbing it. They pointed to how dress codes often reflect society's biases about Black femininity—and Black feminine bodies, in particular.

"[My school] is a baby version of a [community college] and it's very, very strict. It's mostly Black and Latino," Jeneé said. "It's just really strict, that's why I transferred. Three hours of homework each night . . . If you came with black shoes on, but they had a certain label on them, it was just [minor] stuff that they got us in trouble for, and nobody felt like explaining to me why I got in trouble for something. I didn't see it. We had to wear uniforms . . . there was no creativity. I know schools that have uniforms where people come out of uniform and you could have that freedom, but the days that we had to come out of uniform, there was still that strict rule. And at that school, there were no White people at my school."

Patrice said, "In my school, we don't wear a uniform. So, of course, schools are strict on their dress policy. So it be like, when it gets hot outside or warm, girls like to wear their shorts, their dresses or whatever. So, if you know, an African American female comes in with some shorts, they're too little. But if another race comes in—it could be the same exact shorts—they're fine. So that's how like, a lot of African American girls at my school get angry and rebel because they feel like you say to the African American girl, 'You cannot wear these. These are not school-appropriate.' But you didn't tell the other girl that it's not appropriate. Oh, she can wear it. [Black girls] feel like it's unfair, so they rebel and wear what they want to wear because it be like at our school, the students feel like, if you tell one student, oh, they can't wear those shorts, then nobody should be able to wear them. You shouldn't tell a specific person that, whether [or not] the body shapes are different . . . you should just keep it fair."

I was feeling energy from all the girls in the group that this was a familiar experience. In fact, in every city that I visited I heard this same story organically emerge from conversations about dress codes (official and unofficial ones) in schools. One Black girl after another felt barred from wearing clothing that other girls could wear without reprimand.

"We don't have a dress code, period," Catherine said. "We don't even have gym uniforms, so you know . . . we get to wear whatever we want. So, my freshman year, I came with this kind of sporty top on for gym since we didn't have [gym uniforms]. I just went out and bought stuff for gym. The gym teacher was like, 'Oh, that's not gym-appropriate' . . . and then somebody else came in with the exact top I had on. She was just smaller up here," Catherine said, motioning to her chest. "She just had smaller breasts. So, I was like, 'What's the difference? I just had that top on the other day.' [The teacher] was just like, 'Leave me alone.' She got an attitude with me! See, this is why teachers get disrespected a lot. I don't like when people catch attitude with me because it was only because of my race or my breast size that I couldn't wear it."

In California, Deja talked about what happened one day over a pair of shorts she wore to school. "I came to school with shorts on. It was like, when school first started, so it was, like, one of the hottest days ever. And I was going to have a heat stroke, so I put some shorts on. So I walk in the office, and they're like, 'You need to go back home and change.' But this [White] girl walked in the office, and her shorts were shorter than mine, and she was kinda thicker than me so, like, you could see everything, like her butt cheeks were hanging out kinda and everything. And then they gave her a pass to class!

"I was like, 'You didn't just see what she had on?' " Deja continued. "And then they was like, 'Yeah.' So I was like, 'Why do I have to get sent home for wearing shorts and she just had shorts on and she way thicker than me?' And they were like, 'That's not the case here. I'm trying to help you out.' . . . I said, 'Well you need to be trying to her help her out, too, 'cause my shorts are not even that bad.' Like, it wasn't bad at all. It was just some shorts. And then she was like, 'Anyways, do you think your grandmother will bring you some clothes?' I [wasn't] having her come up [to the school] to bring me some pants [when the woman in the office] didn't just say something to [the White girl]. I was finna go to class, [but] she was like, 'You can't go to class like that.' I was like, 'I'm going to class.' And then I went to class. And she had them send me to the office. I was like, 'If y'all send me home, I'm not coming back because this is unfair.' . . . I was talking to the principal, and she was like, 'What's unfair?' I was like, 'This lady, the attendance lady, just seen some girl who was way thicker than me with some shorts on, but she gave her a pass straight to class and then she seen me with some shorts on, she told me I gotta go home.' And then she looked at the attendance lady [and said], 'I'm going to give you a pass this one time, but please don't be letting the boys feel all on you and stuff.' I'm like, 'I don't . . . I'm not going to do that. I like my personal space.' And then I went to class, but I wouldn't [have] been able to if I didn't say nothing, like people just take that stuff. I don't. I need a reason why I'm getting sent home."

Wearing short shorts on a hot day almost got Deja sent home. The fear, as suggested by the principal's comment, was that Deja's shorts might elicit inappropriate touching and behavior among the boys. Instead of focusing on developing a climate in which boys are taught not to touch girls' bodies, girls are sent home to change their clothes.

I asked the young women in Chicago to share with me their ideas about why they thought schools might be reacting to them in this way. Not surprisingly, the girls pointed to popular characterizations of Black women's bodies as part of the problem.

"This is based off of media and how it portrays us as Black young females," Carla said. "If you see a [Black] girl in a movie even, if you see a girl wearing short shorts, and you see a guy, you automatically know they're going to hook up. If you see a White girl wearing short shorts, you automatically know she's going to the beach or something. . . . They have no reason to do it school-wise. You don't know everybody's story, everybody's reason for what they have on."

In the public imagination, assumptions about the sexuality of Black people make clothing style a socially accepted (though unsound) predictor of behavior.

"I feel like [there's] a distinction between what Black and other race girls can wear," Dee said. "Not only because of their body shape, because most of the time, Black girls' bodies are built . . . like, we're a little more thicker, if you know what I mean—in all the right places . . . your bottom, your boobs. So, people—like the adults at my school—will say, 'You're Black. You can't wear those because you're showing much more skin because your body weight and your body shape is different.' . . . But they automatically think that other race girls can wear it because it's not, like, a sexual thing. They're not wearing the short shorts to try to entice guys. . . . I feel like it's double standards and I feel like there shouldn't be a rule on how short your shorts are unless you can see the actual bottom. If you can't see the actual bottom, who cares how short they are?"

In each city, most of the girls that I spoke with wore clothes that met her own standard of beauty. They wore clothes that they thought were cute and felt unfairly stigmatized by the differential way adults responded to them when they wore trendy clothing styles.

"I think the reason they do that is the boys . . . sometimes the boys could be more attracted to the Black girls, especially when it comes to body shape, and they think it's going to distract the boys, so they do tell the Black girls to cover up, because that's who the boys are looking at," Shamika said. "They are looking at the Black girls. They are looking at the White girls [too], but they're looking at their faces. They're not finna really cover up the White girls."

It's notable that Shamika felt boys were attracted to White girls' *faces* but to Black girls' *bodies*. And that she didn't pause or skip a beat in explaining as much.

"So if they're not looking at your face, what do you think are they looking at?" I asked.

"They're looking at your butt or your boobs," Shamika responded.

"Can you feel that when you're walking past them?" I asked.

The group came alive with a resounding "Yes," sprinkled with the comments "Grown men!" and "Every day!" But it was not something that only affected more curvaceous girls.

"Even though I'm a small . . . very flat . . . African American female . . . a petite female," Charisma said, "I still feel that no matter what a Black girl do, no matter how small she is or how big she is, a man is going to always look at her sexually. No matter what. That's how I feel."

Shamika agreed, saying, "It's like . . . they're all men. Men are going to be men regardless. White girls are going to be White girls regardless. Black girls are going to be Black girls regardless, okay? It's just the way that social media is portraying us, it's just wrong . . . music videos, for instance. I don't see no White girls in the music videos half naked. You don't see no skinny White girl half naked dancing on some dude drinking . . . you don't see none of that. And then you ask yourself, why do they put big Black girls in videos? Everybody want to be thick. . . . Why you just can't be yourself and be the size that you are? I feel like media is influencing everybody."

Shamika's critique of media's representation of Black girls bodies was impressive. *Why do they put big Black girls in videos?* Good question. The fixation with Black women's bodies, which have been increasingly used as ornaments for rappers and petite pop singers alike, has become the latest commercial iteration of objectifying Black women's bodies. Videos tell a story. They also reflect fantasy, which most often reduces Black femininity to the size of her backside—and how fast or forcefully she can make it gyrate.

We continued to talk about this objectification in the context of schools' reactions to Black girls' bodies, especially their feeling that no matter their size or age they were vulnerable to a particular type of sexualization that rendered Black girls as objects of desire, even without their permission. These girls felt that Black girls were constantly sexualized. This is a profound concept that bears repeating: *No matter what a Black girl does, no matter her age, and no matter how small or big she is, a man is going to always look at her sexually.*

If that doesn't make you want to holler . . .

This issue is anything but new. One Black mother wrote in an anonymous 1904 autobiography, "Few colored girls reach the age of sixteen without receiving advances from [men]—maybe from a young 'upstart,' and often from a man old enough to be their father, a white haired veteran of sin."[20] I asked the group of young women how being perceived in this way affected them, if at all, in school.

"For me," Dee said, "when people comment on how short something [clothing] is, it makes me feel really bad and I have a short temper, so it's almost like I want to get up out of my [wheel]chair and do something to them, probably strangle them, because I feel like everything is not sexual! I want to wear these clothes because I want to be me and I want to be comfortable. Every girl that wears short clothes is not promiscuous, as they want to call it. I'm not looking for a boyfriend. I'm not looking to hook up with anyone. Just leave me alone . . . I keep doing me."

Dee's confidence, though wrapped in strong language, was admirable. She was clear that other people's judgmental gaze was not about her. For Shamika, the terms were a bit different.

"I have a big butt," she said. "And everybody knows it. The whole school knows it. My nickname is 'Big Booty Mika.' When somebody sees me, they say, 'Hey, Big Booty Mika.' And it's like, [teachers say], 'You need to go change, go put on some gym shorts,'" . . . I be like, my butt is *big*. Either way it's going to show! Right now, I have on jeans. My butt is still big. If I have on booty shorts, my butt is still big. So, at the end of the day, you're not paying for my clothes. I'm paying for my own clothes, and in the summertime, before I go to school and I pay to buy a whole bunch of booty shorts, best believe that I'm going to school with those whole bunch of booty shorts and I'm going to wear them. Unless you want to go to Forever 21 and buy some shorts for me, then shut up about it."

Shamika talked a good game. She sounded confident and certain that she was entitled to wear whatever shorts she wanted. But I pressed her a bit to get a more complete sense of how she sees herself.

"Do you *like* that people call you Big Booty Mika at school?"

"It depends on the person," she admitted, looking down at the table in front of us. "I'm so serious. If it's a girl, then it's like, she's just being funny . . . but if it's like an athlete or a whole football team, like [the] captain of the football team being like 'Big Booty Mika,' It's like, 'No . . . my name is Shamika . . . just move on.' "

"So what makes the difference for you?" I asked.

"The difference is the point of respect," she said. "The football player probably don't even like me like that. He just sees a big butt. The other people, like, know me inside, but they just want to play around. Like, the football player, he only sees my butt, he doesn't see my personality."

Shamika described a continuous, incessant state of sexual harassment. She was coping, but the adults in her life owe her a safer environment than that—at school and elsewhere.

"Like when I'm walking down Stony Island, literally *old* men be like . . . trying to hit on me. It's mostly old men, and they don't want to say nothing to me when I walk past, but as soon as they turn around and see my butt, they be like, 'Oh, hold up, shorty. What's your name? Can you talk to me for a minute?' Like . . . that's disrespectful. And then, when I don't want to talk to them, it be like . . . like two days ago, [a man] was like, 'Uh, can I talk to you?' I didn't feel like talking to him, so I just stayed quiet or whatever. Then, he went ahead and walked past and he was like, 'Oh, but you got a fat ass though.' Like, that is *so* disrespectful. You shouldn't tell nobody that."

I wondered aloud if he had known how old she was.

"No, they don't," she confirmed. "No, and some of them, I tell my age . . . I be like, '[I'm] fifteen!' And they be like, 'You lying. You look like you're at least seventeen or eighteen.' . . . I'm like, 'I can show you my [high school] ID right now!' "

Shamika was fifteen years old at the time of our discussion, and she had just described a snapshot from her life under a constant barrage of sexual harassment. Every day, even after she disclosed her age. *Every day.*

This is the cloud of abuse and harassment under which many girls who look like Shamika live. This is the climate in which girls are trying to negotiate their safety and discover their identity as students.

"I feel like you can look at somebody's face and tell, like, if they're older or they're younger," Shai said. "I can look and see, she ain't nothing but a teenager . . . she's just tall. People like me, I hit my growth spurt in sixth grade. So, I was in sixth grade looking like I could be eighteen or something . . . it's like, when I finally got in high school, it got worse."

"I feel like sometimes they don't care," said Charisma. "This guy was twenty-four with kids . . . So then, I was looking at him like, 'Sir, how old are you?' He was like twenty-four. I asked him, 'How old do I look?' He was like, 'Nineteen or twenty.' . . . But in the back of my head, I was like, 'I do *not* look that age.' . . . So then I was like, 'I'm seventeen." He was like, 'We still can't talk?' . . . No!"

Whether in the community or at school, age compression (discussed in Chapter 1) is a phenomenon that is often thrust upon Black girls. However, these girls are girls, not fully developed women in younger bodies. They are adolescents, and like most in their age group, they may test boundaries—particularly with respect to clothing—that are established by those with authority or by institutional rules. Yet they have seen that doing this, the normal stuff of teenagers, can make them targets for exclusionary discipline or additional surveillance. Unless they fight back.

Transitions

For Paris in New Orleans, who was transitioning from male to female in high school, the dress code along with the castigation of her identity expression from staff and faculty were a particular nuisance that caused her to question whether her school was a "good fit."

"Every day that I came into school, I had to stop by the office just for the person in the office to approve what I had on. Now, I'm not going to lie and make it seem like I'm this perfect person, or whatever, 'cause I did push the uniform guidelines."

"So, you had to wear uniforms?" I asked.

"Yes," Paris confirmed. Ninety-five percent of the public schools in New Orleans require students to wear uniforms—the highest percentage in the nation.[21] "And the boys and the girls had different uniforms . . . like the girls had to have plaid skirts . . . I never did understand why they didn't make plaid for boys. I would love to see some plaid for boys, because I know a few boys that may like to wear plaid. All the boys had a basic Dickies or basic cotton shirt with the school logo. . . . But I would push the school, as far as dress code. Like, if they say your skirt ain't supposed to be past three inches above the knee, I may push it to four inches above the knee. I would try it, just because I knew I was different. I knew that I was going to cause controversy anyway. They were never happy with me.

"With me [gender] transitioning from middle school to high school, I had an assistant principal who hated my guts. She hated my guts. She didn't really like LGBT individuals, particularly gay young men, and that's what I identified as [in middle school] . . . before knowing myself further. I thought I was happy because I was leaving middle school, but this [administrator] followed me. She went from being our middle school's assistant principal to being our high school's principal, and she thought that she was going to be able to wear it out . . . but she didn't know that I had a supportive mother who fought my battles, who stood behind me.

She didn't know I had that type of support in my family. So we had to go to the school board. . . . [They could not] deny [me my] education because of [my] sexual orientation. [They] can't do that. . . .

"Once that [principal] heard that she could not do anything, that the power she thought she had was crushed, her dreams, her hopes, her aspirations were gone . . . at that very moment, I got up and I swung my hair, and I said, 'Thank you.' I didn't have any problems [after that]."

I applaud Paris. She was determined to complete her education, and she did. But for other Black girls, the marginalization that occurs from being sexualized (or reduced to their sexuality)—in and out of school—may be too intense to handle, especially without adequate support.

From the pullout of girls who are being trafficked to the oppressive school dress codes that irrationally institutionalize adult panic over the morals of girls both cis- and transgender, we see how Black girls continue to live with the burden of under-protection, where a girl's virtue certainly is "not an ornament and a necessity."

4

LEARNING ON LOCKDOWN

I got a pain in my stomach . . .'cause my baby is comin'
(oo-ahh)
I got a pain in my side . . .'cause my baby is alive (oo-ahh)
I got a pain in my back . . .'cause my baby is Black (oo-ahh)
I got a pain in my head . . .'cause my baby is dead (oo-ahh)

Individual desks were arranged in forward-facing rows toward a whiteboard at the front of the class. On the institutional walls were vocabulary words and images of prominent African Americans. Computers, all of them older models, lined the back wall of the classroom. Near the exit was a chair for the uniformed institutional staff member who accompanied the girls to and from their units, and who watched over them during class to help maintain order. Steel doors had already been slammed shut and locked behind me, restricting access between the corridor and the classrooms. On each side of the narrow hallway was a row of classrooms, but in only two of them were classes in session at any given time. The remainder were dark and seemingly not put to any use, though decorated with desk chairs and large blackboards. Displays of student work filled in the wall space not taken by inspirational drawings and photographs of Black leaders.

I asked sixteen-year-old Portia and thirteen-year-old Mia what they thought of their education in detention.

"I can't learn here," Mia said, letting out a heavy sigh.
"Depressing," said Portia.

Twenty-one.

That's the percentage of juvenile court detention cases that involve girls nationwide. This number, low when compared to the
79 percent of cases involving boys, is often used as an excuse to
ignore or dismiss the experiences of girls in this system.[1] More
often than not conversations about incarceration leave girls out, or
add them as an afterthought lest someone take offense to the lack
of gender inclusiveness. It's true—the majority of all juvenile cases
involving secure detention, or other forms of incarceration, are
brought against boys and men. However, the plight of girls in confinement is more severe than any single number suggests.

In fact, while the rate of arrest and detention has declined overall for boys, rates have increased for girls.[2] Between 1996 and 2011,
the proportion of girls arrested declined by 42 percent, compared
to a 57 percent decline among boys.[3] Girls (37 percent) are more
likely than boys (25 percent) to be detained for status offenses
and technical violations rather than for crimes that actually present a danger to public safety.[4] Girls (21 percent) are also more likely
than boys (12 percent) to be detained for sexual assault (cases
that may include commercially sexually exploited children) and
public disorder cases, including those that may include public
drunkenness or scuffles.[5] These statistics amount to a situation
where girls who do not present an immediate and significant threat
(because of having committed violent offenses like homicide, robbery, or false imprisonment) are being held in confinement, despite
research that shows the negative impact of detention on educational
achievement.[6]

More than 70 percent of girls in juvenile detention facilities
have a history of trauma, and at least 60 percent have experienced
rape or the threat of rape—a number that reflects reported inci-

dents and is likely an underestimation.[7] Other studies show that up to 90 percent of girls in detention have experienced some form of sexual, emotional, or physical abuse.[8] We cannot ignore the very real impact of trauma.

In the late 1990s, Isis Sapp Grant, herself a former gang member in New York, launched the Blossom Program for Girls at the Youth Empowerment Mission. Through this program, she worked with girls who were gang-involved or in contact with the criminal legal system for other reasons. Blossom, now a program primarily serving New York schools, facilitated the recovery process for more than two thousand young people and their families. Most of these girls came to the program in search of a way to rehabilitate from an addiction to violence. However, Isis discovered that many of these girls and young women were actually responding to much more.

Juanita came to the Blossom Program through her school after she was expelled for fighting every day. She had been fighting to protect herself from other girls who would jump her for flirting with their boyfriends or being perceived as disrespectful to them in some way. When Isis met her, Juanita was considered very promiscuous. Juanita, who was living with a foster family, would get into trouble for having sex in the bathroom at school or even engaging in sexual acts in the hallways. She claimed to be a gang member, and though there was some question about her actual affiliation, she suffered from compounding conditions that fueled violent behaviors that ultimately brought her into contact with the criminal legal system. One day she was arrested for stabbing another girl who went to her school, which landed her in confinement. While in juvenile hall, officials discovered that her mother suffered from addiction and had abandoned her at birth. At the time, her foster mother of nine years was refusing to take her back into her home.

To Isis, Juanita looked like many of the girls she had worked with who were a part of both the social welfare and juvenile justice systems, dual-jurisdiction children who have multiple institutional "parents." She was unusually thin for her age, afflicted with a severe case of acne, and lacking the ability to focus on a single issue or task. Isis remembers how frequently her eyes would jet from one direction to another—and on top of all that, her hair was falling out, which kept her agitation near a boil. Isis remembers "a lot of attitude and a lot of cursing."

As a part of the Blossom Program, girls and their family members met for joint counseling, but the tensions between Juanita and her foster mother were too chaotic to manage in a typical therapeutic space. Before they could reach any common understandings, Isis remembers, Juanita couldn't keep still—she kept moving around the office until her foster mother threatened to beat her. Finally Blossom staff intervened, and a social worker was able to stabilize the situation by ordering a series of evaluations that resulted in Juanita being clinically diagnosed with bipolar disorder. Her foster mother and the Blossom team also discovered that Juanita had been previously diagnosed and prescribed medication, which she was not taking. Staff diligently worked with Juanita and finally persuaded her to take her medicine. Within a week, everyone began to notice a difference in Juanita's behavior. She could sit still, she started showing up at school, and Blossom was able to assign a mentor to work with Juanita and help her establish better intimate relationship practices. It seemed that all was on the mend.

Then an incident occurred between Juanita and her foster mother at home. Her foster mother was a woman with a kind heart—she was caring for at least two other foster children while Juanita was there—but she ruled with an iron fist. She was operating a day care center for babies, and given the demands on her schedule and her life, she lacked the capacity to adequately respond to Juanita's needs. And the fact that she would threaten physical violence as a way to curb Juanita's lapses in judgment only made

Juanita act more belligerent. After a while, mounting stressors impacted Juanita's reliability in the Blossom Program.

Isis noticed that she hadn't seen Juanita in a few weeks. When the young woman did finally appear, Isis reached out to her.

"Juanita, I haven't seen you in a while. Come here and talk to me," she said.

Juanita walked into Isis's office to talk to her, but Isis could tell that something wasn't right. Juanita was rambling and shifting from side to side.

"Are you taking your medicine?" Isis interrupted.

"I don't want to take it!" Juanita insisted. "It makes me slow down. I'm not going to go back home if she's going to make me take it."

Isis later discovered that not only was Juanita rejecting her medication as an act of rebellion against her foster mother, but she was also being teased by other students in her school for being on psychotropic medication. As long as students were calling her "crazy," she didn't want to take the medicine. Blossom counselors and mentors were ultimately able to convince Juanita that if she wanted to experience a life where she was not on probation or under other forms of surveillance from the criminal legal system, she would need to make different decisions—and they were committed to seeing her through it. Her mentor, Davina, made it a personal goal to help Juanita make new meaning of her life. They became so close that Juanita spent most afternoons after school working for Davina; if she was having trouble at home, she could find refuge at Davina's house. Though trauma and mental illness propelled Juanita toward contact with the criminal legal system, these conditions have not dealt a fatal blow to her future. It took Blossom four years to stabilize Juanita through medicine, counseling, education, employment, and intense mentorship. But they did it.

Black Girls in Trouble with the Law:
A Historical Perspective

Black girls in trouble with the law have a long history of being assigned to institutions that fail to adequately respond to their marginalization from school. The institution of slavery constructed a social and penal environment that reinforced the idea of Black female inferiority, and this setting primarily allowed for the development of a girl's domestic skills rather than the development of her intellect. This focus has maintained its imprint on the quality of education that girls receive in confinement—girls who are disproportionately Black.

In the past, correctional facilities, training schools, and residential houses of refuge were designed to "correct" the behaviors of "bad" Black girls in ways that failed to prioritize education as a rehabilitative practice. In general, these institutions demonstrated a lack of concern for the ways in which race and gender informed Black girls' unique vulnerabilities to involvement with the criminal legal system. Schools designed to address the needs of "wayward girls"—those considered "uncontrollable" by their parents or "in danger of being morally depraved"—responded to the sexual histories of girls without consideration of the ways in which their status as Black females rendered them particularly vulnerable to poverty, violence, sexual exploitation, and/or early sexual activity.

Since the eighteenth century, girls who were in trouble with the law, even as part of the enslaved population, were confined in semi-penal institutions: asylums, jails, reformatories, and other homes. Between 1825 and 1828, the United States opened its first juvenile reformatories in New York, Boston, and Philadelphia, for the purpose of providing "food, shelter and education to the homeless and destitute youth and to remove juvenile offenders from the prison company of adult convicts."[9] Children in these facilities participated in activities that were deemed appropriate for their moral rehabilitation at the time, meaning many children were assigned domestic chores, and some even attended school four hours each day.[10] However, because Black children, including Black girls, were not deemed suitable for such facilities, their alternative reality often involved mob lynchings or placement into punitive adult correctional facilities. It was not until 1835, following an intense, racially charged debate between reformists and racial justice advocates about the rehabilitative promise of troubled Black youth, that the New York House of Refuge, in Hudson, became the first juvenile reformatory to accept Black children. However, in these early days, the blueprint for "reform," as reflected in the practice of reformatories across the nation, included plans to prepare Black girls for lives as "cooks, maids, and seamstresses," and to provide them with religious (Christian) instruction, which was believed to support their moral development.[11]

At this time, the confinement of Black girls was in response to their being labeled prostitutes, drunks, mentally ill, and criminals of other sorts deemed socially unacceptable (particularly for girls).[12] Little has changed over a hundred years later. Girls dismissed as "delinquents" struggled to be included in discourses on correctional education and its role in returning them to their home communities and rebuilding their lives. Black girls were denied opportunity or granted only a limited form of access to private institutions that were designed to "reform" children. But once Black girls were accepted into these institutions, access to services remained unequal. Black girls tended to stay in juvenile justice facilities longer, and experience fewer positive outcomes, than their White counterparts.[13] This is a trend that was exacerbated by formal segregation throughout the Jim Crow era. Classrooms in correctional facilities mirrored the intense segregation of school classrooms in surrounding communities—a trend that continues to this day.

For Black girls who were placed into public reformatories, the rehabilitative emphasis was not on making them more productive students, but rather on forming them into better servants for social elites. This was largely in response to the prevailing early twentieth-century practice of institutionalizing Black girls for their perceived sexual deviance (not for any threat they posed to public safety).[14] According to Mary White Ovington, a sociologist and co-founder of the NAACP, "the depravity among [Black] girls and improper guardianship" compose "the race's most serious defects," which suggested not only that Black mothers were to blame for the perceived sexual deviance of Black girls but that the courts were the only institution that could correct these offenses.[15] Ovington and other scholars who produced work that informed the direction of juvenile justice and public discourses on race, gender, and justice characterized the sexual activity of Black girls as a reflection of promiscuity that was "inevitable" given that Black women are "slow to recognize the sanctity of home and the importance of feminine virtue."[16] As Khalil Muhammad notes in *The Condemnation of Blackness*, "Black women's perceived moral shortcomings or racial 'defects' disqualified them from the protective status of the law . . . the problem was 'located in Black women themselves.'"[17] Never mind that many Black women, including educators and political activists such as Fannie Barrier Williams, Nannie Helen Burroughs, and Mary McLeod Bethune, were calling for an elevation of Black girls' dignity not through the policing of their sexuality (and incarceration) but rather through the implementation of equal rights and economic or educational opportunity. To say these women were facing an uphill battle understates the case.

In scholarly circles, Black girls who were in trouble with the law were depicted as being a part of the "submerged tenth," a term coined by W.E.B. Du Bois to refer to those in the "criminal classes," including prostitutes and "loafers."[18] They were also regarded as "incorrigible" and "neurotic," suggesting that their form of criminality or delinquency was innate and not something that could be critically examined and corrected in the context of their environment.[19] As a result, these Black girls were often disregarded as throwaway children, described by Geoff Ward as children who "experienced prolonged stays in confinement, compared with those of white youths, and [whose] prospects remained constrained by limits on educational and labor market opportunity."[20] As such, apprenticeship programs and other opportunities to improve life outcomes through education and work were not as available to Black children as they were to White children.

Several decades later, in the early 1930s, following the end of the Progressive Era, juvenile reformatories or locked "training" institutions had been established across the country, many of them now housing Black girls. In 1933, there were 1,803 Black girls whose delinquency cases were disposed in sixty-seven courts and eight Black girls whose cases were "handled by federal authorities."[21] However, these girls were still expected to rehabilitate in separate and inferior environments that failed to support their educational development. For example, in 1936, at the New York Training School for Girls in Hudson, New York, Black girls—who were 19 percent of the girls in the facility at the time—were segregated from White female residents and forced to reside in two of the most "crowded and dilapidated of the reformatory's 'cottages'"[22] Jazz legend Ella Fitzgerald was once assigned to this facility for being an "ungovernable" teen.[23] Here she was quarantined, tortured, and excluded from participating in the choir, as it was reserved for White girls only.[24]

The popular perception of Black children as unruly, incorrigible, or inherently ungovernable has affected society's conscious and unconscious responses to Black girls who get in trouble with the law. Black girls are at once female and Black, and their presence in correctional facilities has always been informed by their status as both. All of the traits that were previously described as being a core part of social expectations for "good" girls found a particularly nebulous existence among "bad" girls. Black women and girls were subject to a masculinization of their behaviors if they challenged authority, asserted independence, or attempted to mitigate their impoverished and sometimes violent physical environment by striking back (or, in some cases, first). In 1910, Black girls were four times more likely to be incarcerated than foreign-born White girls, and five times more likely than native-born White girls.[25] Black girls were also more likely than White girls to be found delinquent for person, property, and status offenses—a trend that was particularly prevalent in the southern states.

According to criminologist Vernetta Young, "Black women in American society have been victimized by their double status as blacks and as women. . . . Information about black females has been based on their position relative to black males and white females. . . . Knowledge about [Black] women is based on images that are distorted and falsified. In turn these images have influenced the way in which black female victims and offenders have been treated by the criminal justice system."[26]

Essentially, the criminal legal system never developed clear educational pathways to success for Black girls in confinement—and this has now come back to threaten the legitimacy of a juvenile justice system that is supposed to prevent future involvement with the criminal legal system. Black girls are confronted with the usual hurdles to educational success in a correctional setting: the highly punitive nature of the facility and trouble reconciling school credits. Yet their Black girl identities subject them to a brand of systemic discipline and victimization that mirrors, and in some cases surpasses, the mundane and everyday ways that the full humanity and potential of Black girls is confined.

Criminalized Education

Today Black girls in juvenile correctional facilities have continued to endure hypersegregated and inferior learning conditions that prevent their full rehabilitation and fail to support their healthy development. In 2013, the latest year for which data on youth in residential placement are available, more than 6,000 girls were detained or committed on any given day in U.S. secure juvenile correctional facilities, group homes, boot camps, and long-term secure facilities.[27] Among these girls, 35 percent were Black girls, 40 percent were White, 21 percent were Latina, 3.6 percent were Native American, and less than 1 percent were Asian or Pacific Islander.[28] It is worth remembering that Black girls are less than 14 percent of all girls in the United States; given that 35 percent of those confined on any given day are Black, the term "disproportionate" is putting matters mildly.

The racial disparities described here are a function of multiple factors: socioeconomic (unemployment, poverty), educational (poor performance, truancy), juvenile justice (differential handling, lack of gender-responsive treatment and alternatives to detention), and family and community (an incarcerated parent, living in high-crime areas), among others. Between 1997 and 2011, Black girls experienced assignment to residential placement at a rate of 123 per 100,000 youth, one of the highest in the nation. This racial isolation, coupled with an increase in the number of girls being placed into these facilities, has had a tremendous impact on the development of an effective, culturally competent learning continuum for these girls—and the way they enhance their own self-esteem and academic performance.

The juvenile hall in which I based the majority of my discussions with detained girls was home to about thirty girls on average each month. In the juvenile court school where the detained girls were educated, classrooms were organized into two units, with the size fluctuating according to the number of girls confined in juvenile hall each day. The girls rotated between history, language arts, math, and science classes each day, and attended library or physical education (PE) courses throughout the week.

From my conversations with the young women detained in this facility, it was apparent they understood the importance of their participation in school. Many were seeking credit recovery after having missed significant periods of school in the community. However, their desire to learn was quickly quashed by an emphasis on discipline, uninspired teaching, and a curriculum that was often driven by simple worksheet packets that each student was required to complete every day. There was little opportunity for them to collaborate with each other, learn from each other, or interrogate the material through inquiry and discussion.

"I don't like school," Portia, an eleventh-grader, declared with conviction. "It's not because I just want to do what I want to do. It's because I feel like it's *way* too easy for me. Like, the math in here is like I already know it. . . . Like, I could get easily 4.0s and stuff. It's just that I don't do the work because I feel that it's unnecessary for me to learn the same thing that I already know. . . . It seems like a waste of my time to just sit there and do stuff I already know. . . . I think I'm very advanced in school. I passed my [test] on the first try. So if I take a high school exit exam, I could easily be done with high school."

Portia was very confident about her *ability* to perform well academically, even while she admitted that her *performance* may not have reflected as much. Her response to me signaled that she just wasn't motivated to complete school while in juvenile hall. The simple nature of the work, by her own account, was leading her to disengage even though she knew that school was an important part of the journey toward reaching her career objectives.

"Honestly, for the career that I want, I would say that [education] is very important," she said. "My career is a veterinarian . . . that's where I want to go with my life, so I have to go to school." It's hard to see how the lack of nurturing, inspiration, and available resources would conspire to set Portia on a path to graduate studies in veterinary medicine. So what, exactly, are these schools designed to accomplish?

Schools in juvenile detention facilities are often punitive. Though many operate with the intention or stated mission to be rehabilitative, the approach is often one that punishes children who have made mistakes. Many institutions nationwide offer only a few programs and services that adequately respond to the risk factors associated with the delinquency of girls, particularly girls of color. Facilities are designed to increase surveillance, and programs and approaches often subject children to emotional and physical abuse that produce immediate and long-term harmful effects. According to the Center for Children's Law and Policy, more than one-third of detained youth nationwide report that staff have used unnecessary force in their interactions with them, and half reported that they were punished by staff "without cause."[29] For girls—the majority of whom are being held for status offenses and other nonviolent offenses and among whom 74 percent have a diagnosed psychiatric illness—we have to ask, is this how we facilitate their ability to access a better life?[30]

Portia and many girls like her who attend these schools, despite their bad choices and the equally bad ones made for them along the way, still have hopes, aspirations, and goals for their future selves. But these are children in trouble with the law, and the monitoring and surveillance that go hand in hand with systems of punishment extend well beyond their cell walls. The supervising staff that work alongside the teacher—a preemptive measure in the event that there are disciplinary problems among the students—are ever present. This emphasis on discipline does not go unnoticed by the girls.

More Discipline, More Problems

Over the course of three years, nearly every girl in confinement that I spoke with (more than forty detained girls) at some point had been removed from her juvenile court school classroom. In a study that I conducted in 2013, I found that one-third of detained Black girls—like Faith—believed that it was because they simply asked the teacher a question.[31] Even when girls were "talking back," they often felt that they were responding to an unprompted, negative comment made by their teacher.

Discipline and surveillance are important conditions impacting the learning of girls in confinement. They were on lockdown, and learning there was difficult. Their narratives reveal that learning in the juvenile court school is not perceived as an extension of quality learning from district or community schools. Instead, many of the girls I spoke with expressed that the material was not only repetitive but also unrelated to their future goals or interests. For these girls, the juvenile court school *increased* the counterproductive exclusion to which they were already exposed in their district schools.

"You can't learn," Mia shared. "Like . . . it's even more of a struggle than regular schools, 'cause everybody in here for a certain thing. Either somebody come back from court and they hella mad . . . you say something to them, they have a bad attitude, so you like, 'Hold on.' And then it's like, a fight. Or, you know, I don't know, like . . . sometimes, like this teacher, she don't know. . . . Like when I say this, I'm so serious. If you sat in her class, you'd be like, 'Oh my gosh. She don't know how to teach.' Like, why did they hire this lady? She know how to teach science. That's what she knows. She don't know how to teach math. They put her for science and math, so when she does math, it's like, she ask the kids up in our class, 'Do you know this?' And we're like, 'Aren't you the teacher? Aren't you supposed to know this kind of stuff?' And [the teacher] was like, 'No, you guys are.' . . . You're supposed to be teaching us, not just thinking out of nowhere. She . . . a lot of times she kicks us out because we don't know stuff."

"What has gotten you kicked out of class in here?" I asked.

"One time I was in class . . . I was telling her that I was done, because I get done with my work fast if I know how to do it. So I was like, I'm done. She was like, 'Okay, you're always done before the class, what does that mean?' So, I'm like, 'Well, I have an hour to go before I go back to the unit.' So I'm telling her like, 'What, you want me to just sit here for an hour?' She was like, 'Yes, put your head down.' So I'm just like, 'All right.' So I just sit there, you know, like . . . then I'm like, 'Can I write or draw? Something? I mean, it's a whole hour to go.' She was like, 'No, you can't do anything. You're always getting done before the whole class. You know what, get out. Give me your pencil and get out.' I'm like, 'Because I do my work, I'm actually trying to do my work now, and now you want me to get out?' Hella shit. She blame hella shit on us, like . . . some of the class is badder than the others. So like, some of the class will take off the erasers and throw it at her, and the whole class gets in trouble because of it. 'Oh, I'm going to let your staff know that you guys have been taking off the erasers, and whoop-tee-whoop.' She act like we want to steal a fucking eraser. What's an eraser?"

When girls were "kicked out" of class, they were relegated to sitting out in the hallway until they were invited back to the classroom or the class period was over.

"And sometimes she gives us suspension for that," Mia continued.

"What does suspension look like in here?" I asked.

"You just got no free rec. Free rec is when you, like, come out at nighttime . . . you don't got none of that. You don't . . . really, you don't get to do nothing. You got to eat all your meals in your room."

No recreation, eating in isolation—"suspension" seemed akin to a form of solitary confinement.

For Malaika, who struggled with managing her triggers to fight, school in the punitive environment of juvenile hall was particularly challenging.

"Well, I don't like [this teacher]," she said. "She don't need to be here because it seem like she don't want to be here. And it seem like she miserable and don't got no life, and just come here to, you know, torture us . . . Like you could just sit in the hallway . . . She don't even know the work. She teach [the subject], but she don't know how to do it. Like, she'll teach one student one way, and then teach the other student this way. Then we all just be confused. Then she don't even be knowing the answer. Some of the kids be correcting her. Like, 'Why did you get the job and why did

you volunteer to do that subject if you don't even know how to do
it?' And then, for [the other subject], it's like basically, she don't
teach. All she do is give us a packet in the book. The packet goes
with the book, so it's like, the packet comes out of the workbook,
you know? So, all you got to do is just look in there, it's going to
tell you the answer . . . we're not really learning anything. She's not
even going over it with us. We're just doing the work and put it in
our folder. She don't even check the work. Like, she shouldn't be
no teacher. . . . If you ask her a question, she's going to get mad
'cause *she* don't know [the answer]! 'Cause she don't know it, she's
going to get mad and take it out on us. I be getting hecka irritated.
One time she sent me out of class because I didn't know the answer. And she was going to send me out of class! I'm like, how is
you going to send me out of class 'cause I don't know the answer?
That's stupid."

Teachers in juvenile hall face the tall order of managing girls
with significant histories of school absence and failure, which are
compounded by their histories of trauma and abuse. I have never
met a teacher who actually "didn't care" about the education of
girls in juvenile hall, but many teachers that I have encountered
over the years have admitted to feeling overwhelmed and often
emotionally unprepared or insufficiently trained to deal with
the myriad issues that prevent them from forming meaningful
relationships—even if temporary—with the girls they educate
in juvenile hall.

Where Credit Is Due

"I mean, I know they still want us to get our credits and stuff while
we're in here," Portia said. "But I think it's just, like, a waste
because somebody do something, the whole group got to suffer for
it, which means we all got to go to our rooms. . . . It's structured.
Like military structured. . . . It feels like it's a waste of my time for
me to be here and try to get my credits, if I'm not going to get
them correctly. I feel like if you're going to go to school here, then

you should get the same amount of credits you get in a regular school. 'Cause these little one, two, five credits . . . I mean, it's helpful, but it don't really do nothing."

For Portia, credit recovery was an important motivator for her attendance and participation in the juvenile court school. However, she was aware of the mismatch between what she was doing in the classrooms, and what might actually prove to be useful in the long-run. The No Child Left Behind Act (2001) required all schools, including juvenile court schools, to report "adequate yearly progress" (AYP). The aim was to monitor and evaluate student progress with respect to achievement, accrual of school credits, readiness to transfer to a "regular program or other education program," completion of secondary school or employment, and, as appropriate, postsecondary education or job training efforts.[32] One study by the Juvenile Justice Enhancement Program found that as many as nineteen states were not including juvenile court schools in their AYP reports.[33] This is an issue that many educators understand as problematic, yet feel powerless to address.

I asked a school district official about the credit alignment process and how to facilitate a more seamless process for children in detention. I was specifically interested in how system leaders might better respond to the nature of educating youth in detention—the short stays versus the long stays, reconciling the student's ability versus the design of the curriculum, and other considerations. Other professionals in the department had observed the problem and devised unofficial strategies, such as using smaller increments for the credit accrual process that prevent youth from losing credits if they stayed less than a week in custody. I offered these suggestions and other ideas to engage school board members in a conversation on this topic.

After listening to me talk for several moments, the administrator smugly looked at me and said, "If you can figure that out, then you'll get a major award."

I'm certain he meant it as a joke, but credit recovery is a serious concern for girls who have a history of particularly contentious relationships with school. The uncertainty with which a number of the young women I spoke to approached the topic of credit accrual and recovery left little question that the inconsistent manner for earning and tracking student credits undermines their trust in the juvenile court educational system.

Additionally, the transient nature of the population in confinement, combined with local (district) variances in the credit accrual processes, was confusing for the majority of girls. As Stacy shared, "My mama tried to get . . . credits, but she couldn't do it. . . . I'm going to have my mama come up here, try again and see if she can switch my credits back to my school. I have some credits . . . I think."

Stacy was uncertain. Of this I was sure.

Well Enough to Learn

When I met Portia, she was struggling to maintain her sanity among other girls who were also impacted by mental illness. Nationwide, 81 percent of girls in the juvenile justice system suffer from a mental health disorder.[34] In California, the percentage of youth with a mental health disorder ranges between 40 and 70 percent.[35]

"Other girls' attitudes [make it hard for me]," she said. At that moment, we could hear other inmates banging on their cell doors. The clanks and bangs echoed loudly through the unit.

"Like that," she continued, referencing the banging. "Everybody's different. I mean, you're put in a place with a bunch of girls you don't know and it's hard for you guys to all fit together without wanting to kill each other . . . so I mean, like me, if I'm feeling sad, I hide my feelings. I cover it by being goofy. I do that to the other girls to make them laugh, but they're not used to how my personality is, so then they get upset about it. But then I have to tell them, 'I'm not doing it to make you mad. This is the way I am.'

And they be like, 'Okay' . . . and then they get used to it. Like one of the girls, she reminds me so much of my sister . . . She talks back to me on purpose, [and] that's just our relationship. I call her by my little sister's name, so it's like, that's just me and her . . . So we could be in class and just talk to each other like, acting like we're having an argument. And the teacher think we're having an argument, but we're laughing at each other."

In my experience, children in carceral settings will create family structures in order to normalize what can be an otherwise dehumanizing experience. Youth who are peers in age might appropriate a family structure by calling another inmate their "mother" or "sister" to help normalize the living space and to provide familial supports for each other that may not otherwise exist. When teachers are not aware of these relationships, or when they respond to them with discipline, they undermine these relationships and instead perpetrate a hyperpunitive learning environment. A more productive and effective approach might be to facilitate collaborative learning spaces where girls are encouraged to explore their relationships with each other along with why they reenact "arguments" as a way to demonstrate familial bonds.

Like Black girls who are high achievers, many of those in trouble with the law understand the value of a quality education, even if it has never been offered to them. In my conversations with detained Black girls, they understood that education was an important part of their time in juvenile hall. However, most did not consider their juvenile court school to be a model learning environment. In general, they agreed with youth nationwide who view the quality of correctional education as "poor," inadequate by state standards.[36]

As described in earlier chapters, schools' punitive response to girls' truancy, experience with bullying, and learning disabilities reinforces relationships that further marginalize girls who are struggling to survive. For girls who live in poverty and who have

a history of contact with the criminal legal system, schools reproduce dominant ideas of power and privilege in ways that push
them away from school and toward other environments that increase their risk of confinement. Historically, this vulnerability is
further increased when teachers, administrators, and institutional
policies project low expectations onto Black girls who have been
labeled as delinquent.[37] Notwithstanding their status as "juvenile
delinquents" with significant histories of victimization, these girls
know that an education is their best chance for a good job—that it
is their "passport to the future," as Malcolm X stated.[38]

Girls in confinement know that the juvenile court school provides a special opportunity to reconnect them with school. Still,
too often the poor quality of instruction, combined with racial
isolation, a punitive climate, and an inability to successfully
match their district school credit with the credits they earned
while in detention, has left them at a loss and further pushed out
of school. These tangible, symbolic, verbal, and nonverbal cues
communicate just how tenuous their rehabilitative status really
is. For some girls—like Mia in the Bay Area, who found her family's
conflicting messages about how she should behave in school
confusing—all they have to rely on is self-motivation to attend
school and perform well; being treated as expendable serves to
reinforce her understanding of education as an optional activity,
and school as a place that she could (and in her mind perhaps
should) live without.

The majority of the girls I have spoken with over the years have
reported a lack of confidence in the teaching ability and/or commitment of at least one instructor in their juvenile court school.
Almost half of them have perceived that a teacher in their juvenile
court school had routinely refused to answer their specific questions about the material they were learning.

When girls have not been actively in school prior to their incarceration, they express concern about the perceived skill set of their

instructor having an impact on their future. As Janis once said to me, "I don't even know my credits. They [juvenile court school] don't be helping me out with nothing. . . . I know I really want to go to college, though. But I don't want to go far, because I don't want to be away from home. Like, I get homesick."

Janis was another runner. She ran away from home and group homes and even cut off her electronic ankle monitor because it made her feel enslaved. So, I found her statement about being "homesick" very interesting.

"You run away, but you get homesick?" I asked.

"Yeah," Janis said. "I really get homesick. . . . I don't know. . . ."

She chuckled and then continued, "I just get homesick. I don't want to go far, but . . . I want to have a good education. I know for sure I'm going to go to college for four years."

Her statement piqued my interest. Detained African American girls have been found to express a desire to continue their education after their period of incarceration.[39] Previous research also found that while detained Black girls often have experienced depression and trauma, they demonstrate more self-efficacy and lower levels of delinquency than their male counterparts—all of which has an impact on whether Janis's interest in going to college actually materializes. To this point, Bonita Veysey wrote:

> Girls with histories of physical and sexual abuse are extremely vulnerable to trauma reactions, and typical justice and treatment procedures, such as a pat down by a male officer, can be re-traumatizing and trigger trauma responses. . . . Girls who meet the criteria for conduct disorder, for example, have a higher risk than their male counterparts for developing more severe psychopathology. . . . Similarly, the long-term prognosis for girls with antisocial behavior who fail to receive treatment is dismal. For example, more than half of the girls committed to state training schools reported attempting suicide, and of these, 64 percent had attempted more than once.[40]

Research has also found that having greater levels of family and community involvement may increase student academic potential.[41] Allowing girls to explore their experiences and conditions in the context of their learning environment would give them space to reconsider the value of education. What these young women learn and whom they are learning with, therefore, are just as important as the fact that they are learning.

"Do you know what you want to study in college? Do you know what interests you?" I asked Janis.

"Not yet," she said.

"Have you ever talked to a counselor . . . like a college placement counselor or anything . . . who could help talk to you about how to get to a community college or get you on the road to a four year college?"

Janis shook her head. "No."

Though there are concerns about the low success rate of students who enter college without the necessary pathways to success, when students have a team of stakeholders invested in their academic success and financial stability while in school, they perform well. Janis was full of youthful exuberance (and a fair amount of rebellion), but she was clueless about her own educational trajectory. I looked at her and asked, "How do you think schools could better prepare you to get to college?"

She sat back in her chair and thought about my question for a few seconds.

"They need to tell you your credits," she finally responded, focusing specifically on the juvenile court school. "How much you need [and] what you need. Like, you know how some colleges are like, you got to have this together, or you got to have this grade point average . . . they could help us out with that. Or tell us, 'If you want to go here, you got to go do this,' you know, like . . . we need to learn stuff. I don't want to go to college and just be dumb, thinking I've been learning all this time, and I've been learning

Little League stuff, you know?" Janis was searching for a pathway from confinement to college.

The punitive learning environment that many Black girls experience in their district schools is often exacerbated in their juvenile court school. The girls who spoke with me were removed from the classroom, suspended, or subjected to a written reprimand for acts of insubordination ("talking back" or refusing to read a book) or for acts that signaled a mismatch between their skill set and the material being taught, such as completing work early or persistently trying to ask a question about the material. Being excluded from their learning environment for asking questions or challenging authority—rather than for posing an actual physical threat to their own safety or to the safety of other students—further criminalizes Black girls in their learning spaces. Worse, it fuels them being disproportionately labeled as "defiant," "disruptive," and "uncooperative," all of which may result in a written reprimand that can lead to more severe sanctions in the hall, including solitary "room time" or loss of recreation privileges. The exclusionary discipline that is often indirectly related to school pushout becomes more direct and pronounced in juvenile court schools.

"We're Inmates, but We're Still Kids"

Jennifer had been sex-trafficked, and her sexual victimization and three-year absence from school facilitated an academic lag. Her relationship with educational institutions needed a lot of nurturing. The juvenile court school was the location inside juvenile hall with the most potential to begin this repair. This was particularly important in light of how Jennifer envisioned her future.

"I care about kids," she said. "[When I get older] I want to, like, teach somebody instead of locking them up. 'Cause I feel . . . I mean, we're inmates, but we're still kids. You know, a lot of these kids in here go through a lot of stuff."

Jennifer understood the key role of teachers and wanted
to present a different environment for young women who were
"going through a lot of stuff." Her persistent frown suggested that
she had firsthand knowledge of the ways in which girls were routinely subjected to dehumanizing treatment, both in and out of
the classroom. One morning when I was waiting outside of the classroom before a meeting, an institutional staff person walked past me
with Jennifer in tow. She had been called out of class for a court
appearance, and the staff person had to pause to speak with another
staff member. Jennifer's expression and body language were meek,
but the staff person leading her had a different tone.

"Sit your ass down," the staff person said, pointing to a seat in
the general meeting area.

Without a word, Jennifer sat down. She knew how to take
orders. Her knees were pressed together as she sat with perfect posture, her hands clasped and resting in her lap. At first, she avoided
eye contact with me, but she must have felt my gaze, because she
finally looked up.

We had spoken a few days prior about the ways in which
those who were supposed to protect her had triggered her, and I
wondered why this staff person felt it necessary to bark "sit your
ass down" instead of saying "take a seat" or something more
appropriate.

"Are you okay?" I quickly mouthed.

She nodded and smiled as if there was nothing wrong. I did not
plan to intervene, nor did I have the authority to do so, but I was
curious about why this staff member would speak to her this way.
I nodded back to her and looked down at my notepad.

Juvenile detention centers are not trauma-sensitive, I thought.
And they never will be.

"The teachers' attitudes [could be better in here]," Jennifer had
said when we spoke. "They [could] explain stuff to us and not get
irritated so bad. Not all of them, but some of the teachers think,
like, 'cause we're inmates, like, if we say one little thing wrong,

they're going to send us to our room or something. Like, it's just . . . 'cause we're inmates, they feel like they have power because they're outsiders. That's the problem. If they weren't so mean like that, it would be better . . . make [girls] care more about their education.

"I think they should have a thing, a program about why education is important," Jennifer continued. "You have to go through a process to get what you want. . . . When you're home-schooled, it's more better. When I'm in the classroom, I can't do my work because I get nervous. . . . It's just that I don't like to be around a lot of people. Plus in here, they be arguing over the dumbest stuff ever, like who sit by who, or . . . I look better than you . . . but you in the same suit, so . . . I can't be in no classroom with a boy. You know how little boys make dumb remarks? I'll get irritated really fast."

I asked if Jennifer preferred the same-gender learning environment that she had while in juvenile hall to the coed classrooms of her district school.

"No, not really," she said. "I like my own environment."

For Deja, integration into the juvenile court classroom was less bumpy. She saw it as an important part of her daily routine. At the time of our conversation, she had been in detention for a week and was feeling acclimated to her new learning environment.

"Okay," Deja said. "About seven, you wake up, get ready to come out and eat. You go back in your room for about another ten or twenty minutes, then walk over here to school. You go to that first class for about, like, two hours [and then] come back for a break for like, thirty minutes . . . we might go to PE or to the library after that. Maybe, if it's our day. And then go to the other class for two hours. Then, go eat lunch, come back and go to this one last class. Then, we go back over [to the unit] and then it's shift change, which means we get different staff. So then, we come out and we go work out for like, an hour, thirty minutes or whatever. We eat dinner. Take showers. Then we have an hour rec or whatever . . . you know, they might have a program set up for us. You know, volunteers come up or whatever. Weekends are different. We wake, we eat, clean our rooms, and then like, the staff might have a movie for us."

When I asked her what she thought of school in juvenile hall, she responded, "Well, I like that one teacher, she does take her time and listen. She's really helpful and like, she . . . explains and she goes into more details, versus that other teacher where she just . . . I don't know what's her problem. . . . She just crazy or something."

"How does she act?" I asked, noting that she positively responded to the teacher who she said "took her time and listened."

"If you're asking her too many questions or something like, if you keep asking her for help or something, she'll get mad. She'll make up a little thing, make a big deal out of it, and then try to write you up."

"So do you ask questions when you actually need help?" I asked. "Or do you ask questions just because you want to know more?"

"I don't like to be bothered . . . I really don't. I ask questions when I really don't understand something. Like, I really just try to do it myself before I ask somebody else for help, and then later on do it to see if I got it wrong. . . . It would be better if [the teacher] were to help sometimes. She don't want to help. She just want to give you work and expect you to know how to do it."

Again, the inability for girls to ask questions—clarifying or otherwise—was perceived as a problem by multiple girls getting their education in juvenile hall. Credit recovery was also a hurdle for Deja to overcome.

"Like, every fifteen days, you only get one credit," she said. "I almost didn't pass the eleventh grade, 'cause I was just so far behind. [The juvenile court school] needs to fix their school system or something to make it like regular school because . . . you have this school and then when you go back to regular school, [it's hard]. . . . If I were going to [another] school, it would have been harder for me to get all back my credits 'cause I was just so far back. I almost had to take night classes and everything. . . . I'm missing something [in here]! Like, I feel like [this school] just [takes] a lot from me . . . it wasn't even worth doing the work."

Stacy had a more intimate relationship with school discipline. As a self-described "problem child," she often responded to authority in a very negative manner. Specifically, she often called people at school "bitches"—teachers, students, and security guards.

"Why would you call the security guard a bitch?" I asked.

"I had a pass to go to the bathroom . . . She [stopped me and was] going to take my pass . . . and then she took my pass! I looked at her . . . and said, 'That's hella irritating.' Then she went to my class, so I was like, 'Bitch, you're hella irritating.' She [said], "You going to make me lose my job." I was like, 'Okay, we can just fight 'cause you seem like you threatenin' me, talking about "you going to make me lose my job." I got a mama that will beat your ass' . . . I'm like, yeah . . . so she [took] me to the office. And then when we get to the office, she [said] that she didn't say that I was going to make her lose her job. I was like, 'Why is you lying, 'cause the principal right here?' . . . I will tell them what I said . . . I'ma admit to what I said. Ain't no reason for me to lie. I'm like, 'Why you can't admit to what you said?' "

I looked at Stacy as she cocked her head to the side, folded her arms, and slumped into her chair.

"She know I don't take smack from nobody," Stacy said, still visibly irritated by that experience.

Remember: hurt people hurt other people.

These girls' stories remind us that a classroom inside of a locked facility is not exempt from being a location for the use (or abuse) of suspension and other disciplinary actions that remove children from their learning environment. We are also reminded that for girls accustomed to using violence as a response to feeling disrespected, being in a hyperpunitive environment may only reinforce negative behaviors that result in marginalization from schools. For confined Black girls, the juvenile court school can further alienate them from their education, sometimes for the most minor "infraction," such as asking a question or making a comment to themselves. The problem is that this hyperpunitive classroom management structure affects girls' perceptions about the function of school and their relationship with it. This practice may trigger girls who are in trouble with the law and who are already marginalized from school in any setting. The structure fails to meet girls where they are and guide them through their problems, which in all likelihood leads to exacerbated challenges on the other end instead of leading them down healthier, safer paths.

A majority of the girls I spoke with perceived the level of the coursework to be below their grade level. Irrespective of age or grade level, girls in the juvenile court school were educated in a single classroom and learned the same material. This was a source of great discontent and anxiety among the girls. Those who felt that the work was beneath their skill level were concerned that they were not learning enough to recover credits and return to school with the necessary information to successfully reintegrate into the classroom.

"School here's really frustrating for me," Destiny said. "The teachers here know that we're here temporarily, so I feel like they don't make sure that we're really learning."

Another student said, "[This school] don't teach you nothing. I'm in high school. They're teaching middle school stuff."

The work in the juvenile court school was described by several young women as "the same," or repetitive, and the girls felt that their learning was stagnated by the absence of challenging material. However, for the younger participants who felt the work was above their grade level, there was a concern that they had missed critical information that might impact future learning and performance in their district school. For example, Mia said, "You're teaching tenth grade while I'm still really in the seventh and the eighth . . . so you're not helping me. You're teaching me tenth-grade stuff and yeah, I get that stuff because you're teaching it to me *now*, but what's going to happen when I don't know the other stuff? You know what I'm saying?"

"I'm Not Retarded, I Just Got a Learning Disability"

Mecca was a seventeen-year-old foster child who had been committed to juvenile hall five times by the time we spoke in 2013. In our conversation, she admitted that she was afraid to leave juvenile hall because she was uncertain about where she would go or what her future might bring. Though she was often perceived as a "bully" because of her size—she was a larger girl—Mecca believed that she was actually the victim of bullying. For Mecca, "bullying" was part of the hyperpunitive learning environment in confinement. It was a condition that affected her learning because it was coming not just from students, but also from teachers.

"I don't want to be in school in jail. . . . School in here is, well, you're just still locked up. School on the outside, it's just better. They got more education. Like the teachers, they've got more background about them. The things they're teaching . . . it's just better," Mecca said. "I hate school in juvenile hall. I feel like they're too hard on us. Like, we get stereotyped. I feel like every time I come in here, we're doing the same thing, and I don't come in here, back to back."

She offered specific observations about what made school in juvenile hall different than district schools, in her experience. "The school in here is different than the school you usually go to. On the outs, you have partner work in school. You can talk. If you're stuck, you can ask for help. But in here, it's almost like if you ask for help, they fuss about wanting to help you, and then you just don't want to ask for help. It's going to become a big argument and you're going to get kicked out. In juvenile hall, nobody really

wants to sit in their room all day, so you really don't want to get
kicked out of class. And then there's the bullying."

Nationwide, 28 percent of students in grades six through
twelve have experienced some form of bullying.[42]

"Once, we were doing math in class, and they were teasing me
because I didn't know my multiplication," Mecca continued.
"Instead of trying to help me, they teased me. . . . I had a teacher in
here, she called me 'retarded' in front of everybody because I asked
her for a calculator for my test!"

"What?" I asked. "How did this happen?"

"Well," Mecca said, "a girl asked [the teacher] if she could have
a calculator, and the teacher said no, and [told her] that the only
reason I had a calculator was because my IEP said I could have
one.[43] The girl said, 'Well, how do I get an IEP?' The teacher said,
'Oh, you have to be retarded.' So then I told her, 'I'm not retarded.
I just got a learning disability!' Then the teacher said, 'Say another
thing, and I'm going to suspend you.' I was like, 'How are you
going to suspend me for sticking up for myself?' So . . . it's not only
the kids. Teachers do it too."

Just as in district schools—as discussed in previous chapters—
Black girls are confronted by teachers who argue with them, avoid
answering their questions, and label them as "difficult" for standing up for themselves or others they believe have been treated unfairly. However, while students perceive this relationship to be
problematic, they also want to be engaged by their teachers, to
be loved by them.

"Things could be different in here if the teachers would actually
teach us," Mecca said. "It's not just this unit. It's all the units.
Teachers want to just sit down and give you work when you come
in. 'Oh, do this work, stop talking,' this and that, and you're like,
'Damn, when I finish the work I have nothing to do, and now
you're telling me to stop talking! And now you're focused on discipline.' Then I'm getting sent out of class. They need to focus on
teaching the kids, that's what nobody understands. They're not

teaching the kids anything. This place is set up to fail you. Honestly. If this school was set up to bring you up and help you through your community, then okay, they could do that. But they need to change their perception of what's going on here; because they think they're doing good, and they're actually doing wrong." For Mecca, like for Deja, the effort to recover credits was a hurdle that was exacerbated by the perceived poor quality of instruction, the use of exclusionary discipline, and the inconsistent way in which districts accounted for credits.

For the girls who participated in this project, the student-teacher relationship is a tremendous obstacle to their rehabilitation and full engagement with school. Many teachers are struggling to provide a meaningful educational experience for girls in the criminal legal system who are experiencing multiple risk factors that affect their well-being. Even if the desire to connect with their female students is present, some teachers may be shutting down communication or rejecting the notion that they should teach more than the curriculum because they have not been adequately equipped to handle the downpour once it's invited. These girls' narratives illustrate us that it's crucial for the learning environment to be a place where openness and respect can flourish in order for children to trust that education is their pathway to success. Each girl I spoke with signaled in her own way that she wants to be treated as a human being who is capable of thinking on her own. Her ideas are not lost, her consciousness does not subside, and her hopes may not be quashed simply because she is in juvenile hall.

The experiences of Faith, Mecca, and others in juvenile court school reveal how girls' behaviors are sometimes triggered by the words and actions of the adults around them. To be labeled as "disrespectful" or called "retarded" is problematic because it reinforces a stigma and trauma that these girls have spent their lives rejecting, and it also suggests that often there is no space for interrogating how those with authority instigate or intensify conflict. Not only has rejecting girls' voices failed to teach them what they need in order to learn and reach critical milestones, it does little if anything to restore their faith in educational systems and the power of knowledge. Shutting down girls' voices reinforces their deeply negative associations with school and with other authority figures who have shut down their voices, their spirits, and their bodies for years. If a girl doesn't understand the material, why can't she ask a question? Why must she stay silent and work alone, especially if that is inconsistent with her best learning style?

For a majority of detained girls, juvenile court school did not serve to repair their already problematic relationships with school. At best it was a missed opportunity. Each girl, in her own way, found the schoolwork to be repetitive and unrelated to her interests and goals. Each girl, in her own way, found most of her instructors to be punitive and impatient. A U.S. Department of Education study found that 43 percent of incarcerated youth who received remedial education services in detention did not return to school after being released, and that 16 percent of these youth enrolled in school after their confinement but then dropped out after only five months.[44] Other studies have discovered similar trends, all leading to the conclusion that detention facilities can be, and often are, harmful places. Most of the girls I spoke with had experienced school suspensions, expulsions, or both prior to their confinement in juvenile hall, but what they had not expected—what was in fact counterintuitive given the stated objective of the juvenile court school to *prevent* dropping out—was for their suspension, removal, and general exclusion from the classroom to *increase* in the juvenile court school. Indeed, these girls had learned negative behaviors that fueled a number of mistakes. Though they were cast as the "bad" girls, what was evident from their comments about school was that these girls want to learn. Their complaints, frustrations, and hurt—and sometimes their exact words—reflected their awareness of how important an education is to their ability to succeed. They were also painfully aware of the conditions in juvenile detention that prevented them from trying to put their academic lives back on track.

Histories of victimization and addiction, poor student-teacher relationships, being subject to zero tolerance and harsh discipline along with uninspired and poorly executed curriculum, and the school credit mismatch—independently and together, all these factors function to push Black girls in juvenile court schools further away from all schooling. While few would disagree that the ultimate goal is to prevent more girls from going to correctional facilities at all, more often than not juvenile court schools exacerbate the problems more than they contribute to the solutions. They should be serving as an important rehabilitative structure for detained girls. The schools inside juvenile hall represent the first chance for girls to reenter their home communities successfully and on a different track. They are in a position to shift the girls' perception of what school is, especially for girls whose educational lives have been largely defined by truancy, avoidance, or bullying.

These girls are not a "submerged tenth," but rather our forgotten daughters. They are those among us who have suffered tremendous obstacles and personal traumas. They are the ones we adults have harmed and failed the most. They are the ones who have unsuccessfully attempted to improve life's conditions—often harming themselves and others in the process—but they are also the ones with the greatest opportunity for improvement. Education is likely to be their best chance to shape a better life—their best chance to rebound from their conviction histories and emerge as productive, engaged citizens capable of charting new paths toward redemption.

What happens today in juvenile court schools is a matter of equity. They are structurally inferior, and they are failing to interrupt school-related dropout and pushout. The moral and legal obligation to improve the quality of education for all youth extends even to young people who are in trouble with the law.

For more than half a century, education has been constitution-
ally acknowledged as the primary tool for restructuring social hierarchies and elevating the conditions of historically oppressed
peoples. Prior to that, this understanding engendered fear and
shaped the poor quality of education afforded Black girls under
the wardship of the court for some two hundred years. The education their modern-day counterparts receive raises the question of
whether we want to restructure the social hierarchies or whether
we want to leave the status quo intact.

Thurgood Marshall wrote in his opinion for *Procunier v.
Martinez* (1974), "When the prison gates slam behind an inmate,
he does not lose his human quality; his mind does not become
closed to ideas; his intellect does not cease to feed on a free and
open interchange of opinions; his yearning for self-respect does
not end; nor is his quest for self-realization concluded."

Though these girls are in confinement, their minds are alive.
They are interested in and capable of more than mindless busy-
work. They all can learn, many of them want to do so, and like
anyone whose life has veered off track, they are eager for a second
chance. If we can improve the accountability and performance of
these schools, alongside their district counterparts, we will inevita-
bly move toward a more comprehensive approach to reducing the
impact of policies and practices that criminalize and push girls out
of school. We will, in essence, begin the process of maintaining
these girls' human quality—an essential component of their successful rehabilitation and reengagement as productive members of
our communities. To Black girls in trouble with the law, the juvenile court school has never been a beacon of academic hope. It's
time for a paradigm shift. As long as there are juvenile detention
facilities, the schools inside must uplift the potential of each student, not her deficits.

As potential places for developing the whole person, schools,
whether in facilities or communities, can and should be transformative environments that help girls make better decisions in their

lives. A school with professionals devoted to developing, not unraveling, Black girls' academic well-being *and* their mental health would provide a foundation for cultivating new ways to respond to their emotional, physical, and sexual trauma so they don't repeat mistakes (in relationships with friends, teachers, family, and sexual partners) that spiral them further into poverty, crime, addiction, violence, or worse. Chapter 5 explores how we can begin to do this.

5

REPAIRING RELATIONSHIPS, REBUILDING CONNECTIONS

If you're more confident, then you've got more hope.
—Leila, eighteen years old, Chicago

Heaven had the kind of piercing, attentive stare that responded to your every word. If only she'd been able to focus on school the same way. When we met, it was her first time in juvenile hall—but she hadn't been to school in five months. She was seventeen years old and was supposed to be in twelfth grade, but as a runaway, she had been more concerned with surviving than with attending school. It was still her intention to join a Job Corps program and then complete her high school diploma, but getting that diploma would prove more of a challenge than she thought.

"I don't want a GED," she said. "I feel like it shows that you can't complete something, or you can't finish something, so it's going to be very hard to get a job or a career. [They'll] say, 'Well, you couldn't complete high school . . . so why should we accept you here?' So that's why I really want my high school diploma because the GED still shows that you didn't complete high school . . . I still want to get my high school diploma."

Heaven had been running away from home for years, staying with friends, other family members, and mainly her boyfriend, who was two years older than she was and renting his own apartment. She claimed to have never liked school and said, "It's boring . . . and I feel like . . . I don't know, it's too many hours. The work schedule and school . . . certain classes you're not going to use them in real life."

Like the majority of her counterparts, she knew that school was an important part of her life, even though she did not enjoy going.

"I'm willing to push through that to start my future," Heaven said. "You can't get nothing without [an education]. . . . That's one thing they can't take from you . . . your knowledge. . . . I'm very smart, and I know, like, through all the schools, I didn't pass because I didn't stay long enough to complete them, not because I didn't know [how to do the work]."

Heaven's favorite subjects were English and history, and she felt confident about her ability to learn.

"My teachers always told me that I was smart and capable. . . . They always said that when I came, I always did my work and it was good, but I was the type of student that didn't always come [to school]. Or I came to school and didn't go to class. . . . Sometimes I would come, like, in the morning and then I'll leave for the rest of the day. Or I'll come and then I'll leave . . . I'll probably leave at lunch and not come back. . . . It really didn't matter. Certain periods, like if I really didn't like the period, I wouldn't go to that period. I'd go to the next one."

Heaven had many distractions.

"Which periods did you cut most?" I asked.

"Math and physiology. I loved physiology class because I loved learning about the human body, but I didn't like the teacher, and so that's why I never went to that class. . . . Every time I went to that class, I either cussed her out or something. I got a referral, which made me have to sit in one room for a long time."

For Heaven, positive encouragement from her teachers was an important dynamic for her continued learning. But those relationships were not there, so she looked for reinforcements elsewhere.

She lamented her disconnection from school and thought about the distractions that kept her from engaging, including a preoccupation with looking good at school—the "fashion show," she called it—and getting high with her friends.

"I regret my whole high school years, to be honest, because I was *capable* of completing high school as a normal high school student," Heaven said. "But I *chose* to do other things, which led my life in a different way. I'm still going to get to the roses and the flowers at the end of the path, I just took the rockier path than the straight and narrow. . . . If I would be able to go back, I would not take it for granted. I'm learning [that] love and school are the only things you get for free when you're young, and I took it for granted. And now, if I don't get into a program that will help me get my high school diploma for free, I will have to pay, 'cause I took it for granted when I had the chance of getting it for free."

Heaven was nervous about her prospects of being able to get back on track—especially since she felt that she was primarily on her own. She seemed to fancy herself a good person. For the most part, she claimed, she tried to do the right thing. At age fourteen, she ran away from home and went to live with her sixteen-year-old boyfriend. She was even a good girlfriend to him, especially when he made the decision to get his life back in order and take advantage of programs that were designed to help young men reintegrate into school.

"I always wanted a relationship. . . . Even when I was fourteen, I wanted a relationship. . . . But it took a toll on me in another way. It made me feel like a grown woman, because I was staying with him and I was taking care of a man, so it was like, I was doing everything my mom did for her boo, for my boo. And so . . . now I wasn't going to school. But I made sure *he* went to school and he got *his* high school diploma. . . . You know, I was never really worried about myself. I was always the kind of person who cared about others more than me."

"Why did you sacrifice your own education so he could go to school?" I asked.

"Honestly, I don't know . . . because it wasn't smart. But I know I didn't want him to be like the rest of these boys standing out here on the street . . . and it was so crazy because we started off going to school together. And when he went on the run . . . he used to come to juvie . . . and when he went on the run and cut off his ankle [bracelet], I went with him because I knew that he wasn't going to come to school, and since I wanted a serious relationship, I knew that relationship wouldn't continue unless I was with him all the time, you know. I was one of those . . . I was very insecure. And so I wanted to be with him all the time, and he wanted the same thing. And so if he went to school . . . say if he went to school and I was doing something, he would always want to come and meet me, or I would want to come and meet him . . . while we were in school. So when he went to juvie, I was in school but I was stressin'."

"About what he was doing?" I asked, still processing the fact that she was willing to sacrifice her own education to make sure that her boyfriend had his.

"Yeah. How was he, and things of that nature. But then when he went to a group home and he wasn't able to go places or do nothing, he utilized all of these programs, these youth programs and school, and so every program, every time he went to school, who was there? Me. And so, instead of me being at *my* school, I was up at *his* school bringing him something to eat, giving his security guard sandwiches . . . so he'd be able to leave."

Heaven started laughing, as if she could hardly believe her own naiveté. She shook her head slowly.

Then I asked, "Did anybody ever ask you, 'What are you doing here? You're here for *his* program' . . . did anyone ever turn to you and ask for your story?"

I wanted to believe that the adults running a program for young men might have seen this young woman who was clearly standing by her boyfriend in all respects, yet still experiencing many of the same conditions for which he was getting help.

Her commitment to her boyfriend could be understood as powerful love. If only she had been able to focus some of that love on herself.

Heaven paused for a moment and then shook her head. "They always liked that I was on his team, that I was motivating him to do better. He didn't have nobody else pushing him to do right . . . and I knew that if I wasn't there, he wasn't going to stay that whole time, 'cause he was going to come looking for me somewhere. So I tried to make sure that he stayed on that program. So it messed up *my* program. It's bad and good at the same time. But it's bad for me. I don't regret doing that, to be so honest, because he wouldn't be the person he is now. I'm mad at myself that I couldn't juggle both, but I don't regret it."

I'm mad at myself that I couldn't juggle both. Black girls internalize very early on the idea that their well-being comes secondary to others'. Our policies, our public rhetoric about healing, even our protests all make the pain of Black females an afterthought to the pain of Black males. Heaven blamed herself for not being able to be with him all day and manage her own daily obligations. She blamed herself for essentially not being able to be in two places at once. The idea that Black girls have to hold the pain of Black boys, even at their own expense, is a form of internalized sexism. But when it's couched as a matter of being a "ride or die" girlfriend, many girls never see that by accepting these conditions, they become complicit in their own oppression. For girls like Heaven, getting an education is not only a rehabilitative act; it's an act of social justice.

Education, particularly formal education, is a primary avenue for accessing greater opportunity. Those who are pushed to the margins are often rendered too powerless to manage a clear vision of what a truly inclusive learning environment even looks like, let alone how they might participate in ways that support their well-being as learners, as Black girls, and as negotiators of their own destiny.

Over the years I've come to see how the expressive nature of Black girls has been both a blessing and a curse. Educational policies and practices that politicize dress or hair, that undermine or forgo learning in favor of hyperpunitive disciplinary actions, or that implicitly grant Black girls permission to fail all penalize characteristics and modes of being that could instead be built on and shaped into healthy tools for success.

To date, the conditions of Black females in the United States have been obscured by a racial justice agenda that persistently prioritizes males. The sometimes similar but frequently *not* so similar ways that Black girls are locked out of society become lost. The domestic gender justice agenda has also obscured experiences of struggling Black girls by steering the focus toward colorblind efforts that organize, invest, and develop strategies that purportedly support *all* women and girls—as if all girls are uniformly impacted by sexism, racism, and the consequences of patriarchy. The rather naive logic here parallels the cries that emerged shortly after "Black Lives Matter" unified millions in the wake of protests against routine police misconduct toward Black people: almost predictably, some people, including many well-intentioned ones, switched to the refrain "All Lives Matter." The problem, of course, is not that all lives don't matter. Of course they do. But substituting "All" for "Black" obscures the specific resistance to the anti-Black racism and bias that are frequently at the root of police violence, use of excessive force, harassment, and other injustices. So yes, *all* girls experience injustice, and all of it matters. Boys, specifically boys of color, are incarcerated at unjustifiable rates. And that matters too. But addressing any of these shouldn't come at anyone else's expense. Yet that's what we've tacitly allowed to happen—and in some cases explicitly supported—when it comes to Black girls.

Still, amid these challenges, Black girls possess a resilience that points the way to how we can provide meaningful opportunities for their development. Heaven knew that her own learning suffered because of her decision to put her boyfriend's well-being before her own. Without critical self-reflection—an engagement of her own thought process—she would not be able to see these actions as problematic. In her narrative is a cry for permission to center herself, and to know how and when to do it. Her education should facilitate and validate that process, not work against it, as is so frequently the case.

From the lessons, patterns, and insight gathered through speaking with Black girls from coast to coast, six themes emerged as crucial for cultivating quality learning environments for Black girls: (1) the protection of girls from violence and victimization in school; (2) proactive discussions in schools about healthy intimate relationships; (3) strong student-teacher relationships; (4) school-based wraparound services; (5) an increased focus on student learning coupled with a reduced emphasis on discipline and surveillance; and (6) consistent school credit recovery processes between alternative schools and traditional district or community schools.

At the root of these themes is the need to revisit "education as usual" and relationships that are facilitated, nurtured, and/or damaged in educational institutions. Increasingly, school districts across the nation are seeking alternatives to the alienating and punitive climate that informs negative interactions between schools and Black girls, as well as other girls of color. Many states have now acknowledged that the disparate use of exclusionary discipline among children of color is unconscionable and unsustainable if our nation is to truly implement an educational system that prioritizes teaching children over punishing them, and pushing them out of school.

Envisioning Schools Designed to Achieve Equity

Imagine a future for Black girls that is filled with dignity and where their learning spaces are places they are invited to critically engage, alongside educators, in the construction of their education and in the redemption of their lives. Imagine a Black female student identity that is not marred by stereotypes, but rather is buoyed by a collective vision of excellence that should always accompany the learning identities of our girls.

As we've seen, Black girls' educational lives are dynamic and complex, and too often follow a school-to-confinement pathway. They are affected by school-based decisions and practices that reinforce negative stereotypes about Black femininity and facilitate pushout, and their vulnerabilities increase once their connection with school has been harmed or severed. But pathways to criminalization are clear, often eminently clearer than any other pathway. The failure to fully understand or make space for the wide-ranging gender identities that many of our girls embrace sets up a criminalizing pathway for girls. The absence of culturally competent and gender-responsive methods of teaching—approaches that respond to girls who stand at the crossroads of racism, sexism, transphobia, homophobia, and poverty—sets up a criminalizing pathway for girls. Blanket discrimination against detained or formerly incarcerated people, or those suspected of being involved with the criminal legal system in some way, sets up pathways that further criminalize girls who have made mistakes and want to recover from them. Alongside these criminalizing pathways, external forces—the kinds of influences educators and systems have little control over—all but ensure that Black girls with the deck stacked against them will indeed take these paths, ill-equipped as they are to see and create better ones.

The criminalization and social marginalization that have been described throughout this book go hand-in-hand with society's expanding prison-industrial complex and the increased abandonment of a basic tenet associated with juvenile justice: redemption.[1] It's established and widely accepted that education is one of the greatest rehabilitative and protective factors against delinquency for girls.[2] When we take education away from them, Black girls are exposed to more violence, and they are more likely to be victimized and exploited, to become incarcerated, and to experience a lack of opportunity overall. When we prioritize discipline over learning in our educational institutions, we engage in a reactive politics that maintains a status quo of inequality.

As parents, educators, and concerned community members, we must examine the ways in which our educational institutions are underserving our children—and pushing our girls out of school alongside our boys. Changing the conversation about school discipline is not about excusing abhorrent behavior. Implementing alternative reactions to negative student behavior and developing relationships that teach young people about who they are and how they should behave in a safe learning environment doesn't conflict with developing personal responsibility. In fact, quite the opposite is true.

Rarely is there reflection upon the extent to which our reactions to girls' behaviors are rooted in whether they are being "good girls" or whether they have actually presented a harm or threat to safety, personal or public. We must also consider how expressions of Black femininity (e.g., how girls talk, dress, or wear their hair) are pathologized by school rules. In our haste to teach children social rules, we sometimes fail to examine whether these rules are rooted in oppression—racial, patriarchal, or any other form. Ultimately such a failure undermines the full expression and learning of Black girls.

Black girls need teachers, administrators, and school policies that do not see their Black identity as inferior or something to fear. Their Black femininity must not be exploited, ignored, and punished. Their words need not be seen as problematic, and their questions need not be seen as inherently defiant.

School-based policies and practices that expose Black girls to the disproportionate application of discipline, that emphasize society's dominant and negative constructs of Black femininity, or that seek to punish them for clothing and/or hairstyle choices must be eliminated and instead replaced by a pedagogy that embraces the healing and liberative power of talking.[3] The intention should be to provide learning spaces for Black girls to thrive without feeling that they have to reject their own identity to do so.

When Nancy, a teacher from California, stated that in order to prevent school-to-confinement pathways she must "teach more than the curriculum," she was putting forth a call for educators to see beyond the perceived attitude and the stereotypes that render too many of our girls invisible or unsuitable for the classroom. She was calling for a community response and an unapologetic rejection of the notion that our girls' learning is in any way less important than anyone else's.

There are no throwaway children. We can, and must, do better.

To eliminate the pushout and criminalization of our girls, the first step is for all those investing their time and energy in the fight for racial justice—advocates, scholars, organizers, and others—to stop measuring the impact of the criminal legal system simply by the numbers of people who are incarcerated. Incarceration is now framed as our generation's greatest civil and human rights challenge. We argue (and among like minds generally agree) that prisons and other carceral institutions are overused. We see the buildings, razor wire, and armed guards and understand them as physical monuments to inequality and pain. Prisons are tangible. They also hold more males than females; thus a racial justice agenda framed by the lens of incarceration elevates male endangerment. It leaves little room to consider the ways that females are also subjected to institutionalized harm and a prevailing consciousness that favors punishment over rehabilitation.

Focusing on criminalization, rather than just incarceration, would enable greater understanding of how institutions impact girls and facilitate important shifts in our thinking and decision-making processes. We could see women and girls in their *shared* spaces with men and boys, and develop strategies that are responsive to the conditions that threaten the futures of female and male children. Being more inclusive would save us from a lot of head-scratching about why it is so hard to break harmful cycles, the negative patterns in student outcomes, and contact with the criminal legal system.

Our nationwide culture of surveillance and criminalization is much more pervasive and life-threatening than even the largest prison. Its reach into our schools and our classrooms has reinforced latent ideas of Black inferiority and cast our girls as angry little women who are too self-absorbed and consumed by themselves and their faults to participate in school communities.

We know it's more complicated than that.

A Race-Conscious Gender Analysis

A race-conscious gender analysis may sound like an esoteric academic theory, but it's not. In essence it is the process of acknowledging that Black women never stop being Black people, nor do they stop being women. Thus they are affected by the policies and practices that undermine their development and progress as both. Every intervention that schools, communities, and lawmakers design for our girls has to recognize that gender expression and identity—and sexual expression and identity—must figure prominently in order to support their well-being. During institutional slavery, Black women, like their male counterparts, picked cotton, constructed railroads, and were whipped, flogged, and mutilated under oppressive and dehumanizing conditions. These were deplorable conditions that affected men and women alike. However, the *gendered* way in which racism has played out in their lives also meant that they were routinely raped and forced to serve as wet nurses to the newborn children of slave owners. Racialized gender stereotypes about Black women and other women of color shape how they interact with the world today, and how the world perceives and interacts with them. We are at a moment in history that lends itself to informed community building. The failures of the past are haunting us, and truthfully, there are enough narratives and data to justify a new approach to curbing troublesome behavior in schools. Also, our dominant social narrative—informed by a growing critique of mass incarceration—presents us with an opportunity to do more than just let people out of prison. At this juncture, we can choose the road less traveled and revisit the criminalization that has fueled a culture of incarceration in all its forms. An agenda for Black female achievement does not undermine or preclude any agenda or narrative on Black male achievement. An initiative for Black women and girls is not an affront to the efforts for Black men and boys—so it's time to bridge conversations.

Our girls, boys, and gender-nonconforming youth are sharing communities, institutions, homes, and lives with each other. Efforts to support women and girls of color are imperative to the successful navigation of any condition that places whole communities at risk. Programs to address family structures must not vilify single-female-headed households or assume that by supporting men and boys only, our schools and other institutions are meeting the needs of young women and girls. It's time to stop ignoring the very real conditions that push girls and young women to the margins of society and render them vulnerable to exploitation, abuse, and debilitating legal issues.

What We Should Really Mean by "Respect"

Our work on behalf of Black girls cannot be about respectability politics. Etiquette lessons can be a part of other social practices and agendas, but if our anti-criminalization efforts are to have teeth, schools must look far beyond whether our girls are wearing tight pants, crop tops, or pink extensions in their braids. The crisis of criminalization in schools is an opportunity to focus on the policies, systems, and institutions—in other words, the *structures*—that place women and girls at risk of exploitation in private and public domains. Intervention strategies are needed that respond to the unique ways that women and girls of color are affected by these structures. The safety of girls in schools will not be addressed only through metal detectors and the presence of security guards. Our challenge is to think through the very real triggers for girls, particularly those who have experienced sexual victimization or other abuse, and develop innovative approaches that reach out to girls through a holistic and healing lens (such as restorative processes that protect them from further exploitation and volunteers in the schools to help maintain a culture of respect and safety for girls), rather than a punitive one. Girls' learning can and should be positioned as an act of social justice and self-discovery rather than simply a mandate from the state. We cannot add ribbons and bows to a program, strategy, or agenda that has been developed in response to the circumstances of young men and assume that it will work for young women. Just because young women and girls are *affected* by similar conditions as their male counterparts doesn't mean that they *experience* these conditions in the same way. I hope the narratives in this book make the difference clear.

A new normal is in order with respect to efforts to support the healthy development of Black young women and girls. We need a radical shift in how we examine educational and punitive laws, policies, institutions, and systems—using rigorous race- and gender-conscious frameworks—so that we know how best to understand and remedy their impact on our girls.

We should examine these policies and ask the following central questions:

1. What assumptions are being made about the conditions of Black girls?
2. How might Black girls be uniquely impacted by school and other disciplinary policies?
3. How are organizations, systems, and policies creating an environment that is conducive or not conducive to the healthy development of Black girls?

These questions are important to prevent Black girls from being ignored in policy decisions and the impact of those decisions at every level—in schools, in communities, in cities, and beyond.

A Centered Response to Victimization

Black women, and other women of color, bear scars that are both visible and invisible. Their rates of victimization and experiences with abuse and exploitation are higher than for most other women. And yet, despite these and other statistics, we have yet to center their voices in our public discussions on victimization. The assumption that Black women and girls should be able to "handle it all" dominates our consciousness. But in doing so, we mistake the resiliency of our sisters for the absence of harm, and we miss girls like Heaven, who then blame themselves when their actions fall short of this unrealistic and contrived ideal. Our responses to Black girls must embrace a strong anti-victimization narrative that produces safe learning environments—physically, emotionally, and spiritually—and fosters a creative and expressive pedagogy to combat racial and gender oppression in the twenty-first century. And our actions must be swift and forceful. For too long we have only reacted to the persistent murmur of sexual harassment (instead of trying proactively to prevent it), turned our heads away from the threats to sexual and physical assault, or shamed our girls into believing that their victimization is their own fault.

Prevent and Disallow "Permission to Fail"

To revoke the "permission to fail" that has been granted to too many Black girls, schools must provide ongoing professional development that emphasizes reducing implicit bias and engages all manner of staff in the school's process of institutionalizing fair discipline policies. Teachers need the opportunity to unpack their own unconscious decision-making processes and co-construct tools to help them better respond to students in crisis. Teachers in low-performing schools are subjected to a high degree of stress associated with inadequate resources, pressures to teach to standardized tests, and fluctuations in student attendance, skill sets, and wellness. Regular professional development for the teachers that helps support their ability to more effectively manage the classroom using alternatives to exclusionary discipline is important for moving the dial toward an end to zero-tolerance policies. Also, ongoing professional development for teachers and administrators on how to shape the teaching of students and responses to their problematic behavior will only enhance learning, and will likely reduce the need for discipline related to students' low engagement in the work.

The majority of the young women who engaged in this inquiry mentioned poor student-teacher relationships as a concern. Teachers would benefit from training on the use of culturally competent and gender-responsive discipline protocols, objective decision-making training, and alternative practices that increase their capacity to utilize harm reduction strategies and promote safety, respect, and learning in the classroom. The protocol should be explicit and clearly define the actions that warrant removal from the classroom, such as fighting or threatening another student or the teacher with physical harm. The category of "willful defiance" should be eliminated by state and local governing bodies, such that schools are required to exhaust all other remedies before removing a child from school for failing to follow the rules. Instead, schools should develop an internal continuum of responses and agreements—created in partnership with students—that allow for tailored responses that promote learning and inclusion, rather than punishment and banishment.

Understand and Examine the Impact of Dress Codes
Dress code policies must be revised and new ways of regulating student behavior developed that do not unfairly target Black girls or facilitate their objectification. Dress code policies are designed to encourage respectful student presentation, but as the narratives

in this book demonstrate, many Black girls perceive these codes to affect them differently because of subjective enforcement and/ or assumptions made about their sexuality. First, schools should examine the purpose and impact of their dress codes and remove all references to hairstyles that are historically associated primarily with Black cultural traditions (e.g., dreadlocks, braids, Afros, etc.). Second, schools should seek to remedy the differential application of dress code violations by developing an objective decision-making tool that provides administrators and staff with a rubric by which to gauge the acceptability of student dress. This tool or body should be co-created with a representative group of students and then communicated via peer-led processes that facilitate student buy-in and acceptance of school norms. Champions of these policies and practices should not only be adults. Likewise, students should also help design remedies to dress code violations that do not include suspension or being sent home.

Engage in Practices That Facilitate Healing Opportunities for Black Girls

To lead on campus is too often an elusive experience for Black girls. Our schools should provide ongoing examples and models of leadership. We should promote their engagement in school-based sporting and club opportunities, both to encourage their positive connection to school and to hone skills associated with the cultural norms of speaking out and asking questions in a healing and holistic way.

In my work with girls, sacred inquiry* provided a framework

---

* Peter Reason described "sacred science" as a method of human inquiry that involves "nurtur[ing] the growth of love, beauty, wisdom and compassionate action." My previous research has asserted that applying this lens to Black girls in contact with the criminal legal system may generate a path toward holistic responses to the harm and trauma these girls may have experienced in their educational institutions, as well as in other "systems" to which they are exposed (e.g., health, justice, etc.).

for learning through discussion, experience, representation, understanding, action, and engagement.[4] This foundation is capable
of advancing us beyond a punishment lens to one that embraces
transformation, shifting the emphasis to healing those relationships that have been harmed, along with the anger or frustration
that may have led to the harmful action in the first place. A
trauma-informed practice understands that for a person who
has experienced a severe or extremely harmful event or series of
events, there are certain behaviors, words, and conditions that
trigger in her or him a negative reaction—reactions that are often
responses to past abuse and/or neglect.[5] Developing a trauma-
informed learning environment provides considerations for
these triggers and offers protections for girls, and those who work
with them, against further harm. In such environments, there is
an emphasis on physical and emotional safety. For example, inappropriate touching is not just disallowed as a rule; there is also
constant education of students, faculty, and staff about how to
develop healthy intimate relationships that do not include unsolicited comments and touching.

Emotional safety is supported in learning spaces by emphasiz-
ing a respect for the diversity of thought and the rigor that comes
from positive, appreciative reasoning and engagement with material. Ultimately the vandalism of school property or a school-based
altercation must be seen as an opportunity to understand and respond to the conditions that underlie this plea for help, rather than
just an act worthy of suspension or expulsion. Treating a girl's ideas
or "smart mouth" as violent when they are reflective of her critical
thinking is outside the parameters of being trauma-informed. It is
worth noting that community-based organizations are increasingly embracing a healing-informed approach that positively flips
the trauma frame, focusing on the journey *toward* healing rather
than on past experiences of trauma.

Have "The Talk" with Girls, Not Just Boys

"The talk" with Black girls and young women is also a discussion about racism in America, and as with boys, it should include tips for how to be safe in the presence of law enforcement and include clear instructions about how to behave when they are suspected of wrongdoing in the presence of someone with a gun, stun gun, or other weapon. But "the talk" also requires a candid discussion about sexism and patriarchy in our society, along with the justice movements that work to combat these forces. Our girls need to know how to identify sexism in all its forms, how to understand the ways in which it intersects with racism to create problematic narratives about the femininity of Black girls, and how their own education and self-determination can change these narratives and the devastating effects of biased policies and practices associated with education, justice, and the economy.

Most importantly, we must all recognize that a racial justice practice without a gender-inclusive thrust is nothing more than a moot exercise. Only when we develop a national, fully funded investment in *all* of our young people will we finally breathe life into Maya Angelou's simple phrase: "Equality, and I will be free."[6]

From Punishment to Transformation

For many of these girls, my interactions with them were the first time that an adult had asked them about their future goals and their experiences with schools. Most of the girls in this discussion did not know how they learn best, and were deeply disturbed by the extent to which they were being labeled and tracked as behavioral concerns. They were also aware of others' projections onto them that were leading them to a place of alienation.

By asking why it is so difficult for Black girls to "simply survive," Nikki Jones reminds us that there are structures, social conditions, and individual acts that prevent our girls from fully participating in this nation's promise of opportunity.[7] Ultimately, the failure to include Black girls fully in the articulation of American democracy has relegated them to the margins of society. Though many have achieved remarkable heights and their presence may be found on the front lines of activism and protest, their presence at the center of decisions about policy and practice is at best limited and underdeveloped.

This book's exploration into the criminalization of Black girls in schools provides an opportunity to center Black girls in our discussions about zero tolerance, school discipline, dress codes, child victimization, and the impact of increasing surveillance in our nation's public schools. The hyperpunitive climate of many educational environments, particularly those that have adopted zero-tolerance policies, is antithetical to the cultural norms associated with Black feminine expression (e.g., the use of verbal and nonverbal cues to process information, or the practice of speaking up in the face of adversity).[8] Black girls desire a safe space in which to learn, where they can earn credits toward graduation, where they can heal from harm and develop skills to support healthy relationships, where there is a reduced emphasis on discipline, and where positive student-teacher relationships are reinforced through dialogue and engagement by individuals with whom they can share historical and cultural experiences.

New Futures

Literature on the structure of dominance and the socially reproductive function of schools tells us that schools may reinforce and reproduce social hierarchies that undermine the development of people who occupy a lower societal status.[9] For the Black girls we've met on these pages, the majority of whom live in poverty and under the normalized surveillance of law enforcement in their communities and schools, these socially reproductive structures constitute educational experiences that guide them to, rather than direct them away from, destitution and escalating contact with the criminal legal system. Their vulnerability is compounded by the individual biases that inform the ideological thrust of teachers and underscore their negative responses and low expectations for children who have been labeled as "delinquent."[10]

Our girls have ideas about how to change these conditions.

Sociologist William Corsaro introduced the notion of children's *interpretive reproduction*, the act of combining their peer culture with an adult-centric culture to generate new social constructs and norms, in order to explain how the social worlds of children evolve.[11] Black girls will co-construct their learning environments whether or not we acknowledge that it is happening. They want to see themselves as fully integrated into the content being taught in schools, and they want to feel that their voices are not only heard but *respected*. These girls want to talk, and they need a learning culture that encourages them to talk as part of building community in the classroom or school.[12] They must be allowed to ask questions, to respectfully offer their opinion (even if it differs from the instructor's opinion), and to learn through an extended epistemology that honors their multiple ways of knowing and learning. Stripping Black girls of the ability to ask questions and process information through dialogue is culturally incompetent and antithetical to their development as critical thinkers. It reflects a reduced expectation for learning and generates feelings of hostility and alienation. That the majority of the girls in this discussion requested educational programming that was respectful, collaborative, and tied both to preparing for their futures and to building relationships signals their interest in a praxis anchored in the power of sharing one's story and perspective—a learning process that has the added benefit of being restorative.

Notwithstanding a history of negative experiences in school, girls can sometimes envision positive learning experiences—traditional and alternative—that bring them closer to their objectives, both academically and in terms of their options for the future. The girls I have spoken with identified specific elements that they considered to be important to the development of a culturally competent and gender-responsive environment for them. Leading the list is the quality of their teacher. Black girls are most interested in being educated by qualified teachers who teach from a curriculum that acknowledges the role of women from similar conditions in shaping the nation's discourses on equal opportunity. They also want to be treated with dignity and to learn from a curriculum that provides opportunities to discuss and apply their learning to future career or academic goals.

Girls felt that caring and qualified teachers, along with other positive school leaders, should be a part of an effective and desirable learning environment. For example, Mia believed that educators could establish a better climate for learning by releasing some of their fear. "The teachers . . . I want them to stop being scared," Mia said. "They just so scared. . . . Y'all so afraid to just send us out of class, y'all just letting us get away with hella shit. If y'all not going to send us out of class, y'all just letting us get away with anything." It's telling that Mia has been socialized to see being pushed out as the only option for dealing with challenging classroom situations. What she is really asking for is an effective, supportive space to learn.

Our girls want structure, but not in a punitive, non-rehabilitative way. For Destiny, the reform she sought was to have someone, preferably a teacher that would monitor her progress in school. "I just need to be checked in on more often. Like that progress . . . [someone to ask], 'How are you doing with school?' So, like, I can make sure I have my focus on school and not on what are my friends doing this weekend . . . I'd probably want it to be one of my teachers, so that it could be more, like, immediate. It'd be right there in the classroom instead of it being, like, a counselor and I can tell him one thing and then go to class or not go to class. Yeah . . . 'cause I feel like if it was put more in my face, I'd be like, yeah, more focused."

Others felt that classes, speakers, and volunteer opportunities that enhance their ability to advance their personal academic and career goals would be an essential component of their quality educational experience.

For example, Faith said, "You know how they be having computer classes? They should have a class on jobs and stuff. Research on jobs, like what job you want to do. Like they should research it with you and help you, you know?"

Girls also suggested that the instructors for these courses should possess knowledge of "street" culture and be willing to share information about how to overcome the common obstacles (poverty, parental drug addiction, etc.) that they have found overwhelming in their own lives.

This was stated poignantly by Stacy, the self-described "problem child," who felt that any intervention program needed to "have people that can relate to the young people . . . to help them talk about whatever they need to talk about," adding that parental involvement was key.

This same notion was reinforced by Samantha, an eighteen-year-old emancipated foster child in Southern California who was homeless and in search of resources to help her complete high school.

"We need people who been there," she said. "And I really hope [they] can do this, because I really need it."

Power at its best is love implementing the demands of justice.
—Martin Luther King Jr.

For love to implement "the demands of justice," as Martin Luther King Jr. called them, we must shift our lens. We must consider what social innovations might arise when we come together and mobilize our collective wisdom, and thus begin to maximize the power of our input toward social change. Building an adaptive platform for innovation, one that allows us to rethink what we "know" and what we think works, will reduce the criminalization of our children in schools.

This process will include a transformative, collective decision-making process that removes our public officials from the center of the discussion about how to initiate change and really begins to distribute the locus of accountability in ways that give our local jurisdictions—where these decisions are made—power to build community around girls. If our goal is really to interrupt the practices leading to the criminalization of our girls, then we want to disrupt "business as usual" and take on processes that give us an opportunity to work alongside girls toward implementing plausible, shared long-term visions and opportunities.

Part of this process requires us to envision a new ecosystem for our girls. Whom do we invite to help develop this process? Ultimately, we would want people with multiple and varied experiences to come together and examine the issues from multiple angles. We want girls, their parents, educators, health professionals, sexual abuse and trauma experts, justice professionals, the business community, artists, faith leaders, scholars, and advocates to work together toward a shared vision of collective uplift, of cooperative investment in the well-being of Black girls.

Our goal is to develop schools that our girls don't describe as "jails" or "prisons." This terminology has become so ingrained in their consciousness and experiences that it can be difficult for them to consider what a school that is not governed by discipline looks and feels like. Our expectations for our young people need to elevate. While many of our girls are in school districts where violence and victimization present real concerns for student safety, for a large number of girls the *fear* of violence is greater than the actual demonstration of it. Sociological theories about the ways in which violent conditions flow between institutions and public spaces suggest that our society may need to reconsider how it views the school, its function, and its relationship to the community in which it is located.[13] As a locus of learning, our schools can serve a greater purpose than just indoctrinating our girls with the politics of surviving racial, class, and gender bias. These institutions can be

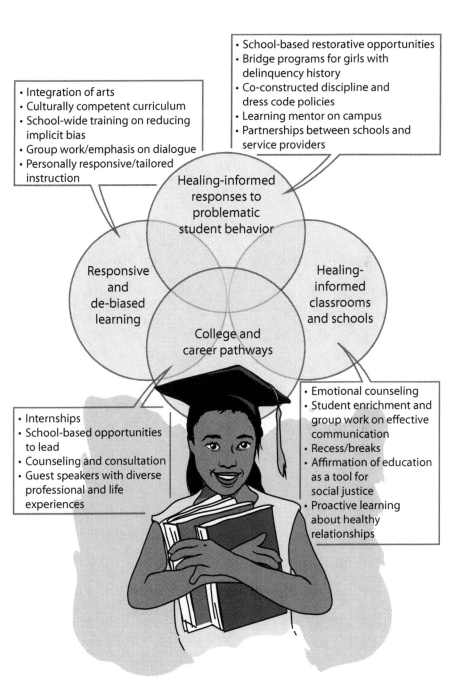

- Integration of arts
- Culturally competent curriculum
- School-wide training on reducing implicit bias
- Group work/emphasis on dialogue
- Personally responsive/tailored instruction

- School-based restorative opportunities
- Bridge programs for girls with delinquency history
- Co-constructed discipline and dress code policies
- Learning mentor on campus
- Partnerships between schools and service providers

Healing-informed responses to problematic student behavior

Responsive and de-biased learning

Healing-informed classrooms and schools

College and career pathways

- Internships
- School-based opportunities to lead
- Counseling and consultation
- Guest speakers with diverse professional and life experiences

- Emotional counseling
- Student enrichment and group work on effective communication
- Recess/breaks
- Affirmation of education as a tool for social justice
- Proactive learning about healthy relationships

bastions of community building, where healing is at the center of their pedagogy and where our girls learn more than just how to behave in the presence of adults to be considered "acceptable" in a school environment.

Historian Manning Marable wrote, "Freedom is first and foremost a public understanding among the members of a society to protect and defend any opinions that are unpopular or at odds with opinions held by those who actually exercise power and privilege. Freedom is the fragile flower that must constantly be protected—not from those at the bottom of the social order but from the whims and desires of those at the top."[14] How we address the conditions facing Black girls—and protect the "fragile flower"—must include more than just slogans or symbolic marches. Defining freedom cannot amount to simply substituting it with inclusion. Countering the criminalization of Black girls requires fundamentally altering the relationship between Black girls and the institutions of power that have worked to reinforce their subjugation. History has taught us that civil rights are but one component of a larger movement for this type of social transformation. Civil rights may be at the core of equal justice movements, and they may elevate an equity agenda that protects our children from racial and gender discrimination, but they do not have the capacity to fully redistribute power and eradicate racial inequity. There is only one practice that can do that.

Love.

EPILOGUE

This book presents the voices of Black girls on the margins. It offers their perceptions of what contributes to their poor academic and behavioral performance in school and how that relates to their risk of incarceration. Together, their stories form a larger narrative that I hope inspires us to include our girls in the broader racial and gender justice movements, making them an integral part of the healing that will ultimately forge a path toward reaching real equality.

I closed this book with a call for us to embrace an alternative paradigm for exploring how our schools respond to Black girls in crisis, but I also recognize that a broader set of policy reforms is apropos. Reports referenced in this book, including those produced by the National Women's Law Center and the NAACP Legal Defense Fund, the African American Policy Forum, the Human Rights for Girls Project, the Georgetown Law Center on Poverty and Inequality, and the Ms. Foundation for Women, each contain a comprehensive set of policy recommendations aimed to address data collection, referral and decision-making processes, and legal remedies that may transform the way that schools and their surrounding communities treat and respond to Black girls. I am also keenly aware that I did not fully engage in a critique about the role of media and entertainment in reproducing negative images of Black femininity, or focus on the issue from the vantage point of law enforcement or campus-based security.

Though connected to the topics covered in this book, in many ways these perspectives were outside the scope of inquiry.

There is still so much to explore about the lives of Black girls. We need scholars to center Black girls in their research, educators to immerse their pedagogy in intersectionality, and advocates and policy makers to measure impact outside of a linear framework. I sincerely hope that within the next five years, we are able to develop a robust and coordinated strategy to change the racial justice narrative in a way that authentically and earnestly includes girls and women.

In these girls, I see a raw and uncultivated version of myself. As a preadolescent, I participated in cultures of school-based and after-school-based violence. Like many of the girls in this project, I became a survivor of sexual assault as a child, and throughout my adolescence I had to negotiate the traumatic experience of responding to unwanted stares and touches. But for the empathetic educators who sought to cultivate my intelligence as a clear path toward personal freedom, who knows where I would be. In many ways, I empathized with the girls who shared their narratives with me. What I learned and now know with certainty from this experience is that the education of Black girls is a lifesaving act of social justice.

I think often about the girls whose voices are represented in this book. They trusted me to share their words with integrity, and for that trust (which I consider a gift) I am thankful. It was my intention to be honest in my representation of how these girls articulated their experiences, which in some cases may differ radically from what might be described by the adults in their lives. But we owe it them to listen and respond.

I leave you with this last reflection, a moment that I shared with Jennifer in a California detention facility. We were wrapping up our interview, and I asked her, as I did with all of the girls I spoke with, if she had anything else she wanted to add or ask me.

She cocked her head to the side, folded her arms, and asked, "So, what you gonna do with all this again?"

"Well," I responded, "some people think I should write a novel, and others think I should write it as nonfiction. . . . What do you think?"

She didn't respond at first, but then she relaxed her arms and stood up, responding to a prompt from the detention center staff that our time was up.

As we approached the door and moved toward her cell, she said, "I think you should tell the truth . . . Yeah, just tell the truth."

APPENDIX A
GIRLS, WE GOT YOU!
A Q&A for Girls, Parents, Community
Members, and Educators

I want Black girls to know that they are that important,
that powerful.
—Yejide Ankobia, Bay Area

Our girls are sacred, and they are loved. With a deeper understanding of the complex challenges and dynamics encountered by Black girls, and a framework from the final chapter for altering and expanding our vision of their education, it's time for a closer look at the everyday concerns and obstructions Black girls grapple with in order to shape the path forward. The collected wisdom gathered here is intended to aid anyone searching for insight on how to improve conditions for Black girls.

What follows is a series of questions and answers, organized into three sections: one for girls and young women, one for parents and the extended community of loved ones that embrace girls' healthy development and well-being, and one for teachers and educators working with Black girls. Share this appendix, especially the first section, with the young women and girls whose experiences mirror or relate to the ones included in this book—and the adults who support them.

For Girls

Why should I care about school? I need to make some money.

How much money do you want to make? Black women who have some high school education and no diploma earn just $861,353 over their entire lifetime; but those with a high school diploma will earn $1.07 million! Black women with a bachelor's degree from college earn $1.86 million in their lifetime, and those with a master's degree earn $2.3 million in their lifetime.[1] In other words, school is about giving you options and the skills that will make you more marketable in the workforce.

Life can sometimes get hard, and that can make school seem less important. But remember that if you want a career, something more than just a job that pays the bills, you have to plan and prepare for it. That planning includes completing your education. Consider it an investment—in yourself, which will produce the maximum return. Once you have an education, no one can take that from you. And in fact, being educated will only make you a stronger candidate for success in life, not just for the moment.

Sometimes I feel like school is not for me. How can I get motivated?

First, take a moment to think about *why* you are feeling this way. Ask yourself: "Why do I feel this way about school? Who is associated with how I feel about school? Is there something about school itself that makes me not want to go, or is it about something else that's happening around me? When did I start to feel this way about school? What happened?" Once you have collected your thoughts, get a piece of paper and draw a line down the middle. On one side, list all of the things you like about school, and on the other, list all of the things that you don't like about school. Now, turn the paper over. Make a list of the things that you want to accomplish in life. Sometimes these can be as basic as "leaving this town" or "having a house of my own," but you can also dream big, like "own my own business" or "become a lawyer." Sometimes women fail to give ourselves as much energy as we offer to others around us. Love is supposed to make you stronger, but sometimes we allow fear to drive our practice of love—and this is more prone to happen when we haven't laid our foundation first. As a young woman, a central part of your foundation is your education. Make a promise to focus on your own well-being. Here are two active steps you can take:

- *Find someone at school, at home, or in another part of your community (such as a community center or agency) who can help you create an educational plan.* Ask this person to help guide you toward fulfilling your plan. Find an academic mentor or coach who can check in on you to make sure you've finished your homework and to encourage you to focus on going to school. Their support will help you to be the strongest student you can be.
- *Surround yourself with people who want to achieve, like you do.* People who encourage you to stay away from school—whether they are girlfriends, boyfriends, family, or other adults with power—do not have your best interest at heart. People who love you want you to have your best chance in life, and that begins with staying in school and taking care of yourself.

What do I do if I feel like my teacher is picking on me?
It's hard to feel picked on or bullied by your peers or your teachers. Truthfully, this is an issue that probably can't be resolved with a few words of advice, or even in the course of a school year. In general, you would be best served by taking the high road. Take control of the situation by documenting (writing down or recording) what is happening and what you are observing. If you're struggling with this, try to find an adult you trust to help you record

your experiences. As you document each incident, be sure to include a careful description of what happened just before the teacher acted or reacted, and what you did in response. Record every detail and be sure to honor how you might have contributed to escalating the situation. Just thinking about what is happening will help you slow down a heated situation and be more aware. Paying close attention to the situation might even cause you to choose or act differently, even if you are being disrespected or treated unfairly. Once you have collected enough information to support your claim, and if you feel safe enough doing this alone, first try talking to your teacher one-on-one about how the situation could be resolved. Schedule a meeting to talk about behavior —yours and theirs. If your first meeting only results in a one-sided rant, or if you do not feel that you otherwise have a respectful enough relationship with your teacher to have a helpful conversation, then try to schedule a meeting to have a conversation that includes you, a parent or loved one, your principal (or a dean or counselor), and the teacher. Keep track of the following questions in this meeting:

+ Is there anything different about how everyone involved is seeing the situation? What is the difference?
+ What is similar about each version of the story?
+ What do I want to change about our relationship?
+ What actions will I take to change the situation between my teacher and me? What or who do I need in my corner to help me do the things I've agreed to do?
+ What actions has my teacher agreed to take to change the situation? Who will hold the teacher accountable?
+ How will we hold each other accountable for our agreements? Is there a written agreement? Are there regular conversations and check-ins? Do we need other people to be there for these meetings?

How should I respond if I keep being challenged to fight in school?

First, stop and breathe. Let's start with some facts: You are the *only* person who controls your actions, no one else. No one can make you hit that other person who is provoking you, and no one is making you walk away. You control your own behavior. Now, let's deal with reality: It is possible that you are feeling pressured to fight. There might be social pressures, or maybe you want to feel in control. You could also be triggered to fight after being bullied by other girls or boys who talk about you, spread rumors about you, call you names (in person or on social media sites), or try to intimidate you in some way (in person or on social media sites). You could be feeling pressure to fight in order to keep your relationship with another person intact. Take a moment to check in with yourself about why you are feeling like you want to fight. Learn your triggers. As soon as possible, find an adult or another friend who can intervene. That adult should be able to guide you both in a conversation that allows you to get to the bottom of why you are fighting and think about how you can overcome the urge to come to blows.

How do I know if I'm in an unhealthy relationship?

Every relationship has its ups and downs. But if a relationship is causing physical or emotional reactions in your body or your spirit that are not positive, then you need to check in to see if this is the right relationship for you. How frequently do you feel upset with your partner? Do you feel jealous, suspicious, or envious of your partner? Is there constant arguing? Do you feel put down, controlled, or manipulated? If you are nodding or answering yes to these questions, then you might take some time to think about why you are in this relationship. These are not feelings that you should feel in a committed and loving relationship. Sometimes the thrill of a relationship, especially if that person is popular or powerful in some way, can make us overlook these feelings. Maybe you feel like you have no one else who understands you, or no one else to rely on. But if you are more unhappy than you are happy, love yourself enough not to ignore your own well-being. In other words, remember that you are sacred and loved. If your relationship does not honor this basic idea *most* of the time, you may want to reconsider if your partner is the right one for you, even if you love or have love for this person.

Why do people call what I do "human trafficking" or "sex slavery"? My boyfriend takes care of me, and I don't feel like a "sex slave."
Love feels good. But it's not love if it brings you harm—physically, emotionally, or sexually. If you are under the age of eighteen and in a relationship with someone who asks you to share your body with them or someone else in exchange for money, clothes, shoes, jewelry, or other goods, then you may be in a situation that is considered "human trafficking." Let's be honest. Prostitution is a hustle—one that gives some people a chance to buy things that make them feel good about how they look, and to be treated (at least at first) like they are not invisible. But human trafficking is a serious thing, and love or "being taken care of" should never come with a price, especially one that requires you to sacrifice your body.

What should I say to people who tease me after seeing me on the stroll?
Don't say anything to them. You are not required to justify your life conditions to anyone. You should, however, find an adult or a friend that you can trust, to help you figure out the best way to remain safe (and free from judgment at school) while you figure out your next step in life. As soon as you can, contact an organization or someone you trust to help you gain control of your life. You *can* get off the streets, but it's really hard to do it alone. You'll need help, and there are lots of organizations that can help you. As soon as possible, contact GEMS (see list at the end of this

appendix) to get a copy of *A Survivor's Guide to Leaving*. Adult survivors of sex trafficking believe this booklet is a very helpful tool as you launch your journey. A list of additional resources is included at the end of this appendix. If you're in a different city, contact one on the list and they will help you find someplace closer that can help.

Why do I get so annoyed when people look at me?

Sometimes, when we feel a little self-conscious, someone's look can feel like a judgmental stare. This stare can feel rude. It can be challenging. It can be sexually provocative. People try to pretend that a look or an expression isn't that important, but those things do matter. They matter because they give us an indication of what someone is thinking about us, and what we are thinking about ourselves. Looks have meaning, words have meaning, and physical actions have meaning—we know this instinctively. But it's our interpretations that give them that meaning. In other words, only if you feel inadequate in some way do looks or words have a meaningful impact on your life. When you feel whole, it's harder to be triggered by another person's problems, issues, or judgments of you.

Here's the thing to remember: Your life is beautiful. Their looks are about them, not you. Just because you may not be where you want to be yet, or have all of the material things you want—and that everyone else seems to think are important—doesn't mean that you are any less worthy of respect than the next person. Find ways to be true to yourself under all circumstances. That doesn't mean lashing out with your own special stare or with words at anyone who seems to be challenging you. It also doesn't mean that you have to belittle people who do have some of the material things that might be nice to have. No matter who has what or where you or anyone else comes from, think about the ways that you can treat everyone around you with respect.

Consider that you might be able to turn what feels like a judgmental stare into something else, by smiling at them. Say hello. Teens are notorious for calling that kind of reaction to something "weird"—but don't worry. Just do you. Don't worry about what others think about you. How do you want to feel about yourself? Are you happy with who you are becoming? If the answer is yes, then that's really all that matters. Everyone else will fall in line. If the answer is no, then think about why. It may help you start to see what's missing or what's not working, and how you might be able to lead a more fulfilling life. Ultimately, approval of your life needs to come from inside of you, not from someone else. Focus on what it takes to make you feel whole. The closer you get the more you'll recognize that what used to feel like a challenging or angry stare might actually be a glance of admiration.

How do I get along better with my mom?
The mother-daughter relationship can be tricky. It can also be one of the most sacred and beautiful experiences in life. It can be a bond like no other, which is why—even when our mothers get on our last nerve or when they make mistakes in their own lives—we forgive them. We are forever connected to them. Remember, mothers are people too. If you can, find a time when you can calmly sit next to your mother and talk about what's going through your mind. Nothing beats a good conversation when you're trying to get at the heart of what is bothering you. Ask her to tell you her story. Maybe she's already told you some things about her life several times, but ask her to tell you what her story is. What was life like for her growing up? What's it like for her now? What did she want to do when she was your age? What was her relationship like with her mother? What are her hopes and dreams for herself? Chances are that the same hopes and dreams that she had for herself growing up, she also has for you. Maybe those are not consistent with the dreams you have for yourself—or maybe they are. But you'll never know unless you talk about them.

The problem with differences usually isn't that they exist. Rather, it's all the assumptions we tend to make about other people—even our mothers. Even if you don't always see eye to eye, talking openly and regularly can transform your relationship. Try to carve out a regular time for the two of you to sit down together and share stories. Once she's done with her story, then you should tell yours. Yes, whether you're twelve, fifteen, or nineteen years old, you have a life story. Sharing with each other builds a foundation for mutual respect and, hopefully, a more fulfilling relationship. This strategy may not work for everyone, but give it a chance. Sometimes it helps to bring in other people—a friend, an aunt or cousin, a therapist or counselor—if it's hard or if it seems impossible to start the conversation on your own. If this strategy doesn't work, or if your mother isn't around for you to talk to, try to find another older woman to connect to. Whether or not you have a good relationship with your mother, focus inward and prepare for when it is time to lead your own life. You can make it.

I am lesbian (or gay, or bisexual, or transgender, or queer, or questioning). How can I stay safe at school?
Your sexual and/or gender identity is your own business. You do not have to share your personal business with anyone. That said, you should never have to hide who you are or live under a cloak of oppression. If you feel alone, please consider forming or joining a group of students who can provide you with a community to share feelings, experiences, or activities of shared interest. Clubs like Gay-Straight Alliances, Campus Pride, or other LGBT youth-led efforts in your area can help you create or develop the right club for you. Your school should not prevent you from being you, and instead it should actively support your full growth and expression. First and foremost, know that you are loved. Second, know your rights. Lambda Legal's website (lambdalegal.org) offers a host of resources that you may find helpful along your journey, including a report called *Out, Safe and Respected: Your Rights at School*. Become familiar with this report and identify allies and supportive adults and/or peers on campus. They can help you co-create safe spaces for your learning. Organizations such

as the Safe Schools Coalition, BreakOUT, and Ambiente Joven (for Spanish-speakers) can offer you additional resources and guidance as you seek to establish or further develop a respectful and inclusive school climate. You've got this!

For Parents and Community Members

How do I start a conversation about the effects that school discipline policies are having on Black girls?
Starting a conversation is a very important part of initiating change. It may be helpful to approach the PTA or other parental leaders to inquire about the impact of a school's discipline policies on Black girls. You may want to begin by just asking questions such as: What are the behaviors or actions that are leading Black girls to get into trouble? What are the typical disciplinary actions that are assigned to Black girls who get into trouble? Talk to your daughter or the student that you wish to support and begin to collect anecdotes that support your interest in exploring broader school discipline issues on campus. Ask the school's principal to collect and review data on referrals and then convene regular discussions about the trends these data reveal. Once you have a clear idea about what may be contributing to these trends, partner with parents to explore possible ways to bring alternative disciplinary practices to your school.

What should I do if my daughter (or sister, or niece) keeps getting in trouble at school?
Be patient and do *not* immediately side with the school or teacher before hearing what the young person has to say. Ask her what is happening at school and why she thinks things are getting out of control. Ask her to tell her story, and then tell the version you got from the school. Ask her to share her experiences and talk through the best and worst aspects of school. Ask her to share what she is feeling and observing about her teachers, about her

classmates, and about herself in school. Ask her to list, in detail, what is happening in school and to keep a log of the things that are triggering her negative behavior, and possibly, the negative behavior of others (students or educators) toward her. She can treat this log as a journal that she reviews once a week with you or another adult in her life. As patterns emerge for her (and you) regarding the triggers, brainstorm together how you all might address behaviors or conditions to keep her out of harm's way. It's important not to jump directly to harsh punishment or accusations, because there will be more to unpack. Give it time, but stay on top of the situation and remain consistent in your efforts to prioritize your girl's well-being, in partnership with the school.

What do I say to my daughter to encourage her to go to school?
This is an opportunity to ask questions and better understand why your daughter might be avoiding school. Is she tired? Does she get enough sleep? If not, maybe you should help her establish a new night routine that facilitates rest and a more balanced diet. Also, ask her why she doesn't want to go. Is her safety threatened? Are rumors about her distracting her from her studies? Once you have ruled out some basic physical health issues, perhaps explore whether there are conditions in school that are making her feel that she doesn't want to go to school. Ask your daughter what she wants to accomplish in life, and when she replies, ask her if she understands why education is important to her ability to achieve this goal. Explain to her that education is a tool to move forward. We all have days when we just need a break, but try to reinforce the importance of staying true to her commitments, and then be clear that education is her commitment to herself for the future. Consistency is very important for children, so checking in on her progress regularly and establishing a routine will be very important. If you sense that she is not comfortable talking with you about what's going on in her life, ask her if there's another adult

she would be willing to talk to or if she would talk to a counselor. It might hurt to feel like she can't share with you, but in the long run finding her someone she can talk to may help her get back on track.

What can we do at home to support my daughter in school?
Establish a routine for your daughter that includes quiet study time and an area where she can devote her attention to studying. While every person has her own study style—and some may respond to the additional stimulation of music—explain to your daughter that most television shows, popular music, and social media are distractions and should be minimized during her study time. If she's strong-willed about it or resistant to the idea, make agreements about one or more hours of the day that are free of all electronic media (even when homework involves computer time). Ask your daughter if she has carefully checked and completed her homework assignments. If you suspect that she is lying about not having any homework or having finished an assignment, then check it. Establish a line of communication with your daughter's teachers so that you know your daughter's progress in school *before* parent-teacher conferences. Prepare at least five specific questions about your daughter before attending a parent-teacher conference so that you can ask more than the general "How is she doing?" or "Why are you failing my daughter?" Often there are many reasons and many people involved—parents included—when a girl seems to be "failing" in a subject or in some other way. Ask your daughter's teachers what they need from you to support your collective vision for the academic success of your daughter. Work out a plan that you create *with* your daughter to determine how she can take the lead in this shared vision for her success. Don't forget, this is about her! She should be just as involved in discussions and planning about her school life as everyone else, if not more.

How do I build trust and get my daughter to talk about what is bothering her?

Depending on your relationship with your daughter, you may or may not be the person your daughter goes to first when she is in trouble. If you're not, that's okay. But you need to know who that person is in her life and build a relationship with that person. There are many ways in which you can build enough trust between you and your daughter to ultimately find out why she may be acting out in school. Begin with setting aside a specific time each week for just the two of you. Initially, you two can decide to do something that just brings you joy—play a game, watch a television show that you both enjoy, or take a walk. Once you have established this rhythm, you can start to share your story—specifically the incidents in your life that shaped your educational journey, and what you have learned from these experiences. Don't be afraid to share the bad with the good, but be sure to discuss the consequences associated with bad behavior and provide a space for your daughter to add her perspective. Remember to breathe through the aspects of her story that may not resonate with your own or that you may struggle with; work through these issues together and always end the conversation with how you are going to resolve the issue. Most of all, try not to judge her. Guidance and judgment can be hard to separate, especially if you are "old-school" and find it important to direct your daughter in the way that she will go (if she knows what's good for her). However, in today's society, where young women are exposed to so much so early, it might be more beneficial to listen to her story with an open mind. If you can't hear it, then ask her to write it. If you can't read it, then ask her to pick a song that captures how she's feeling and then talk to her about why the song speaks to her. Sharing stories in this way can help you both get to the bottom of what might be bothering her and why she is feeling the need to behave in ways that are disruptive to her learning. If you don't get an answer or a response right away, that's okay. Buy some time to do your research. Seek out others in your community who can help you think through what is happening or even ask your daughter if there is someone that you both could talk to that could help to resolve the problem. The important thing is that you establish some way to brainstorm with your daughter ways to deal with what is triggering her bad behavior. Ultimately, express your appreciation for her honesty and ask her to help you to understand how her actions could better reflect her future as a queen. Then ask her how you can help her queen shine. Two lights illuminate the hidden treasure all the more effectively.

For Educators

I want to keep my school and classroom safe. How can I do that without security?
Once upon a time, our schools didn't need armed security guards and police officers to manage the activity of schools. Community accountability and the leadership of principals, deans, counselors, teachers, coaches, faith leaders, and other volunteers helped to create a school climate where the majority of students felt safe. Yes, times have changed and the availability of guns, drugs, and other harmful conditions is a reality for too many of our children. But the most fundamental piece of this puzzle has remained constant—children are still children. They still co-construct their lived experiences by bringing their unique peer cultures to the adult world. They will still respond favorably to interventions that are rooted in a respect for them as people and that address their most basic needs. This can all be done without armed security guards on campus, which is evident in the fact that not *every* school in our nation has this structure in place.

When girls are engaged in violent interactions, it is often in response to them feeling disrespected. So the question we should be asking is, how can my school facilitate a culture of mutual respect? There is no cookie-cutter response to these issues. Each school is composed of a unique collection of young people who can help to think through ways that they might help to keep their schools and hallways safe. As long as there are school resource officers and security guards on campus, they must be extensively trained to respond to and work with victims of sexual exploitation. These individuals should be rigorously screened for their own competence with respect to strategies to prevent and reduce the retraumatiza- tion of girls who have experienced sexual assault and victimization. There should be ongoing conversations with students—female, male, and elsewhere along the gender continuum. Ultimately, while adults should take on a leadership role in the development of these school-specific strategies, youth should have a voice too so that they also are invested in the policies or norms that are developed.

There is ample room for innovative approaches to this dilemma that are already being explored but deserve wider adoption. For ex- ample, schools are asking for grandparents, businesses, and other agencies to volunteer to help schools keep their hallways orderly and safe. One powerful example comes from an elder-volunteer program in a Southern California alternative high school. These community volunteers altogether replaced the "security" formerly found in so many high-poverty schools or schools that educate formerly incarcerated children. Not only did these elders help to tutor the students, but I witnessed these grandmothers also serve as enforcers of school rules when young people got out of line. These elders were respected as authority figures by the schools, and when they intervened, they did so with love, which was well received by the students. When we collectively expect our chil- dren to do better, they rise to the occasion.

How can I manage my classroom without sending a girl for referral?
Classrooms are places of learning. Ensuring the safety of stu- dents should remain a priority, so the question for teachers and all

of us always comes back to how this is done. What we've learned is that ensuring safety for some or many students shouldn't, and doesn't, have to mean creating an unsafe or unhealthy learning environment for others. There are many strategies that are used to manage classrooms, including mindfulness, merit-driven practices, restorative approaches, and buddy systems for accountability. Removing a student from your classroom should be a last resort. Before you start your lesson, establish or revisit norms for the classroom that you co-construct with the class on day one. This means that as the instructor, you can lead a five-to-ten-minute conversation with your class about the way all of you want and expect to engage. If someone speaks out of turn, how should it be handled? If someone has a disagreement with something that's been said, how will the class respond? How will the class respond if a student is being too disruptive? Establishing these norms as early as possible helps to create a culture in the classroom where students feel respected and engaged in the shared-responsibility of keeping a classroom safe and free of major disruptions.

Mindfulness practices that allow students to breathe and get centered before learning are also important to maintaining the safety of the students and the classroom. More often than not, students are disruptive because they have a lot on their minds or are masking something. Providing a space for students to acknowledge the issue(s) that they must set aside in order to be present for class is a first step toward making all children feel that they are in a safe space to learn.

How can I get parents involved in keeping their daughters from fighting?
Before you approach a parent about getting involved, do some thinking about how to structure questions and talking points in a way that doesn't trigger parents into combative behavior. In your conversations with parents, search for common ground and intentionally look to elevate issues and approaches on which you both

agree. Also, talk directly to the young woman or girl at a calmer moment and ask her, "What's going on that makes you come to school so angry?" Parents, guardians, and other caregivers in the life of a child play a significant role in the partnership to keep our girls from internalizing negative behaviors (and ideas)—the kind that lead to them becoming both perpetrators and victims of violence. On your back-to-school nights and at each parent-teacher conference, establish a protocol for reaching out to parents if there is a question about their daughter's performance or behavior. One idea is to collect parents' mobile numbers and send a text update on a regular basis. Be sure not to reach out only when something is wrong. Parents want to know when their daughter has been involved in an incident that requires their attention, but they also want to know when their child has done something good. Each school should establish its own parent-led leadership group, if it doesn't have one already, that can effectively communicate parental concerns about administrative issues, and partner with teachers and administrators. National organizational models, partners, and/or resources in parental advocacy include the National Parent-Teacher Association, PTO Today, Opportunity to Learn Campaign, National Parent Academy, and Tellin' Stories, a program from Teaching for Change.

How can I keep girls from coming to school dressed inappropriately?
More important than whether a girl or young woman arrives at school dressed "appropriately" is whether she arrives at school ready to learn new material and engage productively as a student. Dress codes, as I have addressed earlier in the book, function to stigmatize girls and undermine their ability to attend class. Schools should work *with* their students to construct what is appropriate dress for school. As novel as it sounds, asking girls why they are wearing pants that sag, leggings, short shorts, or tank tops is part

of the process that facilitates leadership and decision making about how they want to present to the world. Also ask girls what kind of attention they think their current clothing attracts and talk to them about whether they are aware of other ways to get the attention they may be seeking. Adults should be prepared to receive answers that may not align with what they expect or want. Develop mutual agreements and compromises that allow a young woman to present in a way that reflects her personality without judgment. However, also engage them in conversations about why their clothing might be perceived as unsuitable for certain environments.

Whatever you do, though, *do not* punish girls for the inability of boys or other girls to keep their hands to themselves. Talk to boys and teach them why unsolicited comments about a girl's developing body are inappropriate in school or elsewhere, and explain that they are responsible for their own respectful behavior in school. Engage teachers and school leaders—female and male—to lead regular discussions about their identities, about racial and gender stereotypes that objectify Black girls, and about how they can unlearn negative behaviors. Importantly, adults and the policies they create should model for girls that it is the development of their brains, not their bodies, that is most salient in the school environment.

What should I do if I suspect that my student is being trafficked?

Sex trafficking involving a minor is sex abuse. If you suspect that a child is being harmed in this way, it is your responsibility as a mandated reporter to report it to a local authority. You should begin by completing a report of suspected child abuse and then work with a school therapist, counselor, or other person trained in providing specialized services for girls who are being trafficked. As the facilitator of the intervention, you should be mindful that a girl, depending on her level of involvement with the trafficker, may be in danger of physical harm if special protections are not in place. Do not assume you know what's best for her; seek the advice of experienced professionals.

Refer to your district policy regarding responding to suspected human trafficking among students. If your district or school does not have a policy, work with other concerned teachers and with school and district leaders to create one. Remember the teacher in Northern California who said that we need to be comfortable with teaching more than just the curriculum? She was right that there is a greater opportunity for schools to get involved in the development of life and social skills that can facilitate a safer learning environment for girls. Schools have the unique ability to engage with students—however they identify and express along the gender continuum—about healthy relationships and personal accountability.

Schools can play an important role in a preventative strategy by educating young people and the adults who work with them about the dangers of human trafficking (both sex- and labor-related). However, school-based training and other events addressing this issue should be consistent with curricula that are premised on liberative principles and that can help to dismantle the oppression that fuels an acceptance of the exploitation of girls. Establishing regular professional development opportunities and training sessions that equip teachers and other school personnel on recognizing and responding to suspected student involvement in sex trafficking is important. Also important are regular conversations with students. Schools can engage guest speakers and others who can bring firsthand experience and knowledge about how they can protect themselves against commercial sexual exploitation.

How can I build trust with the Black girls and young women in my school?
Be there for them. Girls want to know that you will consistently show up for them, have their backs, treat them with respect, and

give them your attention. This can be challenging for some, and it's important to remember that our girls understand more than words. They absorb nonverbal cues as well. Taking the time to build relationships on the front end can reduce the time spent responding to crises on the back end. Other actions that you can take to build trust include greeting them by name when you can and actively working to build relationships with them outside of the classroom. Call them out in front of others for doing something good—and do the same with their peers. Tell girls you teach or work with about your own journey and find a way to connect with them. However an adult identifies along gender, race, and class continua, telling your story is a critical part of making yourself accessible and vulnerable enough to meet the girls where they are. Make time when they want to see you after class, or designate a time when they can reach you to talk about how they are responding to the material. In these conversations, you can share why it is important for them to go to school and why their education is your priority. In other words, demonstrate for them that you care. Small and random acts of kindness are more powerful than you might think.

Each of these actions is also about establishing a climate of mutual respect. Respect is the foundation for developing that relationship. Contrary to the rhetorical refrain in schools throughout the country, respect—especially in the context of schools—is not something that should first have to be earned. It's a human right. It is about engaging each person with dignity and honoring that she or he has valid thoughts, feelings, and actions. While respect can be eroded, lost, and earned back, every child should be granted it. That's important, because to build trust, we need to be standing on the same foundation. Adults in school have tremendous power over students, and they know this. As we observed from many of the narratives in this book, some girls take this basic imbalance of power as disrespect, or an affront to their independence.

I'm a teacher and school counselor and I can develop programming for boys because there is money to support those efforts. How can I support the needs of girls when I don't have the same financial resources?
Not every investment requires money. As the girls in this book have shown, they want to know that people care about them and their well-being. They want to be seen and acknowledged for who they are and what they can contribute to the learning environment. Our collective community can respond to their needs by being there for them. But many schools around the country have also established girls' groups as a way to provide encouragement for girls simply by convening them in regular conversation and sisterhood check-ins. These are good ways to facilitate conversation and to launch the next level of investment—one that does require financial resources. Join efforts to raise awareness about the conditions of Black girls in the racial justice movement.

How can school resource officers and security officers better support girls?
Every SRO should be trained to respond to girls as if they potentially have been exposed to sexual trauma and victimization. Remember, 68 percent of sexual assaults go unreported—the actual number is much higher than statistics reflect. Security officers must understand that they are not in schools to instigate fights between girls or to allow conflict for their own entertainment. All security and law enforcement professionals should be screened and trained in trauma-informed first responding, which prioritizes the physical and emotional safety of the girl and/or young women who are involved in the conflict. The role of law enforcement, as long as it is in schools, should transform so that it is part of the school community and an active participant in efforts to increase the use of alternatives to exclusionary discipline and force. Training for school resource officers could include specific, localized, and tailored protocols involving other informed organizations

and agencies that work with girls and their families. School safety is so much more than enforcement. It involves prevention, nurturing, and collaboration. Work to combat implicit bias by constantly revisiting specific decision-making criteria for actions that are taken against girls in schools, and continue to work with the school administration, teachers, and students—as well as other organizations providing services to schools—to develop partnerships that can result in pre-arrest diversion opportunities.

SROs should also try to experience students in other ways than those that are punitive, by observing and celebrating school per-formances or sporting events, spending time talking to students, and asking them about their weekends or how they are doing in class. They should take a moment to see these children in a dif-ferent setting and consider that when girls act out, they may not be necessarily responding to the SRO—or even the uniform—as much as they are responding to the conditions in their own lives that make them vulnerable, or that inform their harmful actions toward others. Ultimately, SROs need tools and expec-tations so that their responses to student misbehavior are ori-ented toward repairing relationships among peers and between girls and the adults and institutions that are tasked with sup-porting their healthy development.

Resources and Programs for African American Girls

African American Female
  Achievement Initiative
Oakland, CA

Alliance for Girls
Bay Area

Beautiful Black Girls, Inc.
Baton Rouge, LA

Black Girls Code
San Francisco, CA

Black Girls Rock
Youth Enrichment
  Programs
New York Metro Area

Blossom Program for
  Girls
Brooklyn, NY

BreakOUT
New Orleans, LA

Center for Young Women's
  Development
San Francisco, CA

Children of Promise NYC
Brooklyn, NY

Community Works West
Oakland, CA

Delta GEMS Program
Delta Sigma Theta
  Sorority, Inc.
Nationwide

Eve's Circle
Montgomery, AL

GEMS
New York, NY

Girl Power! Rocks
Miami, FL

Girls and Gangs
Los Angeles, CA

Girls for Gender
  Equity
New York Area

Girls, Inc.
Nationwide

Girls Rule
Chicago, IL

Impact Family Counseling
Birmingham, AL

Lead4Life, Inc.
Baltimore, MD

LifeBuilders
Chicago, IL

A Long Walk Home
Chicago, IL

The Mentoring Center
Oakland, CA

MISSSEY
Oakland, CA

National CARES
    Network
Nationwide

National Human Trafficking
    Resource Center
Washington, DC
National Hotline:
    1-888-373-7888

PACE Center for
    Girls
Jacksonville, FL

Rise Sister Rise!
Columbus, OH

A Servant's Heart Youth
    Ministries
Upper Marlboro, MD

She's All That
Chicago, IL

Sisters of Tomorrow and
    Today
Atlanta, GA, & New Haven,
    CT

Southwest Key Programs
Texas, Wisconsin, California,
    New York, Florida, Arizona

Tomorrow's Girls
Philadelphia, PA

True Belles Mentoring
    Program for Girls
Dearborn Heights, MI

Young Enterprising Sisters
Nationwide

APPENDIX B
ALTERNATIVES TO PUNISHMENT

Two of our nation's most prominent alternatives to punitive discipline are Positive Behaviors Intervention Systems (PBIS) and restorative justice. Both systems are an alternative paradigm in which to respond to problematic student behavior, but each also provides its own distinct set of promises and challenges—particularly with respect to their ability to interrupt school-to-confinement pathways.

Positive Behavioral Intervention Systems and Black Girls

There are more than seven thousand schools currently implementing Positive Behavioral Intervention Systems with the support of the National Technical Assistance Center on Positive Behavior Interventions and Supports in the Office of Special Education Programs.[1] PBIS is described as a "systems approach for establishing a continuum of proactive, positive discipline procedures for all students and staff members in all types of school settings."[2] As a tiered, research-based approach that may be enhanced by the use of wraparound services, PBIS promotes "prosocial behavior" among "(a) students without chronic problems (primary prevention), (b) those students at risk for problem behavior (secondary prevention), and (c) students with intensive behavioral needs."[3] The focus of PBIS is to "enhance the school's capacity to prevent disruptive behavior"[4] and, where necessary, modify student behavior, often within an existing paradigm or school climate of punishment. This "socially important behavior change" is at the center of the PBIS program-matic thrust and helps to facilitate institutional responses to the problematic behavior of students.[5]

This model draws upon behavioral and social learning and includes several school-based personnel (typically a school psychologist, guidance counselor, or other adult equipped to engage in behavioral assessments) to institute the multitiered interventions.[6] While presented as an alternative to exclusionary discipline, its implementation at the elementary school level also includes "precorrection" of student behavior, whereby adults remind students of school behavioral norms and expectations using "praise statements" such as "I saw you share with your friend."[7]

PBIS is rooted in special education and behavior modification.[8] As a preferred intervention in federal law associated with the behavior modification of students with disabilities, PBIS also has an established legal framework for its implementation.[9] As such, tools to measure the effectiveness of PBIS include those that focus on how well students adapt to teacher- and school-established norms.[10]

PBIS has worked to improve staff members' perceptions of the schools' organizational health, and it reduced "students' need for and use of school-based counseling services."[11] This suggests that by investing in specific interventions that target student behaviors, there can be broader outcomes that impact school climate and resources. In New Hampshire, for example, the implementation of the large-scale use of PBIS reduced suspensions (in-school and out-of-school), reduced office discipline referrals, increased instructional time, and increased time for "administrative leadership."[12]

PBIS has been noted to have a positive effect on student disciplinary outcomes, in that schools that have been trained in PBIS report a significant reduction in the percentage of children with major and minor office disciplinary events and in the overall rate of these events.[13] Existing research found that schools that have implemented PBIS with fidelity experienced decreases in office discipline reports (ODRs) and total suspensions (TS).[14] The researchers also found that over time, fidelity was less a factor in the rate of office discipline reports.[15] According to the investigators of this research, "regardless of fidelity, schools experienced decreases in ODRs over time, but time alone did not lead to overall decreases in [out-of-school suspensions] or TS."[16] So, it takes time to shift the decision-making climate within a school, which might directly impact the number of discipline reports filed, but other interventions are needed to reduce the disparities associated with the use of exclusionary discipline.

PBIS has also been found to positively impact academic achievement. In New Hampshire elementary, multilevel, and high schools, the implementation of PBIS with fidelity produced "associated gains in math achievement."[17] The researchers of this study found that the math scores improved for 20 percent of middle schools. These scholars also found that in these same schools, 41 percent of the schools that implemented PBIS with fidelity saw improvement in reading and language scores. This is not surprising. When children are in class and focused on learning, they experience better academic outcomes.

In alternative educational settings, typically those that include "alternative middle/high schools, day treatment schools, residential facilities, self-contained schools, and secure-care juvenile justice facilities," PBIS has been found to reduce problem behavior among youth.[18] The use of temporary, second-tier interventions such as check-in, check-out (CICO) or "check, connect and expect," both of which target conflict resolution, social skills development, and mentoring, decreased problem behavior in the "most problematic classroom."[19] According to researchers, "The public health model and logic can be applied seamlessly with implementation of PBIS in alternative educational settings when behavioral supports are matched to student needs, beginning with universal supports and interventions."[20]

Initial attempts to understand the impact of PBIS and the factors associated with its effective and/or ineffective implementation are limited by a dearth of student data captured by referral processes and incomplete documentation of school- and evidence-based interventions.[21] While the populations included in studies on PBIS certainly included Black and Latino youth, studies were not designed to examine the specific behaviors for which PBIS interventions (by tier) were determined and whether those interventions varied in effectiveness by levels of youth cognition, perceived racial bias, stereotype threat, law enforcement reactivity, or other attributional features that may impact student behaviors in schools. PBIS and its outcomes are outliers in comparison to other conditions associated with the disproportionate discipline, exclusion and marginalization of youth of color (e.g., implicit bias in school discipline decision making, or the impact of a school's structure of dominance on students structural change or leadership development to reduce the use of exclusionary discipline). So we still have little information about how PBIS specifically impacts responses to Black girls.

We can imagine how a PBIS-based intervention might have helped to create a climate for the establishment of behavioral norms that would have provided an alternative for Mia when she was agitated by a teacher or student, or how it may have helped Stacy, the self-described "problem child," find language and actions that could help her to present as a more constructive member of the school community. Each of the these girls had developed actions in response to feeling disrespected—cursing and fighting—that a PBIS approach could isolate and provide opportunity to correct (without academic marginalization or criminalization). Taking the time to invest in the development of behavioral adjustments and expectations prevent later outbursts that can negatively impact student achievement. But these interventions, in focusing on modifying the behaviors of children, still might miss the oppressive conditions—present in institutions and in society at large—that place these girls in harm's way.

In our efforts to create conditions to support the learning of
Black girls, it is important to understand the intention of each intervention. PBIS is aimed at correcting student behavior (largely
in association with the use of school discipline), but as we will
explore, restorative justice aims to shift the paradigm of accountability. Because PBIS is a federally supported intervention, there is
a more supportive legislative environment for the adoption of policies and practices that fall under the PBIS rubric.[22] Restorative
approaches are well suited as a community- and school-based intervention that may improve the overall climate for PBIS and other
behavior modification programs among students.[23]

Restorative Justice and Black Girls

Restorative justice is a process by which individuals involved in a
crime or harmful incident are brought together to repair their relationship.[24] Rooted in indigenous paradigms of justice from the
United States, New Zealand, and other world cultures, restorative justice provides an alternative structure by which to correct
negative student behaviors and to build accountability and community.[25] Research on the school-to-prison pipeline shows an un-
derutilization of restorative approaches in schools where Black
students predominate, but there may be growing anecdotal and
local evidence that restorative approaches are a promising strategy
by which to build leadership skills and repair relationships between and among Black youth in schools and communities.[26]
While these studies on restorative justice have typically lacked an
intersectional lens, there are aspects of the restorative approach
that inform this discussion.

Restorative justice is a paradigm that emphasizes the repair of
relationships when a harmful incident has occurred. The repair of
relationship(s) comes by way of tending to obligations, engaging
stakeholders, using cooperative and collaborative processes, and
focusing on harms and needs.[27] Restorative practices prioritize
the relationships that exist in people's conscious and spiritual do-

mains. Howard Zehr, a leading source on restorative practice in the United States, has cautioned against the labeling of all retributive or discussion-oriented processes as inherently "restorative." In other words, just talking out an issue and assigning an action to hold someone accountable does not automatically restore or transform the relationship that has been harmed. According to Zehr, three questions are central to a restorative process:

+ Who has been hurt?
+ What are their needs?
+ Whose obligations are these?[28]

These questions are associated with the core pillars of restorative justice: (1) a focus on harm, (2) the understanding that wrongdoing results in certain obligations, and (3) the understanding that restorative justice requires participation and engagement.[29] Ada Pecos Melton has offered the view that restorative justice is an extension of the "indigenous paradigm" of justice that is based on a "holistic" philosophy, in which "a circle of justice . . . connects everyone involved with a problem or conflict on a continuum, with everyone focused on the same center. The center of the circle represents the underlying problems and issues that need to be resolved to attain peace and harmony for the individuals and the community."[30] This holistic philosophy is consistent with the norms of the African diaspora as well—but this is a practice that has been forgotten and/or obscured by poverty and cultural subjugation in the United States.

While restorative justice is considered an approach, as opposed to a program, there are a number of activities that are typically associated with it. These include victim offender reconciliation programs/victim-offender programs, family group conferences, and restorative circles or conferences.[31] Each of these strategies occupies a unique space in the restorative paradigm. However, some believe that restorative approaches are neither new nor revolutionary. According to University of California, Berkeley, law professor Mary Louise Frampton, "For most of human history, the response to what are now called 'crimes' was restorative justice because people understood that crime results in injuries to victims, neighborhoods, even the offenders themselves."[32]

Numerous efforts have been made to create restorative environments in schools—particularly in states where the restorative justice movement has been implemented as an alternative to punitive school discipline and the common paradigm of criminal and juvenile justice in the United States. In Illinois, Minnesota, California, Massachusetts, and other states, comprehensive and restorative efforts have been adopted and/or touted by state departments of education as effective reforms to school-based discipline processes. According to Zehr, "Schools have become an important place for restorative practices. While there are some similarities to restorative justice programs for criminal cases, the approaches used in an educational setting must be shaped to fit that context."[33] School-based restorative practices such as circles, mediation and counseling, family group counseling, and peer juries have been found to produce restorative school cultures that seek to provide a space for the reparation of harm.[34] These programs have been found to be effective strategies to interrupt student and staff conflict, negative youth behaviors in class, and other problems that might require the involvement of a parent.[35] Restorative practices have been found to enhance youth leadership qualities and to increase accountability, school safety, and the development of prosocial skills.[36]

Research on implicit bias reveals that by virtue of our existence in a racially stratified society, there are certain ideas, racial stereotypes, and norms that affect how we make meaning and decisions.[37] These biases are rooted in our subconscious behaviors, and manifest in our implicit reactions to individuals based upon latent, involuntary preconceptions.[38] Studies have found that in schools where the population of students is predominately African

American and/or Latino, educators and administrators perceive a "racial threat," which has been shown to affect their reactions to problematic student behaviors.[39] Indeed, a recent national study found that the greater the concentration of students of color, the greater the likelihood of a school's reliance on punitive exclusionary discipline in response to disruptive and problematic student behaviors.[40] The use of punitive responses to student behaviors is especially prevalent in schools where principals and other school leaders believe that "frequent punishments help to improve behavior."[41] In short, while some research has found that restorative practices may reduce discipline disparities associated with disproportionate contact with the juvenile justice system,[42] a racial threat "reduces the use of restorative discipline and increases the use of harsh discipline in schools."[43]

The use of restorative practices in urban schools has been found to support a reduction in suspension (even when the rate of suspension is increasing district-wide), to avert expulsions, to resolve conflict between students, and to increase students' skill sets.[44] Researchers acknowledge that restorative practices in response to school discipline may be difficult for both the children and adults involved.[45] The social discipline window, as described by Costello, Wachtel, and Wachtel, captures the "interplay between two axes, one for 'control' or limit setting and another for 'support' or nurture."[46] With respect to striking a balance between these axes, Costello and colleagues wrote, "By engaging with young people, we can hold them accountable in an active way. Then we are doing things WITH them. But when we simply hand out punishments, we are doing things TO them. Or when we take care of their problems and make no demands, we are doing things FOR them. And when we ignore their behavior, we are NOT doing anything."[47]

While zero-tolerance approaches represent the most extreme aspect of the school punishment continuum and are known to facilitate future delinquency and criminalization among youth of color, the use of restorative justice may be related to the willingness of the teachers and administrators to apply sound discipline in schools and raise expectations for children of color, including those among them who are Black girls.[48]

As with PBIS, studies presented in the literature on restorative justice have typically not included a rigorous gender/race analysis, so there is no strong discussion about how racial threat may be informed by gender, or by intersections between race and gender. However, it is important to note that the lack of restorative and holistic approaches (i.e., conferencing circles, mediation and counseling, and peer juries) in the schools where Black populations predominate could be exacerbated by the presence of law enforcement in these environments.[49] Girls in the Bay Area, Southern California, Chicago, New Orleans, the Northeast, and other places I have visited have discussed contentious relationships with security officers and other school-based disciplinarians. They long for "something else." But implementing that "something else" is a challenge, especially when there are so many models of the alternative at play.

According to sujatha baliga, director of the Restorative Justice project at Impact Justice, there are many models of restorative justice; some are more scripted, others are more flexible. However, she has found that the more hands-off the process, the more culturally responsive the practice.

"I train folks on how to facilitate with very little intervention, because we read things that aren't there," sujatha said. "We all bring our cultural biases to whatever work that we do, and for me, the intersectionality of gender and race is powerful in terms of how we are uncomfortable when women and girls step out of the boundaries of what we think a proper girl is. . . . Aggression can be read into situations. If folks are going to read aggression into the [behavior of a girl], then they are limiting her full expression, which is actually damaging to restorative practice. We need to be comfortable with all of the ways that discomfort expresses itself."

In other words, if a Black girl is rolling her eyes, sucking her teeth, or even elevating her voice in a circle, she is demonstrating discomfort that should be engaged by the restorative justice facilitator, rather than punished.

"The other thing is to know yourself," sujatha said. "That's really important as a facilitator. To have an awareness of where you might be missing stuff or seeing things that aren't there—and with Black girls, [society] sees things that aren't there a lot."

School administrators, security guards, teachers, and restorative justice facilitators are not the only ones who are still adjusting to this new paradigm. Black girls also struggle to fit their current expectations into new paradigms that are not being implemented with consistency, or in some cases, with fidelity to the best practice.

In our Chicago conversation about restorative justice circles, Nala offered, "I'm not going to lie, [restorative justice] never worked for me . . . but I'd just forget about the situation anyway."

"Why didn't it work for you?" I asked.

"I don't know. . . . I'm the type of person where I'd [like to] forget about the situation anyway. It happened. It's over with."

In restorative approaches, all parties involved agree to come together and discuss the incident. But for Nala, it appeared that this fundamental practice was dissuasive.

"So, sometimes having the conversation was prolonging it?" I asked.

"Yup . . . I think it makes the altercation go longer. You sit up in a room with people [and] y'all both still beefing right now. If you say something wrong, something's going to happen. I just don't listen. . . . If she wants to keep going off at the mouth, let her do her."

To sujatha, this remaining conflict is the perfect reason to bring the young women together in conference. "If they're still beefing, we should lead them through a restorative process . . . we need an intervention. We want to bring them into the circle, but we can't police their behavior in the circle. We're not going to have active threats, but [we need to acknowledge] that the only way *out* is *through*."

Leila also saw this example as an opportunity for healing.

"What if y'all have continuous meetings?" Leila asked. "I'm pretty sure it didn't take one incident for y'all to be beefin'. So, maybe if they had continuous meetings . . . 'cause in circle, you're supposed to express yourself, she's supposed to express herself, and a few other of your classmates express themselves about how it felt. And so, at least you get your point across, like 'Why don't you like me? What is the issue?' Like, hopefully, it's supposed to break through . . . I don't know how your circle went, but I feel like if maybe we don't get the results, then we should try again. 'Cause we've been doing prisons for over four-hundred-something years, and they *clearly* don't work. So, let's try restorative justice for about one hundred [years]."

The young women laughed, but Leila had a point—and others agreed. Imperfect implementation should not lead to an abandonment of the idea.

"We did circles at my school," Michele offered. "It was two cliques . . . they didn't like each other. [The school administrator] brought all the girls together downstairs . . . I could have been in class learning. They brought all the girls downstairs. Nothing was accomplished. They made us leave because the girls was finna fight. . . . They wanted to start another circle, but they were like, never mind because the girls were too heated. They wanted to fight."

I wondered aloud whether the girls were forced to join the circle. An important principle in restorative practice is that participation is voluntary, although I concede that people respond to the options set before them. If they don't really know restorative practices, then they may not feel confident choosing them.

"I was forced," Michelle said. "[We all went], whether or not you had anything to do with the situation, because they wanted to sit down and talk with all of the girls anyway. So, you had to go down there and they were just telling us what a young lady should do and then they got onto the situation [about] what was going on in the school . . . Then people started speaking up. Some people were like, 'This is a waste of time, because it's not going to get to the real issue at all. I'ma tell y'all right now.' And it didn't."

"It's forced at our school, too," said Nala. "Because after you get off suspension, you got to have a meeting with the person you got into it with and their parents . . . and if your parents don't go, you still got to go. . . . I was talking about this with my dean . . . and he wants us to keep meeting and stuff and start doing volunteer work at places, like working together and stuff with the person I got into it with, just to be around each other, find out more stuff about each other and stuff."

This practice of ongoing communication is closer to the intent and practice of relationship building. I never met with the dean of Nala's school, but it sounded like he was on to something positive.

"I think also," Leila said, "they should change the curriculum a little bit and put in Afrocentric studies because a lot of people have a lot of self-esteem issues and don't even realize that's why you getting so mad [because] she's staring at you like that . . . if you're more confident, then you've got more hope."

Leila was on to something too. In the practice of repairing relationships between Black girls and schools, sometimes attention must also be paid to the curriculum. Low self-esteem and a failure to know themselves and their cultural contributions are important to this discussion about interventions, largely because they engage the student's learning about herself. Knowledge moves from being about others to being about self—which is the foundation for self-appreciation and love. This ancient wisdom anchors on the concept of "know thyself"—not "know others" or "know the dominant culture." When young people's cultural identity is actively integrated into their standard, skills-based learning, they do better. They are more responsive to the material, perform better on benchmark measures of learning, and are less inclined to feel alienated and threatened by peer or teacher conflict.

"Or lashing back because they *think* that's the norm," Leila added. "That's not how a lot of us actually handle situations, but if you feel like, 'Black people [fight] . . . this is me, this is who I am,' then you're taking on that. They say Black people [are] loud. . . . If I think that's a characteristic of Black [people], then I'm not finna be ashamed of being aggressive, because I'm me. But if we go through our history, even our current events—I don't like going too far back in history because we have strong Black leaders right now—we have good role models that we could look at. All we got to do is look at grown folks and see how they handle situations. A lot of youth get mad, and they don't know how to channel that anger. They're taking gym [class] out of [schools] now. They don't have sports, activities. Do something where you can get that anger out."

Black girls are less likely than White girls of similar ages to participate in athletic activities.[50] They're searching for ways to release stress and develop strong interpersonal communications skills, but they are underrepresented in school-based activities that provide an opportunity for them to do that. In district schools nationwide, Black girls are seeking to be woven into the social and academic fabric of their learning environments. They want to learn and know that school is a necessary tool for their overall development. They also know that there are limited opportunities for their full immersion in their learning when they are attending classrooms that emphasize test taking over learning, that silence their ideas and interrogation of the content they are being taught, and that emphasize behavior and dress over engagement with the material.

Successful educators and students alike recognize that at the heart of their positive outcome strategy is a commitment to nurturing the relationships between everyone who is involved in the learning process. When the communication is transparent, the learning can flow. When the expectations are co-constructed and clear, there are no surprises. When the well-being of the student is centered, she is not criminalized or marginalized for making mistakes. Instead, she is engaged as a developing human being—a learning person—and responded to first with love, and then with the intention to support and repair the harm that has been caused. As the girls' narratives suggest, we must begin by getting the girls themselves to understand the value of these conversations. When girls feel these discussions are a "waste of time," they have already assigned themselves to failure and may reject the appreciative approach—which enables them to embrace a worldview of possibility—when participating in restorative practices.

Yejide Ankobia, a restorative justice professional and advocate whose work in the Bay Area has included girls on school campuses and in the criminal legal system, has seen this shift in worldview, though she acknowledges that building these relationships are sometimes a challenge.

"Black girls have felt that they were the least listened to . . . that they were treated worse and responded to least at the high school," Yejide said. "They came into that space and were getting into trouble because of potential fights. . . . Although they don't always like the [restorative] process, they can't resist the process because the outcomes are better in terms of quashing stuff or keeping the peace."

As a former adjunct administrator at a high school, Yejide was able to work directly with Black girls who were struggling to expand their conflict resolution skills to include restorative approaches. In her conversations with these young women, she discovered that at the center of this work was a commitment to "be there" for the young women in ways that adult women may not have consistently "been there" in the past.

"Walking the balance between dean of students and holding the restorative justice process was a challenge. I was always the person that was called in to work with them," Yejide said. "My

intention was to be in good relationship with every kid. It started
with showing respect. I was always the person they knew would
say hello, recognize them by name if I knew them and ask them
why they weren't in class ... I was the one who would say, 'I care
about you and want to know how you're doing, but I also want to
know why you're not where you're supposed to be.'"

Ultimately, Yejide described how she "showed up" for the young
women, who would sometimes disperse when they saw her coming. Still, she knew they were aware that her love for them was
genuine.

"It's about always showing up and wanting to make sure they
were okay, but then holding them accountable," she said. "Even
though they sometimes didn't want that, I realized that [the ones
that scatter] are the ones that would come by my office and just
start talking. Part of what breaks through is when you show them
that you care by approaching them with a certain amount of respect. When I was growing up, it wasn't on my radar, but for kids,
that's at the top of their list—not yelling, not calling them out of
their names, not using profane language with them. I believe they
appreciated that ... I cared. I wasn't faking it. I didn't have any
ulterior motives for being there. They knew I wanted to be there
and that I cared. They would trust that I was going to be fair, that
I was going to listen."

Our girls ultimately want to be engaged as human beings,
and to transcend being referred to with terms such as "female,"
"THOT," or other dehumanizing labels that girls may see as
stripping them of their humanity. Girls in Chicago explained
how these labels impact their ability to develop personal value
and relationships—something that restorative approaches might
be able to improve.

"Some people don't even label women or girls as 'women' or
'girls.' Everybody is a 'female,'" Deena explained. "Everybody is a
'female,' no matter how old you are. You're just a 'female.' So, it's
like, okay, you're not giving us our entitlements. You're not recog-

nizing us for who we are. . . . Now, you have to have a job, be in school, and have a lot of stuff going for yourself just to be recognized as a good girl, or what they call 'approachable,' 'wifey material,' and stuff like that. Otherwise, you ain't really nothing.

"To me it's like, they're degrading us," she continued. "We're not looked upon as the young women that we are, which is something. . . . They want to be called men all of the time, but when you want to say, 'I'm a lady, I'm a young woman,' [they are saying,] 'No, you're just a female.' So basically you're just a piece of meat."

Deena, who was born and raised in Chicago, was processing many of the same issues that Faith and Heaven were wrestling with in the Bay Area. Feeling excluded from discourses and programs that were designed to address the needs of young people, Deena was struggling to see an environment that would be conducive to the implementation of programs and strategies to support young women.

"I think they pay more attention to the males, especially Black men and boys, because a lot of them don't finish high school or don't go on to college, but I feel as though we get left out the loop on a lot of things. Like, [there were] so many scholarships, but [they were] for men. It was like, why aren't there any women scholarships? You know, why can't women be included? They were like, 'Because you know, men aren't doing that well.' Well, girls can get pregnant, so you know . . ."

Deena's statement reflected her understanding that boys are not the only ones who face potential interruptions in their schooling. While only 11 percent of girls in the United States will give birth before they turn twenty years old, Deena's recognition of the hardships that accompany being a teenage mother and student was an important proxy for the myriad interruptions that can negatively, and uniquely, impact girls.[51]

"Have you had conversations with people about those kinds of expectations?" I asked. I recognized her highlighting of the

conditions that uniquely affect girls' ability to finish school—
pregnancy being just one of many. Restorative approaches in
schools might not directly facilitate these new opportunities, but
they might provide girls with a venue to express their concerns
about these identity and communications issues, and build relationships to address their concerns. I wondered if she had ever had
open conversations with people about this, or whether she was
keeping these thoughts to herself.

Deena shook her head and said, "We don't have that many good
role models." In her experience, teachers told students that they
"weren't good for nothing but laying on your back.... [They say],
'You're not going to make it through life out here being fast with
these little boys.' It was always something bad with regards to a
female. You're labeled as a 'ho,' a 'THOT' ... you ain't even got to
be one, they're going to call you that regardless. So you ain't good
for nothing but laying down."

"Even if you're smart," Deena continued, "they be like, 'What
does that mean? If you're so smart, give me some money.' ... That
was in elementary school."

And so we were back to Black girls in elementary school feeling
that if they were smart, they had to prove it by "making money"—a
terrible by-product of age compression. I thought about Danisha
in the Bay Area, who had learned to sell "fruit cocktail" by the
fifth grade, and all of the other young women who have been
pushed into the streets or conditioned to see their struggle to survive as less important than the well-being of others around them.
Our girls are being taught some harmful lessons in their formative
years. It's time to change that.

For those girls whose educational continuum includes juvenile court or other alternative schools, the promise of restorative
justice is relatively undocumented, and so ripe for exploration.
However, in an exploratory study in the Midwest, researchers
Gaarder and Hesselton found that conducting gender-responsive,
restorative programming for girls in detention facilities was par-

ticularly challenging.[52] This should not be surprising given the hyperpunitive nature of a juvenile detention center. When the norm is punitive, concepts of what it means to be "respectful" or "restorative" may be distorted. But learned negative behaviors can be replaced by positive ones. The study also discovered that restorative justice may facilitate "establishing a safe environment" for girls and contribute to the empowerment of young women.[53] Girls who participate in circles may play a strong, participatory role in their own development, and that is important. They have also been shown to recidivate at lower rates than girls who do not experience restorative justice—largely because the focus is on healing the relationships rather than on punishment.[54] Researchers found that girls were able to "gain a sense of control over their lives, contribute to their own rehabilitative process, and strengthen their family and community."[55]

Restorative approaches work best for girls when they are fully engaged in the process through understanding and investment.[56] This investment among girls of color appears to increase when facilitators reflect a similar background or express empathy for their experiences.[57] Circles require an investment of time and trust, which may be difficult to fully implement in carceral facilities, even in their educational spaces. That may be why the study found that restorative circles in a detention facility failed to build trust among young women, that participants lacked respect for the talking stick, and that they failed to pay attention to the need for building relationships among members of the circle.* Gaarder and Hesselton also found that to be responsive to system-involved girls, restorative processes must "address girls' harmful action . . . in a way that encourages them to accept responsibility for making amends."[58] These researchers cautioned against referring to

---

* The talking stick is a communication tool designed to facilitate respect for the person speaking. It controls the environment such that only one person is able to speak at a time, while the others listen.

institution-based programs as "restorative" if they fail to meet the minimum requirements of actually "addressing harm, understanding responsibility, and [making] an effort to include victims."[59]

While the undertheorization of gender-responsive, restorative practices in traditional and alternative learning environments has provided a limited scope by which to examine its promise, particularly for Black girls, an awareness of intersections between race, ethnicity, and class has been observed to improve group dynamics in circle sharing among African American girls. In this research, Black facilitators helped to create a safer space in which the young women were able and willing to share their experiences and generate an authentic healing of relationships. According to Gaarder and Hesselton, "The black facilitator lived in the same neighborhood as some of the girls, which seemed to make it easier for African American girls to share their stories in the circles."[60]

This is the connection that Yejide observed once she was able to establish a relationship with the young women that she has worked with in the past. "Teachers are human too and they need to process their stuff too. I think restorative justice and its utility made it so that I could build *relationships* and there was no one like me on campus. I looked like them and I was giving them something different," Yejide said. "I wish that the world would acknowledge that women hold a lot. Black girls are our future women, and if we do not invest in them, our communities will never be healthy and strong. . . . When I look at these Black girls, I want them to know that they are that important, that powerful. Adults are not pouring that energy back into them; they are not appreciating how important Black girls are to this culture . . . When I look at our girls struggling to be who they are, struggling to fit into these false stereotypes, I just think that they know that these things are false, and yet they don't always have the tools and support to see something else out there. We need to pour more money, more humanity, more passion, more spirituality into our Black girls. For me, the work is very personal in that way." She is not alone.

School-based interventions should prioritize engaging Black women in the development of specific conditions that provide Black girls with the opportunity to engage their healing with dignity—and remove themselves from an external gaze that has miscast them as attitude-bearing, "incorrigible" young women.

Considerations

While largely examined in the criminal justice context, critiques of restorative practices are largely informed by popular notions of crime, justice, and historic interpretations of how to address culpability in modern society.[61] Within the school context, there have been fewer debates about the usefulness of restorative justice.[62] The primary debate with respect to its use centers on the philosophy of school leadership and whether there is a prevailing sentiment of punitive responses being more effective at curbing juvenile delinquency than conversational, restorative, or other alternative practices.

It is also important to note that not all programs or strategies labeled as "restorative" are consistent with its alternative paradigm of justice. In some jurisdictions and school districts, restorative practices are little more than carefully implemented mediation programs that still adhere to a punitive construct wherein the primary objective is not to repair relationships but rather to satisfy the requirements of institutions tasked to maintain public safety. For example, some school districts have experimented with school-based youth courts, wherein discipline is handled through a mock court, in which students assume the roles traditionally held in the U.S. paradigm of justice, such as a judge, attorney, bailiff, and so on.[63] While not characterized as authentically restorative, youth courts have functioned as an alternative to more punitive responses to negative student behaviors.

The intentional use of restorative approaches to reduce contact with the justice system might also be viewed as inherently contradictory, since the primary purpose of restorative justice is to repair

relationships, not necessarily to remove or deter children from contact with the juvenile justice system or formal disciplinary boards
in school.[64] However, it is worth noting that repairing relationships is considered an important protective factor against antiso-
cial behaviors associated with youthful acts of aggression. There is
also the question of how transferrable the findings from previous
studies are to more urban and racially diverse areas in the United
States.[65] There are smaller studies that reveal the promise of restorative practices with youth of color.[66] However, the absence of research and data on the outcomes associated with programs in these
areas—and their impact on girls of color, specifically Black girls,
who experience pushout more frequently than other girls—prevents
a rigorous analysis of the successes and challenges associated with
implementing restorative practices among girls.

Another critique of restorative justice is that it fails to recognize
that not all individuals are seeking to have relationships return to
where they began (if they were negative); rather, some prefer to
transform the nature of these relationships.[67] Some might consider
this an issue of semantics.[68] But others view this as an important
distinction associated with the use of restorative approaches to address the root causes of conflict and harm that produce pathways
to poor academic performance, educational marginalization, and
incarceration.[69]

METHODOLOGY

The study upon which this book is predicated collected narratives from Black girls regarding their experiences in education—including schools in the community and schools in carceral settings—toward the goal of identifying potential policy and infrastructure improvements to support the learning of Black girls in schools. The primary research methods that I implemented for this study were qualitative, phenomenological, and action-oriented, using critical narrative inquiry to explore and describe the educational experiences of Black girls that may facilitate, or reflect, criminalization. Quantitative methods are collected from previously published reports and data sets, and percentages have been rounded to the nearest whole number.

Phenomenological research elevates the meaning of the "lived experience" of those at the center of the inquiry. In this study, I employed qualitative research methods, because they are best suited for inquiries that seek to describe and present a deep understanding of an issue.[1] The intensive nature of the inquiry allowed me to develop relationships of meaning and other patterns that informed how Black girls articulate their understanding of their educational experiences and how I have ultimately interpreted their narrative descriptions of these experiences.[2] As a critical tool in qualitative research, the interview offers an opportunity for the interviewer to explore the phenomenon through the lens of the affected person.[3] Methodologist John Creswell added that interviews allow for the researcher to "control" the line of questioning and possibly steer the person toward providing historical information that may be useful for the researcher.[4] I also note that interviewing allowed for a dialogical engagement that can be liberative and therapeutic for the person being interviewed (i.e., the "storyteller"), particularly if she has not previously been able to release her thoughts and feelings about the phenomenon under study. A similar dynamic was present for the focus groups.

In writing this book, I used a composite narrative method, which represents narrative data and research from my study in a manner that blends the voices of participants with those of the researcher in order to demonstrate our "connectedness."[5] Narratives in this book were collected from intensive interviews and focus groups with girls, young women, educators and justice professionals in California (Northern and Southern), New York, Louisiana, and Illinois. These interviews and focus groups allowed the Black girls at the center of this inquiry to share their educational experiences from *their* perspectives, and in their own words. Specific scenes are described from observations that I conducted in classrooms throughout the San Francisco Bay Area and Southern California between November 2011 and July 2014. The majority of these girls—more than 60 percent, identified as Black, alone or in combination with at least one other race.[6] In the facility in which I located my in-depth interviews, where the length of stay ranged from one day to several months, girls were required to attend school for at least 240 minutes each day. Girls who experienced longer than average stays typically remained in custody because they were awaiting a court-ordered placement, sometimes in another city or state. Academic institutions, school districts and administrators, and the appropriate government and nonprofit agencies that helped to coordinate participants for this work granted permission. Unless already a matter of public record, all names and other personal identifying information have been changed to protect the identity of participants.

A Note on Key Terminology

Black/African American: In this book, people of African descent are referred to as *Black* and *African American*. While *African American* refers to people of African descent who reside in the United States, *Black* is a larger umbrella term that captures individuals throughout the African diaspora (e.g., those of Caribbean and/or Latino descent who belong to the racial group indigenous to Africa). In this document, I prioritize the use of *Black* but also occasionally use *African American*, as data sources use these terms interchangeably.

Culturally competent: Joseph Betancourt, Alexander Green, J. Emilio Carrillo, and Owusu Ananeh-Firempong define cultural competency as acknowledging and incorporating "at all levels—the importance of culture, assessment of cross-cultural relations, vigilance toward the dynamics that result from cultural differences, expansion of cultural knowledge, and adaptation of services to meet culturally unique needs."[7] They also note that a culturally competent system has as its foundation, "an awareness of the integration and interaction of health beliefs and behaviors, disease prevalence and incidence, and treatment outcomes for different patient populations." While cultural competency has largely been framed in the health context, its usage has greatly informed the discussion about organizational responses to people of color in other disciplines, particularly in education and juvenile justice.[8] For this study, I use cultural competency as a measure by which strategies, programs, or individuals consider and reflect the cultural needs of the population they serve.

Gender-responsive: Stephanie Covington and Barbara Bloom define gender responsiveness as a systems response "that, in both context (structure and environment) and content, are both comprehensive and relate to the realities of [women's] lives."[9] The gender responsiveness of criminal justice programs and interventions is also characterized as those that "target women's pathways to criminality by providing effective interventions that address the intersecting issues of substance abuse, trauma, mental health and economic marginality," according to Barbara Bloom, Barbara Owen, Stephanie Covington, and Myrna Raeder.[10] While this definition was developed in the context of building responses to *women* in the criminal justice system, studies find that gender-responsive programs for adolescent girls should also include responses to sexual identity, self-esteem, relationships and relational aggression, health concerns, and victimization.[11]

Juvenile hall: In this book, this term is used interchangeably with "juvenile detention facility."

ACKNOWLEDGMENTS

First, giving honor to the Creator, I would like to extend my gratitude and appreciation to the ancestors and elders who struggled for human dignity and racial justice. Our work is to carry forward your legacy in the spirit of the liberation and uplift of our people and our nation.

I would also like to thank my family for their unwavering support and understanding during the research and writing phases of producing this book. Together, you all provide a foundation more powerful than anything. I love you.

To the many girls and young women who were fearless enough to share their narratives for this book, I offer you my heartfelt thanks and commitment to use your stories as a springboard for change. With love, this book is dedicated to you.

I would also like to express my gratitude to Marie Brown, who has so graciously guided and supported my work. I am equally grateful to my very talented editor, Tara Grove. I am so lucky to work with you two!

As one can imagine, this book is the product of hours and hours of thought partnership over the past four years with many of this nation's most dedicated investors in the lives of Black women and girls. There are many people that I would love to thank for their participation in this project—the administrators, teachers, students, probation staff, juvenile court(s), and law enforcement professionals—but in order to protect their identities and those of the girls that I spoke with, I will not name them here.

To compile and respond to the questions in Appendix A, I consulted with a diverse group of committed people whose personal and professional engagement with and love for our girls and young women is unwavering. These people include Dereca Blackmon, Falilah Aisha Bilal, Isis Sapp-Grant, Nola Brantley, Fran Frazier, sujatha baliga, and Wes Ware. Thank you, friends, for your guidance. Additionally, I am so grateful for the conversations, consultations, and general support that the following individuals have offered me on elements of this project: Fania Davis, Anna Deavere Smith, Celsa Snead, Joanne Smith, Nakisha Lewis, Avis Jones-DeWeever, Susan Burton, Tracey Robertson Carter, Nola Brantley, Larita LaFlotte, K. Jones, Stephanie Bush-Baskette, Alvin Starks, Yejie Ankobia, Shawn Ginwright, Charity Tolliver, JoHanna Thompson, Marlene Sanchez-Roy, Zandra Washington, Camisha Fatimah Gentry-Ford, Mariah Landers, Timothy McCarthy, Geoff Ward, Sonia Kumar, Maria Casey, Lenneal Henderson, Kitty Kelley Epstein, Kathy Tiner, Douglas Paxton, Irma Herrera, Jolon McNeil, Francine Sherman, Lesleigh Irish-Underwood, Erika Irish Brown, Stefanie Brown-James, Cedric Brown, Hector de Jesus, Berta Colon, Jeanette Pai-Espinosa, Agape Adams, and the community of scholar-advocates who refuse to leave our girls behind, including (but certainly not limited to) Angela Y. Davis, Kimberlé Crenshaw, Beth Richie, Coramae Ruchey Mann, Vernetta Young, Stephanie Sears, Elaine Richardson, Jamilia Blake, Simone Drake, Brittney Cooper, Nikki Jones, Priscilla Ocen, and many others upon whose shoulders I stand.

I would also like to extend my gratitude to the Open Society Foundations Soros Justice Fellowship; the W.K. Kellogg Foundation; the Akonadi Foundation; Fielding Graduate University; Girls for Gender Equity; the African American Policy Forum; the Schott Foundation for Public Education; the Advancement Project; the

National Council on Crime and Delinquency; the NAACP Legal Defense and Education Fund; the National Women's Law Center; Impact Justice; the National Urban League; Delta Sigma Theta Sorority, Inc.; the Georgetown Law Center on Poverty and Inequality; the Institute for Research in African American Studies at Columbia University; and other institutions, collaborative efforts, and coalitions that support this work and the public discourse it seeks to engage at the national level.

NOTES

Introduction

1. Ashley Fantz, Holly Yan, and Catherine Shoichet, "Texas Pool Party Chaos: 'Out of Control' Police Officer Resigns," CNN.com, June 9, 2015.

2. Kimberlé Crenshaw and Andrea Ritchie with Rachel Anspach, Rachel Gilmer, and Luke Harris, *Say Her Name: Resisting Police Brutality Against Black Women* (New York: African American Policy Forum and Columbia University Center for Intersectionality and Social Policy Studies, 2015).

3. Eliott McLaughlin, "Tamir Rice's Teen Sister 'Tackled,' Handcuffed After His Shooting, Mom Says," CNN.com, December 8, 2014.

4. Angela Irvine and Aisha Canfield, "Factsheet: The Overrepresentation of Lesbian, Gay, Bisexual, Questioning, Gender Nonconforming, and Transgender Youth in the Juvenile Justice System," Impact Justice, July 1, 2015.

5. U.S. Department of Education, Office for Civil Rights, Civil Rights Data Collection, 2011–12, available at http://ocrdata.ed.gov. Data notes are available at http://ocrdata.ed.gov/downloads/DataNotes.docx.

6. Civil Rights Data Collection, 2011–12.

7. Kevin Koeninger, "Arrested and Beaten for Dozing in Class," Courthouse News Service, May 7, 2013.

8. Tamara Lush, "Kiera Wilmot Will Not Be Charged for Explosion at Florida School," *Huffington Post*, April 15, 2013.

9. Ibid.

10. "Girl Arrested in Texas for Inappropriate Prom Dress," *Capitol Street*, May 13, 2008, http://capitolstreet.wordpress.com/2008/05/13/girl-arrested-in-texas-for -inappropriate-prom-dress.

11. "Palmdale High School Student Battered by School Guard," ABC News via YouTube, uploaded September 30, 2007, http://www.youtube.com/watch?v=3_gr

_VBRhO4. See also Jessica Valenti, "Teenage Girl Beaten, Expelled, and Arrested . . . for Dropping Cake," Feministing.com, October 1, 2007, http://feministing.com /2007/10/01/teenage_girl_beaten_expelled_a_1.

12. Janice D'Arcy, "Salecia Johnson, 6, Handcuffed After Tantrum, What's Wrong with This Picture?," *Washington Post*, April 18, 2012.

13. Bill Bush, "Westerville Police Criticized for Handcuffing Children After School-Bus Fight," *Columbus Dispatch*, November 17, 2011.

14. "Kindergarten Girl Handcuffed, Arrested at Fla. School," WFTV.com, March 30, 2007, http://www.wftv.com/news/news/kindergarten-girl-handcuffed -arrested-at-fla-schoo/nFBR4.

15. Georgia Slave Code, 1848.

16. "Catherine Ferguson: Founder, New York City's First Sunday School, Born 1779–Died July 11, 1854," Early America, http://www.earlyamerica.com/catherine -ferguson.

17. Anonymous, "Katy Ferguson: The Woman Who Loved All Children," OneHistory, http://www.onehistory.org/katy.htm.

18. "Douglas, Sarah Mapps (1806–1882)," BlackPast, http://www.blackpast .org/aah/douglass-sarah-mapps-1806-1882.

19. National Council of Negro Women, Inc., "Mary McLeod Bethune," http:// ncnw.org/about/Bethune.htm.

20. Gerda Lerner, ed., *Black Women in White America: A Documentary History* (New York: Vintage Books, 1972).

21. See, for example, *Brown v. Board of Education of Topeka*, 347 U.S. 483, 1954.

22. See, for example, Wanda Blanchett, Vincent Mumford, and Floyd Beachum, "Urban School Failure and Disproportionality in a Post-Brown Era: Benign Neglect of the Constitutional Rights of Students of Color," *Remedial and Special Education* 26, no. 2 (March–April 2005): 70–81.

23. See, for example, W.E.B. Du Bois, *The Philadelphia Negro: A Social Study* (1898; Philadelphia: University of Pennsylvania Press, 1995). See also Charles S. Johnson, *The Negro in Chicago: A Study of Race Relations and a Race Riot* (Chicago: University of Chicago Press, 1922).

24. Patricia Hill-Collins, *Black Sexual Politics: African Americans, Gender, and the New Racism* (New York: Routledge, 2004), 193.

25. Monique W. Morris, *Race, Gender, and the School-to-Prison Pipeline: Expanding Our Discussion to Include Black Girls* (New York: African American Policy Forum, 2012).

26. Kimberlé Crenshaw, Priscilla Ocen, and Jyoti Nanda, *Black Girls Matter: Pushed-Out, Over-Policed and Under-Protected* (New York: African American Policy Forum, 2015).

27. Daniel Losen and Jonathan Gillespie, *Opportunities Suspended: The Disparate Impact of Disciplinary Exclusion from School* (Los Angeles: Center for Civil Rights Remedies at the University of California, Los Angeles Civil Rights Project, 2012). See also John Wallace, Sarah Goodkind, Cynthia Wallace, and Jerald Bachman, "Racial, Ethnic, and Gender Differences in School Discipline Among U.S. High School Students: 1991–2005," *Negro Educational Review* 59, nos. 1–2 (2008): 47–62.

28. Nikki Jones, *Between Good and Ghetto: African American Girls and Inner-City Violence* (Piscataway, NJ: Rutgers University Press, 2009).

29. Jamilia Blake, Betty Ray Butler, Chance Lewis, and Alicia Darensbourg, "Unmasking the Inequitable Discipline Experiences of Urban Black Girls: Implications for Urban Educational Stakeholders," *Urban Review* 43, no. 1 (2011): 90–106. See also Kristi Holsinger and Alexander Holsinger, "Different Pathways to Violence and Self-Injurious Behavior: African American and White Girls in the Juvenile Justice System," *Journal of Research in Crime and Delinquency* 42, no. 2 (2005): 211–42.

30. Blake et al., "Unmasking the Inequitable Discipline Experiences of Urban Black Girls."

31. Edward W. Morris, "'Ladies' or 'Loudies'? Perceptions and Experiences of Black Girls in Classrooms," *Youth and Society* 38, no. 4 (2007): 490–515.

32. Kathleen Nolan, *Police in the Hallways: Discipline in an Urban High School* (Minneapolis: University of Minnesota Press, 2011).

33. American Bar Association and National Bar Association, *Justice by Gender: The Lack of Appropriate Prevention, Diversion, and Treatment Alternatives for Girls in the Juvenile Justice System* (Washington, DC: ABA, NBA, 2001). See also Monique W. Morris, Stephanie Bush-Baskette, and Kimberlé Crenshaw, *Confined in California: Women and Girls of Color in Custody* (New York: African American Policy Forum, 2012).

34. Cathy S. Widom and Michael G. Maxfield, "An Update on the 'Cycle of Violence,'" Research in Brief, U.S. Department of Justice, National Institute of Justice, February 2001, NCJ 184894.

35. Gretchen R. Cusick, Judy R. Havlicek, and Mark E. Courtney, "Risk of Arrest: The Role of Social Bonds in Protecting Foster Youth Making the Transition

to Adulthood," *American Journal of Orthopsychiatry* 82, no. 1 (2012): 19–31; Barbara Bloom, Barbara Owen, and Stephanie Covington, *Gender-Responsive Strategies: Research, Practice, and Guiding Principles for Women Offenders* (Washington, DC: National Institute of Corrections, 2002), 64.

36. Barbara Bloom and David Steinhart, *Why Punish the Children?: A Reappraisal of the Children of Incarcerated Mothers in California* (Oakland, CA: National Council on Crime and Delinquency, 1993.

37. Lerner, *Black Women in White America*, 574.

1. Struggling to Survive

1. Nikki Jones, *Between Good and Ghetto: African American Girls and Inner City Violence* (New Brunswick, NJ: Rutgers University Press, 2009), 158.

2. Angela Y. Davis, *Women, Race and Class* (New York: Vintage Books, 1981), 6.

3. Jones, *Between Good and Ghetto.*

4. Ibid., 48–49.

5. Gerda Lerner, ed., *Black Women in White America: A Documentary History* (New York: Vintage Books, 1972), 165.

6. Katherine Gallager Robbins and Anne Morrison, *National Snapshot: Poverty Among Women and Families* (Washington, DC: National Women's Law Center, 2014).

7. Bureau of Labor Statistics, *The Employment Situation—December 2014* (Washington, DC: U.S. Department of Justice, 2014). Unemployment rates are seasonally adjusted.

8. American Association of University Women. *How Does Race Affect the Wage Gap?* (Washington, DC: AAUW, 2014).

9. E. Ann Carson and Daniela Golinelli, *Prisoners in 2012: Trends in Admissions and Releases, 1991–2012* (Washington, DC: Bureau of Justice Statistics, 2013); The Sentencing Project, *Incarcerated Women* (Washington, DC.: The Sentencing Project, n.d.).

10. Annie E. Casey Foundation, *Kids Count 2014 Databook: State Trends in Child Well-Being.* (Baltimore, MD: Annie E. Casey Foundation, 2014), 19.

11. U.S. Census Bureau, *People in Families by Family Structure, Age, and Sex, Iterated by Income-to-Poverty Ratio and Race: 2012, Below 100% of Poverty—Black Alone or in Combination (A.O.I.C.)* (Washington, DC: Census Bureau, 2013).

12. National Center for Education Statistics, *Percentage of High School Dropouts Among Persons 16 Through 24 Years Old (Status Dropout Rate), by Sex and Race/Ethnicity: Selected Years, 1960 Through 2012* (Washington, DC: U.S. Department of Commerce, 2013). See also U.S. Census Bureau, *Current Population Survey (CPS), 1967 Through 2012* (Washington, DC: Census Bureau, 2013).

13. Charles Puzzanchera, Benjamin Adams, and Sarah Hockenberry, *Juvenile Court Statistics 2009* (Pittsburgh, PA: National Center for Juvenile Justice, 2012), 26.

14. Melissa Sickmund, *Juveniles in Corrections* (Washington, DC: U.S. Department of Justice, 2004). See also National Center for Juvenile Justice, *Easy Access to the Census of Juveniles in Residential Placement: 1997–2010* (Washington, DC: Office of Juvenile Justice and Delinquency Prevention, 2015).

15. Centers for Disease Control, *Leading Causes of Death by Age Group, African American Females—United States* (Atlanta, GA: CDC, 2011).

16. Shannan Catalano, *Intimate Partner Violence 1993–2010* (Washington, DC: U.S. Department of Justice Statistics, 2012).

17. Margot Adler, "Before Rosa Parks, There Was Claudette Colvin," *Weekend Edition Sunday*, National Public Radio, March 15, 2009.

18. Biography.com, "Claudette Colvin," http://www.biography.com/people/claudette-colvin-11378.

19. Adler, "Before Rosa Parks."

20. W.E.B. Du Bois, *The Souls of Black Folk* (New York: New American Library, 1969), 45.

21. Kimberlé Crenshaw, "Demarginalizing the Intersection of Race and Sex: A Black Feminist Critique of Antidiscrimination Doctrine, Feminist Theory and Antiracist Politics," *University of Chicago Legal Forum* (1989): 139.

22. Audre Lorde, "Learning from the 60s," in *Sister Outsider: Essays and Speeches* (Trumansburg, NY: Crossing Press, 1984).

23. bell hooks, *Black Looks: Race and Representation* (Boston: South End Press, 1992), 115–31.

24. Education is correlated with occupational options. An analysis of census data conducted by Valerie Wilson found that median inflation-adjusted annual earnings for African American women working full-time in 2013 were 3.3 percent below the 2009 level, compared to 0.2 percent and 0.5 percent lower for white and Hispanic women, respectively, for that same period. While Black women consistently earned less than their White counterparts, increases in access to education

were associated with greater earnings. See Valerie Wilson, "Post-recession Decline in Black Women's Wages Is Consistent with Occupational Downgrading," Economic Policy Institute, October 8, 2014. See also Dana Wood, Rachel Kaplan, and Vonnie McCloyd, "Gender Differences in the Educational Expectations of Urban, Low-Income, African American Youth: The Role of Parents and the School," *Journal of Youth and Adolescence* 36, no. 4 (2007): 417–27.

25. Linda Darling-Hammond, "Quality Teaching: What Is It and How Can It Be Measured?," PowerPoint presentation, Stanford University, 2011, https:// edpolicy.stanford.edu/sites/default/files/events/materials/ldhscopeteacher-effective ness.pdf.

26. Jan Hughes and Oi-man Kwok, "Influence of Student-Teacher and Parent-Teacher Relationships on Lower Achieving Readers' Engagement and Achievement in the Primary Grades," *Journal of Educational Psychology* 99, no. 1 (2007): 39–51.

27. Gloria Ladson-Billings, "I Ain't Writin' Nuttin': Permissions to Fail and Demands to Succeed in Urban Classrooms," in *The Skin That We Speak*: *Thoughts on Language and Culture in the Classroom*, ed. Lisa Delpit and Joanne Kilgour Dowdy (New York: The New Press, 2002), 111.

28. Caroline Hodges Persell, *Education and Inequality: The Roots and Results of Stratification in America's Schools* (New York: The Free Press, 1977).

29. Peter Senge, *The Fifth Discipline: The Art and Practice of The Learning Organization* (New York: Currency Doubleday, 1990).

30. Douglas Massey and Nancy Denton, *American Apartheid: Segregation ad the Making of the Underclass* (Cambridge, MA: Harvard University Press, 1993), 18–19.

31. Ibid., 19.

32. Daniel Georges-Abeyie, "Race, Ethnicity, and the Spatial Dynamic: Toward a Realistic Study of Black Crime, Crime Victimization, and Criminal Justice Processing of Blacks," in *African American Classics in Criminology and Criminal Justice*, ed. Shaun Gabbison, Helen Taylor Taylor Greene, and Vernetta Young (Thousand Oaks, CA: Sage Publications, 2002), 229–42.

33. Eugene Genovese, *Roll, Jordan, Roll: The World the Slaves Made* (New York: Vintage Books, 1972), 331.

34. U.S. Department of Education, *Turning Around the Dropout Factories: Increasing the High School Graduation Rate* (Washington, DC: Department of Education, n.d.).

35. Alliance for Excellent Education, *Prioritizing the Nation's Lowest Performing High Schools: Issue Brief* (Washington, DC: Alliance for Excellent Education, 2010).

36. Bureau of Labor Statistics, *Labor Force Characteristics by Race and Ethnicity, 2013* (Washington, DC: Bureau of Labor Statistics, 2014), 4.

37. Ibid., 19.

38. U.S. Census Bureau, "Table 104.20. Percentage of Persons 25 to 29 Years Old with Selected Levels of Educational Attainment, by Race/Ethnicity and Sex: Selected Years 1920 Through 2014," *Digest of Education Statistics* (Washington, DC: NCES, 2014).

39. FairTest, *Racial Justice and Standardized Testing* (Jamaica Plain, MA: National Center for Fair and Open Testing, n.d.).

40. In more than thirteen states, students are required to meet a baseline score on third-grade reading assessments in order to advance to the fourth grade. In Ohio, for example, a student must score at least a 394 to advance to the fourth grade. Four percent of the state's third-graders were prevented from advancing because of it, but the grade retention rate for students increased by 600 percent between the 2012–13 and 2013–14 academic years. Only 32 percent of Black third-grade students scored "proficient or better" on the Reading Achievement Test, compared with 71 percent of Asian Pacific students, 64 percent of White students, and 41 percent of Hispanic students. Performance on the state's high school graduation tests also revealed racial disparities. Statewide, 78.7 percent of Black students scored "proficient" on the Ohio Graduation Test, compared with 92 percent of White youth, 86.8 percent of Asian Pacific youth, 80.9 percent of Hispanic youth, and 72.6 percent of Native American youth. See Ohio Department of Education, "Ohio Graduation Tests Preliminary Results March 2014 Test Administration," March 2014, http://education.ohio.gov/getattachment/Topics/Testing/Testing-Results/Ohio-Graduation-Tests-OGT-Assessment-Results/Highlights-of-March-2014-OGT-2.pdf.aspx.

41. The average national score in reading for twelfth-grade Black girls is 273, which is lower than all other groups of girls taking the test. See U.S. Department of Education, Institute of Education Sciences, National Center for Education Statistics, National Assessment of Educational Progress (NAEP), 1992, 1994, 1998, 2002, 2005, 2009, and 2013 Reading Assessments. http://nces.ed.gov/nationsreportcard/naepdata/report.aspx?app=NDE&p=3-RED-2-20133%2c20093%2c20053%2c20023%2c19983%2c19982%2c19942%2c19922-RRPCM-GENDER%2cSDRACE-NT-MN_MN-J_Y_0-1-0-37.

42. Mark Hugo Lopez and Ana Gonzalez-Barrera, *FactTank: Women's College Enrollment Gains Leave Men Behind* (Washington, DC: Pew Research Center, 2014).

43. Ibid. Recent data show that Black women may be earning degrees at a higher rate than Black men. See National Center for Education Statistics, *Fast Facts: Degrees Conferred by Sex and Race* (Washington, DC: U.S. Department of Education, 2012).

44. U.S. Department of Education, National Center for Education Statistics, *Graduation Rates of First-Time Postsecondary Students Who Started as Full-Time Degree/Certificate-Seeking Students, by Sex, Race/Ethnicity, Time to Completion, and Level and Control of Institution Where Student Started: Selected Cohort Entry Years, 1996 Through 2007* (Washington, DC: NCES, 2011), http://nces.ed.gov /programs/digest/d11/tables/dt11_345.asp.

45. Lerner, *Black Women in White America*, 594.

46. The concept of age compression has largely been framed within the context of commercialization and consumer marketing; however, as I include it in this narrative, its reach extends into other domains as well. See Adriana Barbaro and Jeremy Earp, "Consuming Kids: The Commercialization of Childhood," Media Education Study Guide, 2008, https://www.mediaed.org/assets/products/134 /studyguide_134.pdf.

47. Guadalupe Valdes, *Con Respect: Bridging the Distances Between Culturally Diverse Families and School* (New York: Teachers College Press, 1996).

48. Hughes and Kwok, "Influence of Student-Teacher and Parent-Teacher Relationships."

49. Sherri F. Seyfried and Ick-Joong Chung, "Parent Involvement as Parental Monitoring of Student Motivation and Parent Expectations Predicting Later Achievement Among African American and European American Middle School Age Students," *Journal of Ethnic and Cultural Diversity in Social Work* 11, nos. 1–2 (2002): 126.

50. Tamba-Kuii Bailey, Y. Barry Chung, Wendi Williams, Anneliese Singh, and Heather Terrell, "Development and Validation of the Internalized Racial Oppression Scale for Black Individuals," *Journal of Counseling Psychology* 58, no. 4 (2011): 481–493.

51. Monique W. Morris, "Representing the Educational Experiences of Black Girls in a Juvenile Court School," *Journal of Applied Research on Children: Informing Policy for Children at Risk* 4, no. 2 (2014): article 5.

52. Ibid.

53. Bureau of Labor Statistics, *Employment and Unemployment Among Youth—Summer 2013* (Washington, DC: U.S. Department of Labor, 2013).

54. California Demographic Labor Force, Summary Tables March 2015, http://www.calmis.ca.gov/specialreports/CA_Employment_Summary_Table.pdf.

55. John Ogbu describes Black Americans as falling into two categories: those who descend from involuntary immigrants (those arriving on American shores as enslaved Africans in the seventeenth century) and voluntary immigrants (those of African and Caribbean descent who voluntarily immigrated to the United States). John Obguk, *Black American Students in an Affluent Suburb: A Study of Academic Disengagement* (Mahwah, NJ: Lawrence Erlbaum Associates, 2003).

56. Jacquelynne S. Eccles, Janis E. Jacobs, and Rena D. Harold, "Gender Role Stereotypes, Expectancy Effects, and Parents' Socialization of Gender Differences," *Journal of Social Issues* 46 (1990): 183–210.

57. Toni Falbo, Laura Lein, and Nicole Amador, "Parental Involvement During the Transition to High School," *Journal of Adolescent Research* 16 (2001): 511-29. See also Gwynne O. Kohl, Liliana J. Lengua, and Robert J. McMahon, "Parent Involvement in School: Conceptualizing Multiple Dimensions and Their Relations with Family and Demographic Risk Factors," *Journal of School Psychology* 38, no. 6 (2000): 501–23.

58. Ibid.

59. Ibid.

60. DeMarquis Hayes, "Parental Involvement in Urban African American Adolescents from a Parent's Perspective," *Journal of Comparative Family Studies* 94, no. 4 (2011): 154–66.

61. Jung-Sook Lee and Natasha K. Bowen, "Parent Involvement, Cultural Capital, and the Achievement Gap Among Elementary School Children," *American Educational Research Association Journal* 43, no. 2 (2006): 193–218.

62. Suniti Sharma, "Contesting Institutional Discourse to Create New Possibilities for Understanding Lived Experience: Life Stories of Young Women in Detention, Rehabilitation, and Education," *Race, Ethnicity and Education* 13, no. 3 (2010): 327–47.

63. Ladson-Billings, "I Ain't Writin' Nuttin'," 110.

64. Ibid.

65. Pierre Bourdieu and Jean-Claude Passeron, *Reproduction in Society, Education and Culture*, 2nd ed. (London: Sage Publications, 1990), xv.

2. A Blues for Black Girls When the "Attitude" Is Enuf

1. "Kindergarten Girl Handcuffed, Arrested at Fla. School," WFTV.com, March 30, 2007, http://www.wftv.com/news/news/kindergarten-girl-handcuffed-arrested-at-fla-schoo/nFBR4.

2. Janice D'Arcy, "Salecia Johnson, 6, Handcuffed After Tantrum: What's Wrong with This Picture?," *Washington Post*, April 18. 2012.

3. Judith Brown Dianis, "When Temper Tantrums Become Criminal," *The Root*, April 18, 2012.

4. Talia Kaplan, "8-Year-Old Special Needs Student Handcuffed, Arrested for Tantrum at School," *The Grio*, March 8, 2013.

5. "School District, Alton Police Stand by Decision to Handcuff Child," CBS St. Louis, March 7, 2013, http://stlouis.cbslocal.com/2013/03/07/school-district-alton-police-stand-by-decision-to-handcuff-child; Gabrielle Levy, "8-Year-Old Handcuffed for Tantrum," United Press International, March 7, 2013, http://www.upi.com/blog/2013/03/07/8-year-old-handcuffed-for-tantrum/2621362666107/.

6. U.S. Department of Education Office of Civil Rights, *Discipline Snapshot: School Discipline, Issue Brief No. 1* (Washington, DC: Department of Education, 2014).

7. Daniel Losen and Russell Skiba, *Suspended Education: Urban Middle Schools in Crisis* (Los Angeles, CA: Civil Rights Project at UCLA and the Equity Project, Center for Evaluation and Education Policy, Indiana University, 2010), 7.

8. The highest-suspending school districts included in this study: Memphis City Schools, Tennessee; Columbus City, Ohio; Henrico County Public Schools, Virginia; City of Chicago SD 299, Illinois; Alief Island, Texas; Detroit City School District, Michigan; Fulton County, Georgia; Wichita, Kansas; Oklahoma City, Oklahoma; and Clayton County, Georgia. See Daniel Losen and Jonathan Gillespie, *Opportunities Suspended: The Disparate Impact of Disciplinary Exclusion from School* (Los Angeles: Center for Civil Rights Remedies, Civil Rights Project, University of California, Los Angeles, 2012).

9. bell hooks, *Developing an Oppositional Gaze* (Boston: South End Press, 1992), 115–31.

10. Jan Hughes and Oi-man Kwok, "Influence of Student-Teacher and Parent-Teacher Relationships on Lower Achieving Readers' Engagement and Achievement in the Primary Grades," *Journal of Educational Psychology* 99, no. 1 (2007): 39–51.

11. Ibid.

12. Anthony G. Greenwald and Linda Hamilton Krieger, "Implicit Bias: Scientific Foundations," *California Law Review* 94 (2006): 945–67.

13. Kelly Welch and Allison A. Payne, "Exclusionary School Punishment: The Effect of Racial Threat on Expulsion and Suspension," *Youth Violence and Juvenile Justice* 10, no. 20 (2012): 155–71.

14. Losen and Gillespie, *Opportunities Suspended*, 39.

15. Mary Field Belenky, Blythe McVicker Clinchy, Nancy Rule Goldberger, and Jill Mattuck Tarule, *Women's Ways of Knowing: The Development of Self, Voice, and Mind* (New York: Basic Books, 1997).

16. See John Heron, *Empirical Validity in Experiential Research* (Guildford: University of Surrey, 1982).

17. James Wilson and George Kelling, "Broken Windows: The Police and Neighborhood Safety," *Atlantic Monthly*, March 1982.

18. U.S. Department of Education, *Guidance Concerning State and Local Responsibilities Under the Gun-Free Schools Act of 1994* (Washington, DC: Department of Education, 1994).

19. Angels of Columbine, "Violence in Our Schools: August 1, 1993 Through July 31, 1994." Columbine-Angels.com, http://www.columbine-angels.com/School _Violence_1993-1994.htm.

20. Greg Toppo, "10 Years Later, the Real Story Behind Columbine," *USA Today*, April 14, 2009.

21. U.S. Department of Education Office of Civil Rights, *National Estimations* (Washington, DC: Department of Education, 2000, 2009–10).

22. Black girls without a disability were 39 percent of girls with only one out-of-school suspension. See U.S. Department of Education Office of Civil Rights, *National Estimations*, 2009–10.

23. These states included Wisconsin (21 percent), Indiana (16 percent), Michigan (16 percent), Missouri (16 percent), Tennessee (15 percent), Nebraska (15 percent), West Virginia (14 percent), Arkansas (14 percent), Delaware (14 percent), Ohio (14 percent), Florida (14 percent), Oklahoma (13 percent), Pennsylvania (13 percent), South Carolina (13 percent), Rhode Island (13 percent), Illinois (13 percent), Alabama (13 percent), and the District of Columbia (13 percent). U.S. Department of Education, *Discipline Snapshot*.

24. Edward Smith and Shaun Harper, *Disproportionate Impact of K-12 School Suspension and Expulsion on Black Students in Southern States* (Philadelphia:

University of Pennsylvania, Center for the Study of Race and Equity in Education, 2015).

25. U.S. Department of Education, *National Estimations*, 2009–10.

26. Ibid., 2011–12.

27. U.S. Department of Education, *Discipline Snapshot.*

28. Kelly Meyerhofer, "Special Report: Nearly Three-Quarters of MPS High School Students Labeled 'Truants,'" Milwaukee Neighborhood News Service, November 17, 2014, http://milwaukeenns.org/2014/11/17/special-report-nearly -three-quarters-of-mps-high-school-students-labeled-truants.

29. U.S. Department of Education Office of Civil Rights database, accessed May 10, 2015, http://ocrdata.ed.gov/flex/Reports.aspx?type=district#/action%3D addSearchParams%26tbSearchSchool%3DMilwaukee%26btnSearchParams%3D Search%26cblYears_4%3D1. Milwaukee Public Schools has defined a habitually truant student as "a student who is absent from school without an acceptable excuse under s.118.16(4) and s.118.15, Wis. Stats., for part or all of 5 or more days on which school is held during a school semester." See Wisconsin Department of Public Instruction, 2015, http://wise.dpi.wi.gov/wisedash_glossary.

30. Wisconsin Department of Public Instruction, "Wisconsin School District Performance Report, 2013–14: Milwaukee," accessed April 10, 2015, https:// apps2.dpi.wi.gov/sdpr/district-report.action.

31. Wisconsin Council on Children and Families, *Race to Equity: A Baseline Report on the State Disparities in Dane County* (Madison, WI: n.d.), http:// racetoequity.net/dev/wp-content/uploads/WCCF-R2E-Report.pdf.

32. Leticia Smith-Evans, Janel George, Fatima Goss-Graves, Lara Kaufmann, and Lauren Frohlich, *Unlocking Opportunities for African American Girls: A Call to Action for Educational Equity* (New York: NAACP Legal Defense and Education Fund, 2014), 7.

33. Kimberlé Crenshaw, Priscilla Ocen, and Jyoti Nanda, *Black Girls Matter: Pushed-Out, Over-Policed, and Under-Protected* (New York: African American Policy Forum and the Center for Intersectionality and Social Policy Studies, 2015).

34. Jeremy White, "California Bill Curbing 'Willful Defiance' Suspensions Opens School Discipline Debate," *Sacramento Bee*, August 16, 2014.

35. Chicago Public Schools, "Stats and Facts," 2015, http://cps.edu/About _CPS/At-a-glance/Pages/Stats_and_facts.aspx.

36. Ibid. Statistics have been rounded to the nearest whole number.

37. U.S. Department of Education Office of Civil Right Database, "Discipline

of Students Without Disabilities—Referral to Law Enforcement. Survey Year: 2011," accessed April 10, 2015, http://ocrdata.ed.gov/Page?t=d&eid=32906&syk=6&pid=861.

38. Matthew Steinberg, Elaine Allensworth, and David W. Johnson, "Student and Teacher Safety in Chicago Public Schools: The Roles of Community Context and Social Organization," University of Chicago, 2015, http://ccsr.uchicago.edu/publications/student-and-teacher-safety-chicago-public-schools-roles-community-context-and-school.

39. W. David Stevens, Lauren Sartain, Elaine M. Allensworth, and Rachel Levenstein with Shannon Guiltinan, Nick Mader, Michelle Hanh Huynh, and Shanette Porter, *Discipline Practices in Chicago Schools Trends in the Use of Suspensions and Arrests* (Chicago, IL: University of Chicago Consortium on Chicago School Research, 2015), 13–14.

40. Ibid.

41. See "The Chicago Race Riot of 1919," History.com, http://www.history.com/topics/black-history/chicago-race-riot-of-1919.

42. Ibid.

43. Charles S. Johnson, *The Negro in Chicago: A Study of Race Relations and a Race Riot* (Chicago: University of Chicago Press, 1922), 247.

44. Nathan James and Gail McCallion, *School Resource Officers: Law Enforcement Officers in Schools* (Washington, DC: Congressional Research Service, 2013), 2, 3.

45. Ibid., 9.

46. U.S. Department of Justice, *FBI Law Enforcement Bulletin: Addressing School Violence* (Washington, DC: Federal Bureau of Investigation, 2011).

47. Public Agenda, *Teaching Interrupted: Do Discipline Policies in Today's Public Schools Foster the Common Good?* (New York: Public Agenda, 2004).

48. Simone Robers, Anlan Zhang, Rachel Morgan, and Lauren Musu-Gillette, *Indicators of School Crime and Safety: 2014* (Washington, DC: U.S. Department of Education and U.S. Department of Justice Office of Justice Programs, 2015).

49. U.S. Department of Education, National Center for Education Statistics, *Indicators of School Crime and Safety: 2013* (NCES 2014-042) (Washington, DC: Department of Education, 2014).

50. Chongmin Na and Denise C. Gottfredson, "Police Officers in Schools: Effects on School Crime and the Processing of Offending Behaviors," *Justice Quarterly* 30, no. 4 (2013), doi:10.1080/07418825.2011.615754.

51. See Kathleen Nolan, *Police in the Hallways: Discipline in an Urban High School* (Minneapolis: University of Minnesota Press, 2011).

52. Ibid., 59–62.

53. Ibid.

54. Roberts et al., *Indicators of School Crime and Safety: 2014*, 22.

55. Chicago Public School, *Student Code of Conduct*, 2014, http://cps.edu /SiteCollectionDocuments/SCC_StudentCodeConduct_English.pdf.

56. Ibid., 34.

57. Ibid., 10.

58. Barbara Norvell Hall, "An Examination of the Effects of Recess on First Graders' Use of Written Symbol Representations" (PhD diss., Auburn University, 2006); Jennifer R. Cady, "A Qualitative Case Study on the Impact of Recess and In-Class Breaks, in the American Public Schools, Through the Eyes of Elementary School Administrators, Teachers, and Students" (PhD diss., Capella University, 2009).

59. Olga Jarrett, "A Research-Based Case for Recess," Georgia State University, 2013, http://usplaycoalition.clemson.edu/resources/articles/13.11.5_Recess_final _online.pdf.

60. Laura Ann Wurzburger, "Recess Policy in Chicago Public Schools: 1855–2006" (master's thesis, Loyola University Chicago, 2010).

61. Jarrett, "Research-Based Case for Recess," 2013.

62. Nicholas Day, "The Rebirth of Recess: How Do You Introduce Recess to Kids Who Have Never Left the Classroom?," *Slate*, August 29, 2012.

63. See Jarrett, "Research-Based Case for Recess."

64. Jamilia Blake, Betty Butler, Chance Lewis, and Alicia Darensbourg, "Unmasking the Inequitable Discipline Experiences of Urban Black Girls: Implications for Urban Educational Stakeholders," *Urban Review* 43, no. 1 (2011): 90–106. See also Monique W. Morris, *Race, Gender, and the School-to-Prison Pipeline: Expanding Our Discussion to Include Black Girls* (New York: African American Policy Forum, 2012).

65. Danielle Dreilinger, "New Orleans Public Schools Pre-Katrina and Now, by the Numbers," *Times-Picayune*, August 29, 2014.

66. Ibid.

67. Ibid.

68. "Tulsa School Sends Girl Home Over Hair," Fox23.com, September 6, 2013, http://www.fox23.com/news/local/story/Tulsa-school-sends-girl-home-over-hair /sGcEwBSrm02W8ZSBNnGoXQ.cspx.

69. Shaun Chaiyabhat, "African-American Girl Faces Expulsion over 'Natural Hair': Vanessa VanDyke Told to Cut Hair or Leave School," Local10.com, December 24, 2013, http://www.local10.com/news/africanamerican-girl-faces -expulsion-over-natural-hair/-/1717324/23165492/-/eo6hiz/-/index.html.

3. Jezebel in the Classroom

1. Laura Murphy and Brian Ea, "The Louisiana Human Trafficking Report," Modern Slavery Project, Loyola University, New Orleans, 2014, http://admin .loyno.edu/webteam/userfiles/file/LA%20HT%20Report%20final.pdf.

2. Ibid., 11.

3. Nihal Shrinath, Vicki Mack, and Allison Plyer, "Who Lives in New Orleans and Metro Parishes Now?," Data Center, New Orleans, 2014, http://www.datacenter research.org/data-resources/who-lives-in-new-orleans-now.

4. Malika Saada Saar, Rebecca Epstein, Lindsay Rosenthal, and Yasmin Vafa, *The Sexual Abuse to Prison Pipeline: The Girls' Story* (Washington, DC: Human Rights Project for Girls and Georgetown Law Center on Poverty and Inequality, 2015).

5. Office for Crime Victims, U.S. Department of Justice, Office of Justice Programs, *NCVW Resource Guide: Human Trafficking* (Washington, DC: Department of Justice, 2013).

6. H.E.A.T. Watch, Alameda County District Attorney's Office, "About Commercial Sexual Exploitation of Children," n.d., http://www.heat-watch.org /human_trafficking/about_csec.

7. Adaku Onyeka-Crawford, "New NWLC and LDF Report: African American Teen Mothers Need Support, Not Shaming," *National Women's Law Center Blog*, September 29, 2014, http://www.nwlc.org/our-blog/new-nwlc-and -ldf-report-african-american-teen-mothers-need-support-not-shaming.

8. U.S. Department of Education, National Center for Education Statistics, *Parent and Family Involvement in Education Survey of the National Household Education Surveys Program* (PFI-NHES) (Washington, DC: Department of Education, 2007), http://nces.ed.gov/pubs2012/2012026/tables/table_35.asp.

9. Gerda Lerner, ed., *Black Women in White America: A Documentary History* (New York: Vintage Books, 1972), 163.

10. *The Independent*, September 18, 1902, in ibid., 166–69.

11. Fannie Barrier Williams, "A Northern Negro's Autobiography," *The Independent*, July 14, 1904, in Lerner, *Black Women in White America*, 164–66.

12. "Jezebel" is a term that refers to a sexually promiscuous and seductive woman. Biblical characterizations of the biblical figure Jezebel as a sinner and wicked woman provided a narrative proxy for the perceived immorality of Black women. As discussed throughout the book, the deviance of the Black woman has been rooted in denigrating her sexuality, a practice that was developed and nurtured by the institution of slavery. Over time, the term *jezebel* has been used to shame and degrade Black women's sexual identity, rendering it immoral.

13. Stella Dawson, "U.S. Courts Deny Trafficking Victims Lost Wages: Study," Reuters, October 1, 2014.

14. Monique W. Morris, "Black Girls for Sale," *Ebony.com*, May 19, 2014.

15. Mike Kessler, "Gone Girls: Human Trafficking on the Home Front," *Los Angeles Magazine*, October 14, 2014.

16. Rape, Abuse, and Incest National Network, "Who Are the Victims: Breakdown by Gender and Age," 2009, https://www.rainn.org/get-information/statistics/sexual-assault-victims. A study by the Black Women's Blueprint found that 60 percent of Black girls have experienced sexual assault before turning eighteen. See http://blackwomensblueprint.org/sexual-violence/.

17. Astrid Goh, "Chicago: A National Hub for Human Trafficking," Youth Project, January 22, 2014, http://www.chicago-bureau.org/chicago-national-hub-human-trafficking.

18. National Association of Elementary School Principals, *National Survey of School Leaders Reveals 2013 School Uniform Trends* (Alexandria, VA: NAESP, 2013).

19. Ibid.

20. "The Race Problem—An Autobiography by a Southern Colored Woman," *The Independent*, March 17, 1904, 587–89, in Lerner, *Black Women in White America*, 158.

21. Statistics from U.S. Department of Education, NCES, ECS, NAESP, University of Florida, 2015, http://www.statisticbrain.com/school-uniform-statistic.

4. Learning on Lockdown

1. Francine T. Sherman and Annie Balck, *Gender Injustice: System-Level Juvenile Justice Reform for Girls* (Portland, OR: National Crittenton Foundation, 2015).

2. Annie E. Casey Foundation, *Reducing Youth Incarceration in the United States* (Baltimore, MD, 2013).

3. Sherman and Balck, *Gender Injustice*.

4. A status offense is an offense that is determined illegal due to the status of the person committing the "crime." For people who are under the age of eighteen, for example, status offenses include runaway and truancy—"offenses" that are associated with their status as children, not their threat to public safety.

5. Sherman and Balck, *Gender Injustice*.

6. Barry Holman and Jason Ziedenberg, *The Dangers of Detention: The Impact of Incarcerating Youth in Detention and Other Secure Facilities* (Washington, DC: Justice Policy Institute, 2011), http://www.justicepolicy.org/images/upload/06-11 _rep_dangersofdetention_jj.pdf.

7. Chandlee Johnson Kuhn, "Gender Disparities in the Juvenile Justice System," Coalition for Juvenile Justice blog, October 23, 2013, http://juvjustice.org/blog /598.

8. Leslie Acoca and Kelly Dedel, *No Place to Hide: Understanding and Meeting the Needs of Girls in the California Juvenile Justice System* (San Francisco, CA: National Council on Crime and Delinquency, 1998).

9. Sanford Fox, "Juvenile Justice Reform: An Historical Perspective," *Stanford Law Review* 22, no. 6 (1970): 1187–239.

10. Geoff K. Ward, *The Black Child-Savers: Racial Democracy and Juvenile Justice* (Chicago: University of Chicago Press, 2012), 52.

11. Ibid., 56.

12. Alana Barton, *Fragile Moralities and Dangerous Sexualities: Two Centuries of Semi-Penal Institutionalisation for Women* (Aldershot: Ashgate, 2005), 34–36.

13. Ward, *Black Child-Savers*.

14. Mary White Ovington, *Half a Man: The Status of the Negro in New York* (New York: Longmans, Green, 1911), 67–68.

15. Ibid., 190.

16. Ibid., 190–91.

17. Khalil Gibran Muhammad, *The Condemnation of Blackness: Race, Crime and the Making of Modern Urban America* (Cambridge, MA: Harvard University Press, 2010), 133–34.

18. W.E.B. Du Bois, *The Philadelphia Negro: A Social Study* (Philadelphia: University of Pennsylvania Press, 1995).

19. Russ Immarigeon, "Delinquent Girls Need to Farm," Prison Memory Project, October 30, 2014, http://www.prisonpublicmemory.org/blog/2014/delinquent -girls-need-to-farm.

20. Ward, *Black Child-Savers*, 47.

21. E. Franklin Frazier, *Rebellious Youth: The Negro Family in the United States* (Chicago: University of Chicago Press, 1939), in *African American Classics in Criminology and Criminal Justice*, ed. Shaun Gabbidon, Helen Taylor Greene, and Vernetta Young (Thousand Oaks, CA: Sage, 2002), 99.

22. Nina Bernstein, "Ward of the State: The Gap in Ella Fitzgerald's Life," *New York Times*, June 23, 1996.

23. Ruzz Immarigeon, "The 'Ungovernable' Ella Fitzgerald," Public Prison Memory Project, October 29, 2014, http://prisonpublicmemory.org/blog/2014/02/ungovernable-ella-fitzgerald.

24. Ibid. See also Bernstein, "Ward of the State."

25. Ward, *Black Child-Savers*, 88–91.

26. Vernetta Young, "Gender Expectations and Their Impact on Black Female Offenders and Victims," *Justice Quarterly* 3, no. 3 (1986): 305–27.

27. Melissa Sickmund, Anthony Sladky, Wei Kang, and Charles Puzzanchera, *Easy Access to the Census of Juveniles in Residential Placement* (Washington, DC: U.S. Department of Justice, 2015).

28. Ibid.

29. Center for Children's Law and Policy, "Understanding OJJDP Survey of Conditions of Confinement in Juvenile Facilities, Fact Sheet," August 3, 2010, http://www.cclp.org/documents/Conditions/Fact%20Sheet%20-%20OJJDP%20Survey-%20Conditions%20of%20Confinement.pdf.

30. Bonita Veysey, *Adolescent Girls with Mental Health Disorders Involved in the Juvenile Justice System* (Delmar, NY: National Center for Mental Health and Juvenile Justice, 2003).

31. Monique W. Morris, "Representing the Educational Experiences of Black Girls in a Juvenile Court School," *Journal of Applied Research on Children: Informing Policy for Children at Risk* 5, no. 2 (2014): article 5.

32. David E. Houchins, DaShaunda Puckett-Patterson, Shane Crosby, Margaret W. Shippen, and Kristine Jolivette, "Barriers to Facilitators to Providing Incarcerated Youth with Quality Education," *Preventing School Failure* 53, no. 3 (2009): 159–66.

33. Bruce Wolford, *Juvenile Justice Education: Who Is Educating Youth?* (Richmond, KY: EDJJ, 2000).

34. Jennie L. Shufelt and Joseph J. Cocozza, *Youth with Mental Health Disorders in the Juvenile Justice System: Results from a Multi-State Prevalence*

Study (Delmar, NY: National Center for Mental Health and Juvenile Justice, 2006).

35. Berkeley Center for Criminal Justice, *Mental Health Issues in California's Juvenile Justice System* (Berkeley: U C Berkeley School of Law, 2010).

36. Osa D. Coffey and Maia G. Gemignani, *Effective Practices in Juvenile Correctional Education: A Study of the Literature and Research* (Washington, DC: Office of Justice Programs, Office of Juvenile Justice and Delinquency Prevention, 1994). See also Nicholas W. Read and Mindee O'Cummings, "Factsheet: Juvenile Justice Education," National Evaluation and Technical Assistance Center for the Education of Children and Youth Who Are Neglected, Delinquent, or At Risk, 2011, http://www.neglected-delinquent.org/sites/default /files /NDFactSheet.pdf.

37. Donald Keeley, "Some Effects of the Label Juvenile Delinquent on Teacher Expectations of Student Behavior" (PhD diss., University of Georgia, 1973).

38. Malcolm X, Speech at the Founding Rally of the Organization of Afro-American Unity, March 8, 1964. The full quote is "Education is our passport to the future, for tomorrow belongs only to the people who prepare for it today."

39. Ivory Toldson, Kamilah Woodson, Ronald Braithwaite, and Rhonda Holliday, "Academic Potential Among African American Adolescents in Juvenile Detention Centers: Implications for Reentry to School," *Journal of Offender Rehabilitation* 49, no. 8 (2010): 551–70.

40. Veysey, *Adolescent Girls with Mental Health Disorders.*

41. Toldson et al., "Academic Potential Among African American Adolescents."

42. Stopbullying.gov, "Facts About Bullying," http://www.stopbullying.gov /news/media/facts/#listing.

43. An IEP is an Individualized Education Plan, which is part of the district's special education services.

44. Linda LeBlanc and Alexander Ratnofsky, "Unlocking Learning: Chapter 1 in Correctional Facilities," prepared for the U.S. Department of Education, Office of the Under Secretary, Washington, DC, 1991, http://babel.hathitrust.org/cgi/pt?id =uiug.30112047630717;view=1up;seq=3.

5. Repairing Relationships, Rebuilding Connections

1. The "prison-industrial complex" refers to the "looming presence" of the prison system, both as a function of government and in its privatized state, and

its attraction of capital and service (e.g. health, telecommunications, construction, etc.). See Mike Davis, "Hell Factories in the Field: A Prison-Industrial Complex," *The Nation*, February 20, 1995. See also Angela Y. Davis, *Are Prisons Obsolete?* (New York: Seven Stories Press, 2003).

2. Alan Payne, Denise Gottfreson, and Candace Kruttschnitt, "Girls, Schooling, and Delinquency," in *The Delinquent Girl*, ed. Margaret Zahn (Philadelphia: Temple University Press, 2009), 149.

3. Paolo Freire, *Pedagogy of the Oppressed* (New York: Continuum International, 2012).

4. Monique W. Morris, "Sacred Inquiry and Delinquent Black Girls: Developing a Foundation for a Liberative Pedagogical Praxis," in *Understanding Work Experiences from Multiple Perspectives: New Paradigms for Organizational Excellence*, ed. G.D. Sardana and Tojo Thatchenkerry (New Delhi: Bloomsbury India, 2014), 416–28; Peter Reason, "Reflections on Sacred Experience and Sacred Science," *Journal of Management Inquiry* 2, no. 3 (1993): 277; Monique W. Morris, "Representing the Educational Experiences of Black Girls in a Juvenile Court School," *Journal of Applied Research on Children: Informing Policy for Children at Risk* 5, no. 2 (2014): article 5.

5. "Justice by Gender: The Lack of Appropriate Prevention, Diversion and Treatment Alternatives for Girls in the Justice System," *William and Mary Journal of Women and the Law* 9, no. 1 (2002): 73.

6. Maya Angelou, "Equality," in *I Shall Not Be Moved* (New York: Random House), 1990.

7. Nikki Jones, *Between Good and Ghetto: African American Girls and Inner-City Violence* (Piscataway, NJ: Rutgers University Press, 2009), 158.

8. Elaine Richardson, "My Ill-Literacy Narrative: Growing Up Black, Po and a Girl, in the Hood," *Gender and Education* 21, no. 6 (2009): 753–67.

9. Caroline Hodges Persell, *Education and Inequality: The Roots and Results of Stratification in America's Schools* (New York: The Free Press, 1977); Pierre Bourdieu and Jean-Claude Passeron, *Reproduction in Society, Education and Culture*, 2nd ed. (London: Sage Publications, 1990). See also Kathleen Nolan, *Police in the Hallways: Discipline in an Urban High School* (Minneapolis: University of Minnesota Press, 2011).

10. Donald Keeley, "Some Effects of the Label Juvenile Delinquent on Teacher Expectations of Student Behavior" (PhD diss., University of Georgia, 1973). See also Emanuel Mason, "Teachers' Observations and Expectations of Boys and Girls

as Influenced by Psychological Reports and Knowledge of the Effects of Bias," *Journal of Educational Psychology* 65 (1973): 238–43.

11. William Corsaro, *The Sociology of Childhood*, 4th ed. (Bloomington: Indiana University Press, 2015).

12. Rebecca Carroll, *Sugar in the Raw: Voices of Young Black Girls in America* (New York: Three Rivers Press, 1997). See also Ted Wachtel and Laura Mirsky, *Safer, Saner Schools: Restorative Practices in Education, Restoring a Culture of Community in Learning Environments* (Bethlehem, PA: International Institute for Restorative Practices, 2008).

13. Elijah Anderson, *Code of the Street: Decency, Violence and the Moral Life of the Inner City* (New York: W.W. Norton, 2000).

14. Manning Marable, *Black Liberation in Conservative America* (Boston: South End Press, 1997).

Appendix A: Girls, We Got You!

1. U.S. Census, "Education and Synthetic Work-Life Earnings Estimates," September 2011, http://www.census.gov/prod/2011pubs/acs-14.pdf.

Appendix B: Alternatives to Punishment

1. Positive Behavioral Interventions and Supports, *Primary FAQs*, 2015, http://www.pbis.org/school/primary-level/faqs.

2. Lucille Eber, George Sugai, Carl Smith, and Terrance Scott, "Wraparound and Positive Behavioral Intervention and Supports in Schools," *Journal of Emotional and Behavioral Disorders* 10, no. 3 (2002): 171.

3. Ibid.

4. Catherine P. Bradshaw, Mary M. Mitchell, and Philip Leaf, "Examining the Effects of Schoolwide Positive Behavioral Interventions and Supports on Student Outcomes: Results from a Randomized Controlled Effectiveness Trial in Elementary Schools," *Journal of Positive Behavioral Interventions* 12, no. 3 (July 2010), doi:10.1177/1098300709334798.

5. George Sugai, Robert Horner, Glen Dunlap, Meme Heineman, Timothy Lewis, C. Michael Nelson, Terrance Scott, et al., *Applying Positive Behavioral Support and Functional Behavioral Assessment in Schools* (Eugene, OR: Center on Behavioral Interventions and Supports, University of Oregon, 1999).

6. Bradshaw et al., "Examining the Effects of Schoolwide Positive Behavioral Interventions."

7. Elizabeth Steed, Tina Pomerleau, Howard Muscott, and Leigh Rohde, "Program-wide Positive Behavioral Interventions and Supports in Rural Preschools," *Rural Special Education Quarterly* 32, no. 1 (2013): 38

8. Brennan L. Wilcox, H. Rutherford Turnbull III, and Ann P. Turnbull, "Behavioral Issues and IDEA: Positive Behavioral Interventions and Supports and the Functional Behavioral Assessment in the Disciplinary Context," *Exceptionality: A Special Education Journal* 8, no. 3 (2000): 173–87.

9. H. Rutherford Turnbull III, Brennan L. Wilcox, Matthew Stowe, Carolyn Raper, and Laura Penny Hedges, "Public Policy Foundations for Positive Behavioral Interventions, Strategies, and Supports," *Journal of Positive Behavior Interventions* 2, no. 4 (2000): 218.

10. Note that these norms may not have been created in partnership with the students. Rigorous measurements of PBIS outcomes in elementary schools include randomized controlled effectiveness trials, using the Effective Behavior Support Survey and the Schoolwide Evaluation Tool (SET) to measure the implementation and effectiveness of seven subscales, including (1) behavior expectations defined, (2) behavioral expectations taught, (3) reward system, (4) violation system, (5) monitoring and evaluation, (6) management, and (7) district support. In Maryland, researchers used the Implementation Phases Inventory (IPI), which follows a "stages of change" theoretical model (i.e., preparation, initiation, implementation, maintenance) to assess forty-four key elements of PBIS implementation. Researchers Bradshaw and Pas found that lower performing schools were more likely to use PBIS in Maryland, where participants in PBIS training self-identify. These scholars also found that district factors (e.g., qualified teachers, school disorganization, etc.) were closely related to training in and ultimately adopting PBIS.

11. Catherine P. Bradshaw, Christine W. Koth, Katherine B. Bevans, Nicholas Ialongo, and Phillip J. Leaf, "The Impact of School-wide Positive Behavioral Interventions and Supports (PBIS) on the Organizational Health of Elementary Schools," *School Psychology Quarterly* 23 (2008): 462–73; Bradshaw, Mitchell, and Leaf, "Examining the Effects of Schoolwide Positive Behavioral Interventions."

12. Howard S. Muscott, Eric L. Mann, and Marcel R. LeBrun, "Positive Behavioral Interventions and Supports in New Hampshire: Effects of Large-Scale Implementation of Schoolwide Positive Behavior Support on Student Discipline and Academic Achievement," *Journal of Positive Behavior Interventions* 10, no. 3 (2008): 190–205.

13. Bradshaw et al., "Examining the Effects of Schoolwide Positive Behavioral Interventions."

14. Meeting 80 percent of the fidelity criteria on the overall and subscales related to teaching expectations have the most positive student outcomes. See J. Doolittle, "Sustainability of Positive Supports in Schools" (PhD diss., University of Oregon, 2006. See also Robert H. Horner, Anne W. Todd, Teri Lewis-Palmer, Larry K. Irvin, George Sugai, and Joseph J. Boland, "The School-wide Evaluation Tool (SET): A Research Instrument for Assessing School-wide Positive Behavior Support," *Journal of Positive Behavior Intervention* 6 (2004): 3–12.

15. Brandi Simonsen, Lucille Eber, Anne Black, George Sugai, Holly Lewandowski, Barbara Sims, and Diane Myers, "Illinois Statewide Positive Behavioral Interventions and Supports: Evolution and Impact on Student Outcomes Across Years," *Journal of Positive Behavior Interventions* 14, no. 1 (2012): 5–16.

16. Ibid.

17. Muscott, Mann, and LeBrun, "Positive Behavioral Interventions and Supports in New Hampshire," 202.

18. Kristine Jolivette, Sara C. McDaniel, Jeffrey Sprague, Jessica Swain-Bradway, and Robin Parks Ennis, "Embedding the Positive Behavioral Interventions and Supports Framework into the Complex Array of Practices Within Alternative Education Settings: A Decision-Making Process," *Assessment for Effective Intervention* 38, no. 1 (2012): 15.

19. Nicole Cain Swoszowski, Kristine Jolivette, L.D. Fredrick, and Laura J. Heflin, "Check In/Check Out: Effects on Students with Emotional and Behavioral Disorders with Attention- or Escape-Maintained Behavior in a Residential Facility," *Exceptionality* 20, no. 3 (2012): 163–78.

20. Jolivette et al., "Embedding the Positive Behavioral Interventions."

21. Katrina Debnam, Elise Pas, and Catherine Bradshaw, "Secondary and Tertiary Support Systems in Schools Implementing School-wide Positive Behavioral Interventions and Supports: A Preliminary Descriptive Analysis," *Journal of Positive Behavior Interventions* 14, no. 3 (2012): 142–52.

22. Jessica Feierman, Rachel Kleinman, David Lapp, Monique Luse, Len Reiser, and Robert Schwartz, "Stemming the Tide: Promising Legislation to Reduce School Referrals to the Courts," *Family Court Review* 51, no. 3 (2013): 409–17.

23. Margaret Shippen, DaShaunda Patterson, Kemeche Green, and Tracy Smitherman, "Community and School Practices to Reduce Delinquent Behavior:

Intervening on the School-to-Prison Pipeline," *Teacher Education and Special Education* 35, no. 4 (2012): 296–308.

24. Howard Zehr, *Changing Lenses: A New Focus for Crime and Justice* (Scottsdale, PA: Herald Press, 1990).

25. Ada Pecos Melton, "Traditional and Contemporary Tribal Justice," in *Images of Color, Images of Crime*, ed. Coramae Richey Mann and Marjorie S. Zatz (Los Angeles: Roxbury, 1998), 58–71; John Braithwaite, *Restorative Justice and Responsive Regulation* (London: Oxford University Press, 2002).

26. Thalia González, "Keeping Kids in Schools: Restorative Justice, Punitive Discipline, and the School to Prison Pipeline," *Journal of Law and Education* 41, no. 2 (2012): 281–335. See also Michael Sumner, Carol Silverman, and Mary Louise Frampton, *School-Based Restorative Justice as an Alternative to Zero-Tolerance Policies: Lessons from West Oakland* (Berkeley: Thelton E. Henderson Center for Social Justice, University of California, Berkeley School of Law, 2010).

27. Howard Zehr, *The Little Book of Restorative Justice* (Intercourse, PA: Good Books, 2002), 33.

28. Ibid., 21.

29. Ibid.

30. Melton, "Traditional and Contemporary Tribal Justice," 66.

31. Edgar Cahn, Kerri Nash, and Cynthia Robbins, "A Strategy for Dismantling Structural Racism in the Juvenile Delinquency System," *Poverty and Race* 20, no. 2 (2011): 1–8; William Bradshaw and David Roseborough, "Restorative Justice Dialogue: The Impact of Mediation and Conferencing on Juvenile Recidivism," *Federal Probation* 69, no. 2 (2005): 15–21; Sarah Sun Beale, "Still Tough on Crime? Prospects for Restorative Justice in the United States," *Utah Law Review* 1 (2003): 413–37. See also Carol Chmelynski, "Restorative Justice for Discipline with Respect," *Education Digest*, September 2005; and Wendy Drewery, "Conferencing in Schools: Punishment, Restorative Justice, and the Productive Importance of the Process of Conversation," *Journal of Applied Social Psychology* 14 (2004): 332–44.

32. Mary Louise Frampton, "Transformative Justice and the Dismantling of Slavery's Legacy in Post-modern America," in *After the War on Crime*, ed. Mary Louise Frampton, Ian Haney López, and Jonathan Simon (New York: New York University Press, 2008), 216.

33. Zehr, *Little Book of Restorative Justice*, 42.

34. Chmelynski, "Restorative Justice for Discipline with Respect," 2005.

35. Jessica Ashley and Kimberly Burke, *Implementing Restorative Justice: A Guide for Schools* (Chicago: Illinois Criminal Justice Information Authority, 2009).

36. Ted Wachtel and Laura Mirsky, L, *Safer, Saner Schools: Restorative Practices in Education, Restoring a Culture of Community in Learning Environments* (Bethlehem, PA: International Institute for Restorative Practices, 2008).

37. Russell Fazio and Michael Olson, "Implicit Measures in Social Cognition Research: Their Meanings and Use," *Annual Review of Psychology* 54 (2003): 297–303. See also Justin Levinson, "Forgotten Racial Inequality: Implicit Bias, Decision-making and Misremembering," *Duke Law Journal* 57 (2007): 345–421.

38. Anthony G. Greenwald and Linda Hamilton Krieger, "Implicit Bias: Scientific Foundations," *California Law Review* 94 (2006): 945–67.

39. Kelly Welch and Allison A. Payne, "Exclusionary School Punishment: The Effect of Racial Threat on Expulsion and Suspension," *Youth Violence and Juvenile Justice* 10, no. 20 (2012): 155–71. See also Lionel Brown and Kelvin Beckett, "The Role of the School District in Student Discipline: Building Consensus in Cincinnati," *Urban Review* 38 (2006): 235–56.

40. Welch and Payne, "Exclusionary School Punishment."

41. Daniel Losen, Tia Martinez, and Jon Gillespie, *Suspended Education in California* (Los Angeles, CA: Center for Civil Rights Remedies at the University of California, Los Angeles Civil Rights Project, 2012), 39.

42. González, "Keeping Kids in Schools," 2012. See also Sumner et al., *School-Based Restorative Justice*.

43. Welch and Payne, "Exclusionary School Punishment."

44. Ashley and Burke, *Implementing Restorative Justice*; Wachtel and Mirsky, *Safer, Saner Schools*, 182. See also Bob Costello, Joshua Wachtel, and Ted Wachtel, *The Restorative Practices Handbook for Teachers, Disciplinarians, and Administrators* (Bethlehem, PA: International Institute for Restorative Practices, 2009.

45. Costello et al., *Restorative Practices Handbook*.

46. Ibid., 50.

47. Ibid., 51.

48. Advancement Project, *Test, Punish, and Push Out: How "Zero Tolerance" and High-Stakes Testing Funnel Youth into the School-to-Prison Pipeline* (Washington, DC: Advancement Project, 2010). See also American Psychological Association Task Force, "Are Zero Tolerance Policies Effective in Schools?," *American Psychologist* 63, no. 9 (2008), 852–62; Costello et al., *Restorative Practices Handbook*.

49. Monique W. Morris, *Race, Gender, and the School-to-Prison Pipeline: Expanding Our Discussion to Include Black Girls* (Los Angeles: African American Policy Forum, 2012).

50. Leticia Smith-Evans, Janel George, Fatima Goss-Graves, Lara Kaufmann, and Lauren Frohlich. *Unlocking Opportunities for African American Girls: A Call to Action for Educational Equity* (New York: NAACP Legal Defense and Education Fund, 2014).

51. U.S. Department of Health and Human Services, *Trends in Teen Pregnancy and Childbearing Teen Births* (Washington, DC: DHHS, 2015), http://www.hhs.gov/ash/oah/adolescent-health-topics/reproductive-health/teen-pregnancy/trends.html.

52. Emily Gaarder and Denise Hesselton, "Connecting Restorative Justice with Gender-Responsive Programming," *Contemporary Justice Review: Issues in Criminal, Social, and Restorative Justice* 15, no. 3 (2012): 239–64.

53. Ibid., 249.

54. Nancy Rodriguez, "Restorative Justice at Work: Examining the Impact of Restorative Justice Resolutions on Juvenile Recidivism," *Crime and Delinquency* 53, no. 3 (2007): 355–79.

55. Gaarder and Hesselton, "Connecting Restorative Justice with Gender-Responsive Programming," 254.

56. Rebecca Hubbard Maniglia, "Translating Gender Theory into Juvenile Justice Practice for Girls" (PhD diss., University of Illinois at Chicago, 2007).

57. Gaarder and Hesselton, "Connecting Restorative Justice with Gender-Responsive Programming."

58. Ibid., 258.

59. Ibid., 260.

60. Ibid., 257.

61. Beale, "Still Tough on Crime?" See also Bradshaw and Roseborough, "Restorative Justice Dialogue."

62. Gillean McCluskey, Gwynedd Lloyd, Jean Kane, Sheila Riddell, Joan Stead, and Elisabet Weedon, "Can Restorative Practices in Schools Make a Difference?," *Educational Review* 60, no. 4 (2008): 405–17.

63. Heather Cole and Julian Vasquez Heilig, "Developing a School-Based Youth Court: A Potential Alternative to the School to Prison Pipeline," *Journal of Law and Education* 40, no. 2 (2011): 305–21.

64. Zehr, *Little Book of Restorative Justice*, 2002.

65. David Karp and Todd Clear, eds., *What Is Community Justice?* (London: Sage Publications, 2002). See also Jodi Lane, Amber Schroeder, Susan Turner, and Terri Fain, *South Oxnard Challenge Project* (Santa Barbara, CA: RAND, 2002). Also Paul Takagi and Gregory Shank, "Social Justice for Workers in the Global Economy," *Social Justice* 31, no. 3 (2004): 147–63.

66. Restorative Justice for Oakland Youth, "About," Oakland, CA, http://www.rjoyoakland.org/about.php.

67. Frampton, *Transformative Justice*.

68. Lode Walgrave, ed., *Restorative Justice for Juveniles: Potentialities, Risks, and Problems* (Leuven, Belgium: Leuven University Press, 1998).

69. Howard Zehr, "Restorative Justice: The Concept," *Corrections Today* 59, no. 7 (1997): 68–70.

Methodology

1. Linda Dale Bloomberg and Marie Volpe, *Completing Your Qualitative Dissertation: A Roadmap from Beginning to End* (Los Angeles: Sage Publications, 2008).

2. Clark Moustakas, *Phenomenological Research Methods* (Thousand Oaks, CA: Sage Publications; 1994).

3. Steinar Kvale, *Interviews: An Introduction to Qualitative Research Interviewing* (Thousand Oaks, CA: Sage Publications, 1996). See also Sharan B. Merriam, *Qualitative Research and Case Study Application in Education* (San Francisco: Jossey-Bass, 1998). Lastly, see Irving E. Seidman, *Interviewing as Qualitative Research*, 2nd ed. (New York: Teachers College Press, 1998).

4. John Creswell, *Research Design: Qualitative, Quantitative, and Mixed Methods Approaches,* 2nd ed. (Thousand Oaks, CA: Sage Publications, 2003.

5. Marcia S. Wertz, Marcianna Nosek, Susan McNiesh, and Elizabeth Marlow, "The Composite First Person Narrative: Texture, Structure, and Meaning in Writing Phenomenological Descriptions," *International Journal of Qualitative Studies in Health and Wellbeing* 6, no. 2 (2011).

6. County Probation Department aggregate summary of youth admitted/released to secure detention in January 2013 and March 2013. Data on file with author.

7. Joseph Betancourt, Alexander Green, J. Emilio Carrillo, and Owusu Ananeh-Firempong, "Defining Cultural Competence: A Practice Framework for

Addressing Racial/Ethnic Disparities in Health and Health Care," *Public Health Reports* 118 (July–August 2003): 294.

8. See Isami Arifuku, Monique Morris, Michelle Nuñez, and Mary Lai, "Culture Counts: How Five Community-Based Organizations Serve Asian and Pacific Islander Youth," National Council on Crime and Delinquency, 2003.

9. Stephanie Covington and Barbara Bloom, "Gendered Justice: Programming for Women in Correctional Settings," paper presented at the 52nd Annual Meeting of the American Society of Criminology, San Francisco, CA, November 2000, 12.

10. Barbara Bloom, Barbara Owen, Stephanie Covington, and Myrna Raeder, *Gender Responsive Strategies: Research, Practice, and Guiding Principles for Women Offenders* (Washington, DC: National Institute of Corrections, 2003), vii.

11. Meda Chesney-Lind, Merry Morash, and Katherine Irwin, "Policing Girlhood: Relational Aggression and Violence Prevention," in *Fighting for Girls: New Perspectives on Gender and Violence*, ed. Meda Chesney-Lind and Nikki Jones (Albany: State University of New York Press, 2010). See also Norine Johnson, Michael Roberts, and Judith Worell, *Beyond Appearance: A New Look at Adolescent Girls* (Washington, DC: American Psychological Association, 1999).

ABOUT THE AUTHOR

Monique W. Morris, EdD, has been working in the areas of education, civil rights, and social justice for more than twenty years. She writes and lectures widely on the research, policies, and practices associated with improving juvenile justice and educational conditions for Black girls, women, and their families. She is a co-founder of the National Black Women's Justice Institute and a 2012 Soros Justice Fellow, and she formerly served as Vice President for Economic Programs, Advocacy and Research at the NAACP and as Director of Research for the Thelton E. Henderson Center for Social Justice at the UC Berkeley School of Law.

Morris sits on the National Girls Initiative Expert Panel and on California's Board of State and Community Corrections' Reducing Racial and Ethnic Disparities Subcommittee. She is also an advisory board member for Global Girl Media, Oakland, and a regular contributor to Ebony.com. She is the author of *Black Stats: African Americans by the Numbers in the Twenty-First Century* (The New Press), and her debut novel, *Too Beautiful for Words* (MWM Books), is a favorite among girls in detention facilities and marginalized youth across the country. She lives in the Bay Area with her husband and two daughters.

Publishing in the Public Interest

Thank you for reading this book published by The New Press. The New Press is a nonprofit, public interest publisher. New Press books and authors play a crucial role in sparking conversations about the key political and social issues of our day.

We hope you enjoyed this book and that you will stay in touch with The New Press. Here are a few ways to stay up to date with our books, events, and the issues we cover:

- Sign up at www.thenewpress.com/subscribe to receive updates on New Press authors and issues and to be notified about local events
- Like us on Facebook: www.facebook.com/newpressbooks
- Follow us on Twitter: www.twitter.com/thenewpress

Please consider buying New Press books for yourself; for friends and family; or to donate to schools, libraries, community centers, prison libraries, and other organizations involved with the issues our authors write about.

The New Press is a 501(c)(3) nonprofit organization. You can also support our work with a tax-deductible gift by visiting www.thenew press.com/donate.